Customer Relationship Management

Customer Relationship Management

Perspectives from the Marketplace

Simon Knox
Stan Maklan
Adrian Payne
Joe Peppard
Lynette Ryals

OXFORD   AMSTERDAM   BOSTON   LONDON   NEW YORK   PARIS
SAN DIEGO   SAN FRANCISCO   SINGAPORE   SYDNEY   TOKYO

Butterworth-Heinemann
An imprint of Elsevier Science
Linacre House, Jordan Hill, Oxford OX2 8DP
200 Wheeler Road, Burlington MA 01803

First published 2003

British Library Cataloguing in Publication Data
A catalogue record for this book is available from the British Library

Library of Congress Cataloguing in Publication Data
A catalogue record for this book is available from the Library of Congress

ISBN 0 7506 5677 8

For more information on all Butterworth-Heinemann publications visit our website
at www.bh.com

Typeset by Keyword Typesetting Services Ltd, Wallington, Surrey
Printed and bound in Great Britain by Biddles Ltd, *www.biddles.co.uk*

Contents

Foreword

CRM has confounded the business world since its inception. Indeed, analysts Gartner calculate that 65 per cent of CRM projects failed last year (2001). Yet industry remains committed to CRM: despite an inhospitable IT investment climate, spending projections for the sector remain in the ascendancy.

The reason for the perseverance is obvious: a coterie of businesses is getting CRM right and achieving impressive results. Perhaps more fundamentally, businesses appreciate the inherent logic that underpins CRM practice, and the sense in adhering to its guidelines however maddening this can prove to be at times.

As a CRM technology vendor, my business grapples every day with the realities of what best-practice CRM entails. Quite simply, it is about understanding customers and helping them to satisfy their individual needs. Of course, behind that it is about helping businesses to increase their own value.

With a deft touch, this book unravels the curious mix of social, technological and business changes that have spawned the CRM industry. The scale of the research is breathtaking; it offers insight from the industry's leading thinkers, and is peppered with case study examples from a range of industries.

In *Customer Relationship Management: Perspectives from the Marketplace*, one is left with a real sense of the potential of CRM to deliver business value, provided certain ingredients are in place. Getting senior management to buy into CRM at an early stage is perhaps the most critical of these ingredients. To that end, I could not recommend a wiser starting point than this enthralling book. I hope you enjoy and are as provoked as much as I was from it.

Michael Kelly
Founder and CEO
FINEOS Corporation

About the authors

SIMON KNOX BSc PhD
Professor of Brand Marketing
Simon Knox is Professor of Brand Marketing at the Cranfield School of Management in the UK and is a consultant to a number of multinational companies including McDonald's, Levi Strauss, DiverseyLever, BT and Exel. Upon graduating, he followed a career in the marketing of international brands with Unilever plc in a number of senior marketing roles in both detergents and foods.

Since joining Cranfield, Simon has published over 100 papers and books on strategic marketing and branding and is a regular speaker at international conferences. He is a Director of the Cranfield Centre for Advanced Research in Marketing in the School and is currently leading a research team looking at the impact of Corporate Social Responsibility on Brand Management. He is the co-author of two recent books, *Competing on Value*, published by FT Pitman Publishing in the UK, Germany, the USA and China, and *Creating a Company for Customers*, published by FT Prentice-Hall, in the UK, Brazil and India.

STAN MAKLAN BA MBA
Visiting Fellow and PhD Candidate
Stan Maklan is an experienced marketer and management consultant with senior, international line management experience in blue chip consumer and business marketing companies.

Stan spent the first 10 years of his career in marketing with Unilever Canada, UK and Sweden, where he was Marketing Director of its Toiletries business. He spent the following 10 years largely in consulting, most recently with Sapient, a leading builder of new economy businesses as a senior manager specializing in CRM and marketing strategy. Previously, Stan was a managing consultant with one of the world's largest IT-management consulting firms, CSC Computer Sciences. Stan established CSC UK's Customer Relationship Management practice and then moved to a role within its European Consulting and global management research unit (Research Services). Prior to that, Stan had his own consulting firm specializing in business to business marketing; clients included Motorola, Dell, Santa Cruz Operation, Hong Kong Telecom, Molyncke, Southern Water, Atomic Energy Authority Technology and British Olympic Association.

Stan was awarded honours for academic excellence when he obtained a Masters of Business Administration from the University of Western Ontario (Canada) and has a Bachelor of Science (Economics) from the Université de Montréal. He is a French and Swedish speaker, and a regular contributor to marketing seminars, courses and publications.

ADRIAN PAYNE MEd MSc PhD FRMIT
Professor of Services and Relationship Marketing
Adrian Payne is Professor of Services and Relationship Marketing and Director of the Centre for Customer Relationship Management at the Cranfield School of Management, Cranfield University.

He has practical experience in marketing, market research, corporate planning and general management. His previous appointments include positions as chief executive for a manufacturing company and he has also held senior appointments in corporate planning and marketing.

He is an authority on Relationship Marketing and Customer Relationship Management and is an author of six books on these topics. His research interests are in Customer Retention Economics; the impact of IT on CRM; and Marketing Strategy and Planning in Service Businesses. Adrian is a frequent keynote speaker at public and in-company seminars and conferences around the world. He also acts as a consultant and educator to many service organizations, professional service firms and manufacturing companies.

JOE PEPPARD BBS MSc PhD FICS
Senior Research Fellow in Information Systems
Joe Peppard is a Senior Research Fellow at the Information Systems Research Centre (ISRC). A Graduate of Trinity College Dublin he previously spent five years lecturing at his alma mater, joining Cranfield in 1992. He has held visiting positions at Groningen University in Holland and the University of South Australia and is currently external examiner at a number of institutions. Joe is

a Director of Fineos Corporation and Sophos Development, and a member of the Editorial Board of the *European Management Journal*.

Joe has been involved with the ISRC since its establishment and has worked on many of the centre's research projects. He is a Fellow of the Irish Computer Society, a charter member of the Association for Information Systems and a member of the UK Academy of Information Systems, British Academy of Management, and the Academy of Management. His publications include *IT Strategy for Business* (Pitman Publishing), *The Essence of Business Process Re-engineering* (Prentice-Hall International), *Business Process Re-engineering: Current Perspectives and Research Directions* (Kogan Page), and *Strategic Planning for Information Systems* (Wiley), as well as articles in both academic and general business journals. He is retained by a number of companies as an adviser on IS/IT, e-commerce and strategy related matters.

LYNETTE RYALS MA (OXON) MBA FSIP
Marketing Lecturer

Lynette Ryals began her career in the City as a fund manager and stockbroker trading UK equities, options and futures, and still lectures occasionally on finance issues. She then moved to a marketing company to work on corporate development and acquisitions, subsequently transferring into the consultancy arm of the same business group.

Lynette is a Registered Representative of the London Stock Exchange and is the only woman in the UK to have passed the Fellowship examinations of the Society of Investment Professionals.

She is co-author of *Customer Relationship Management: The Business Case*, a management report in the FT Prentice-Hall series, with Simon Knox and Stan Maklan.

Lynette has also been Director of the Executive MBA programme at Cranfield.

Acknowledgements

The authors would like to thank Margrit Bass, a freelance journalist, for her major contribution to the book – by ensuring that six of the cases were delivered on time and with the appropriate management emphasis. In many ways, writing the cases proved to be only part of the challenge; gaining access to the companies and their managers, agreeing with them what could and should be disclosed and, finally, getting agreement to publish what had been written about the company and its CRM practices all proved to be both time-consuming and requiring considerable diplomatic skills! Margrit proved more than up to the job in developing the case studies for Orange, Homebase, SunMicrosystems, RS Components, asserta home and NatWest.

Jane Simms, a freelance writer and editor specializing in marketing and business management, carried the burden of editing the entire book by joining together chapters in a masterly way and contributing parts of the text. We would like to thank Jane for her patience and professionalism.

We wish to thank Sapient Ltd for its financial contribution and help with the Homebase and asserta home cases, both of whom were Sapient clients.

Finally, our thanks to Gill Glass for her secretarial support in maintaining, updating and formatting the files we created as the book was written, starting with Adrian Payne's strategic framework for CRM, through case study writing to the final chapter on CRM futures. Without Gill's meticulous attention to detail and responsiveness to last minute changes, we could not have delivered the manuscript in such a highly finished format.

With the exception of the case study on Siemens, the cases are the Copyright of the Cranfield School of Management and are published with their permission.

Professor Simon Knox
Stan Maklan
Professor Adrian Payne
Dr Joe Peppard
Lynette Ryals

Note
Please note that the term 'billion' is used throughout this book meaning a thousand million (1000,000,000).

Chapter 1

CRM top of the management agenda

In an era of increasingly transient management themes, few board agenda items are attracting the sustained attention of Customer Relationship Management, or CRM. To provide some measure of the explosion of management interest in CRM, UK market research company Forrester Research searched the Dow Jones' content base of more than 6000 management publications for references about CRM and found 6048 articles in 2000, up from 442 articles in 1998 (Chatham et al. 2001).

This sudden proliferation of references can be partly explained by the lack of a widely accepted definition for CRM: consequently managers and writers use the term broadly to describe all forms of transactions between customers and their suppliers. In this book, we look at CRM as an organization-wide process, which focuses its activities on treating different customers differently to increase value for both customer and organization. In an article on its web site, the European Centre for Customer Strategies quotes Hewson Consulting's definition of CRM as 'a business strategy focusing on winning, growing and keeping the right customers' (European Centre for Customer Strategies 2001). A recent CRM report published by the *Financial Times* (Ryals et al. 2000) suggests that CRM consists of three main elements:

1. identifying, satisfying, retaining and maximizing the value of the firm's best customers;

2. wrapping the firm around the customer to ensure that each contact with the customer is appropriate and based upon extensive knowledge both of the customer's needs and profitability;
3. creating a complete picture of the customer.

The *Financial Times* report identifies the major components for the successful implementation of CRM as:

- a front office that integrates sales, marketing and service functions across media (call centres, people, stores, internet);
- a data warehouse to store customer information and the appropriate analytic tools with which to analyse the data and learn about customer behaviour;
- business rules developed from the data analysis to ensure the front office benefits from the firm's learning about its customers;
- measures of performance that enable customer relationships to continually improve;
- integration into the firm's operational and support (or 'back office') systems, ensuring that the front office's promises are delivered.

Developing a consistent approach to managing customer relationships has been a core objective for the Royal Bank of Canada in implementing its CRM strategy:

EXAMPLE

The Royal Bank of Canada began collecting customer data in 1978 and by the early 1990s had implemented client segmentation in its data warehouse, dividing its customers into three distinct profitability segments. While this provided front-line staff with segmentation codes, these were often interpreted subjectively, resulting in an inconsistent approach at corporate level.

Following research, the bank set about implementing a CRM strategy which allowed it to offer customers an integrated service across its entire product range. To achieve this it needed to measure client offerings, cost management, pricing initiatives and marketing spend. The bank uses five criteria to analyse customer information: income, expense and risk (net interest revenue); other revenue (fees, commission); direct expense (variable cost); indirect expense (overheads); and risk provision. The bank also recognized that profitability was affected by the type and frequency of customer events, their balances and the channels they use.

The Royal Bank of Canada's nine million customers are segmented, however, it has developed strategies not only for these segments but also for hundreds of micro-segments, as it moves towards its objective of one-to-one marketing. It plans to develop individual treatment strategies on small cells of customers to establish what works and what doesn't, and to test refinements on an ongoing basis.

The customer data are also allowing it to move from assessing current customer value to potential value, by taking into account factors such as lifestyle changes. The bank has also recognized that 'there is no such thing as an unprofitable customer' and is tailoring its product offerings to suit what are normally considered to be unprofitable customers. One of the immediate gains was discovering from recalculating customer profitability that its previous measurement metrics had been inaccurate for as many as 75 per cent of its customers.

CRM is not only being written about; big businesses are actively investing in CRM initiatives and technologies. A Forrester report (Callinan et al. 2001) quotes from its first quarter 2001 North America Benchmark study that 82 per cent of firms in the study have CRM implementations planned or in progress. This result is consistent with other published surveys and suggests that most big businesses are actively implementing some facets of one-to-one or relationship marketing.

Popular three-letter acronyms come and go, but we believe that the core of CRM will continue as an enduring foundation of most businesses. Creating satisfied customers at a profit has been espoused as the prime role of business since Peter Drucker first wrote about it almost 50 years ago (Drucker 1954: 'it is the customer who determines what a business is ... the purpose of a firm is to create and keep customers'). However, operationally, the traditional focus of business is improving efficiencies. This focus on efficiency has its roots deep in economic thought. Adam Smith did not write about customer satisfaction, retention and relationships; he developed theories of specialization, division of labour and production efficiencies. Economic theory that originates from his model of perfect markets assumes that competition for undifferentiated products drives prices down to a level necessary merely to sustain investment in continued production. In this model, there are no brands, product differentiation, loyal customers or excess profits. In Adam Smith's world, merely being an efficient producer of commodities, accepting the price and volume dictated by the market satisfies the firm.

Our professional and personal experience suggests that firms in a competitive market are anything but passive price and volume takers. Firms innovate in product design, product function, manufacturing processes, distribution, service and communications to differentiate their offers from those of competitors. Much of this innovation focuses upon creating new and improved products (and services) and reducing costs. Efficiency, coupled with product innovation, drives competitive strategy for most firms.

Long-term social, business and economic trends are having an impact on this efficiency drive and organizations no longer focus *exclusively* upon making better products at lower cost. We observe that many firms strive to help customers in both consumer and business markets become more effective through the goods and services they sell them. For example, improving effectiveness for consumers of financial services may not just be about creating an innovative investment product, it is more likely to centre around helping consumers achieve important life goals such as financial security and increased leisure time. Many financial services providers have segmented their customer base by life stage in order to talk to consumers about these life goals in addition to the products they offer.

A business-to-business equivalent example is found in information technology. Effective use of IT is not delivered through faster computers and new software applications alone; it is more likely to be delivered by helping firms improve their businesses by measures such as moving fixed costs to variable costs, quickly growing the business to scale and developing global reach. Efficiency-driven firms focus on the products and services they sell, whereas effective firms focus on their ability to understand and fulfil individual customers' most important needs. Efficiency-driven firms seek competitive advantage in scale, experience and creating barriers to entry. Effective firms seek competitive advantage in customer involvement, service and superior knowledge of customer motivations and behaviour. Their customers, rather than their technology and production, drive effective businesses. Moving from efficiency to effectiveness represents a big shift in business emphasis, and is one of the drivers behind the surge of attention and investment in CRM.

Long-term forces

Much has been written about the emerging social and economic environment that is enabling this shift in business focus. For the purposes of introducing CRM and current best practice in the area, we wish to concentrate on the three factors we believe are most responsible for creating customer-driven businesses. These are:

1. the evolution of the relationship marketing concept;
2. the impact of information technology;
3. changing customer behaviour and motivation.

Evolution of relationship marketing

Since the early 1990s, academics and consultants have promoted the idea that marketing practice should focus upon identifying and serving the organization's best customers and prospective customers. This may sound highly intuitive, but ten years ago it represented a radical departure from the tradition of marketers identifying and dominating the most attractive product markets. Traditional marketing focuses on resegmenting markets to create and dominate defensible product positions. Product portfolio tools, such as the Boston Consulting Group Matrix, helped firms balance investments across product ranges to maximize profit and long-term growth. Firms allocated scarce resources against competing product investments to ensure that there was a balance of cash generated and attractive investments. In most industries, each product investment was considered on its own merits in accordance with financial analysis tools that tie investment decisions to shareholder value. Firms were free to pick and choose in which market segments they wished to compete on the basis of market and financial attractiveness.

Proponents of relationship marketing challenged the customer and economic logic behind product portfolio management. They argue that:

1. Differences in customer profitability are at least as important as differences in product/market profitability to shareholder value.
2. Customer value is created by customers effectively using goods and services as individuals, as much as by the intrinsic qualities of the goods and services themselves.

In other words, they support the effectiveness versus efficiency argument.

Reicheld's work at Bain Consulting led him to publish findings from research and practice suggesting that differences in the performance of insurance brokers were better explained by examining customer loyalty and retention than by market share, unit cost and scale (Reichheld 1996). He argued that customers become increasingly profitable over time because:

1. customer acquisition costs spread over a larger turnover;
2. customer spending tends to accelerate over time;
3. operating costs fall as customers know the firm's products, services and policies better;
4. satisfied customers make referrals; and

5. loyal customers are less price sensitive, allowing the firm to maintain if not improve its margin.

Garth Hallberg reminds us in the title of his book that *All Consumers are Not Created Equal* (Hallberg 1995). He presents research, which shows that, in most industries, a minority of customers (10–15 per cent) generate the majority of profits. So not only does customers' profitability increase over time, but some customers are potentially far more profitable than others. Peppers and Rogers popularized the expression 'one to one', by suggesting that when considering the differences between customers' profitability and needs, companies must 'differentiate customers, not just products' (Peppers and Rogers 1994). Attracting and retaining the right customer will have a dramatic impact on the business.

Aside from the commercial logic of becoming customer centric, organizations that move beyond short-term, transactional customer relationships can address customers' deeper and broader needs. If customers teach a firm about their motivations and behaviours and the firm responds to this knowledge, the firm can make the customer more effective at the task at hand whilst differentiating and extending its own offer. Over time, this positive cycle of learning and doing 'locks in' loyalty and allows the firm to capture more of the economic value in its value chain. Good products are no longer sufficient to compete. Today, firms must create customized solutions to customers' more profound problems. Reprising the effectiveness argument, companies today must create effective solutions to individual customers' problems, not simply improve their efficiency.

Impact of information technology

The theory of relationship marketing is intuitively appealing, but its widespread implementation has been facilitated by new information technology that permits organizations to identify and manage large numbers of individual customers. New technologies have enabled firms to implement CRM by:

- providing greater individual customer insight;
- allowing firms to effectively respond to individual requirements; and
- integrating the business processes of the firm around individual customers.

It gets cheaper and cheaper for firms to store large quantities of customer information in a format that they can access for customer service and analysis. The cost of data storing and processing continues to fall, while advances in data warehousing and mining software improve a firm's ability to learn from customer data. Firms are creating integrated 'virtual front offices' where all customer-facing staff can access these data so that individual customers are treated in a manner consistent with their individual needs and the firm's customer objectives.

Thomas Cook, the travel agent, was quick to recognize the importance of this facility for customers who had their traveller's cheques stolen abroad.

EXAMPLE

When dealing with a frantic customer calling collect from Azerbaijan to report his passport and travellers cheques stolen, the last thing any travel company worth its salt would want to do would be to put him on hold while the service agent fumbles around trying to extract his details from various databases. The ability to react swiftly in any such situation was at the forefront of Thomas Cook's thinking when it prepared to launch its Global Services Division in 1998. Designed to be a virtual worldwide call centre for the traveller, Global Services' core business is the provision of a complete travel assistance service covering everything from emergency, legal and medical services to hotel bookings and ticket replacement. Given the scope of its vision, Thomas Cook realized that it would need a system which would enable it to handle a high volume of customer contact, not only 24 hours a day, 365 days a year, but in 28 different languages.

From a user perspective, the key advantage of the Global Services which Thomas Cook implemented is that the system controls the call. As soon as the call is picked up, a service agent can identify the customer, and pinpoint where he is and what language he speaks. A map appears on the screen showing where the caller is so they can be directed to the nearest service point. The level of data held on the system includes all previous data on and any correspondence with each customer, enabling Thomas Cook to build an increasingly complex profile of each individual and to offer a more personalized service. For example, if a customer had previously booked a certain hotel in a city and was revisiting it, the service agent could offer to book that same hotel using the customer's preferred credit card.

This enhanced customer insight is only valuable where firms can effectively respond to what they have learnt. A history of mass production and marketing has created structures, cultures and business systems that are not designed to configure products and services according to individual customers' needs. However, modern planning, logistics and manufacturing software and processes enable companies to customize goods and services cost effectively across large numbers of customers. This is often called 'mass-customization'. Because of their cost and complexity, these systems were once the exclusive domain of large companies. But solution providers are now developing lower cost versions for small- and medium-sized businesses, and on a variable, rather than fixed, cost basis. These solutions integrate firms with their suppliers, further increasing the firm's ability to deliver against its promise to individual customers. This integration extends from the individual firm through to its core suppliers, offering whole industries a greater ability to meet individual customer needs. These integrated value chains allow customers to collaborate with advisers, specify products, services or solutions and permit rapid, cost-effective fulfilment through complex alliances of suppliers and logistics firms. Information-rich value chains will be sensitive to individual customer changes and provide real-time information on the progress of individual orders, aggregate demand, forward demand, costs and billing information. The impact of these technologies is to permit businesses, and their suppliers, to 'build to order' cost effectively once the customer and the firm have agreed what is needed.

Changing customer behaviour and motivation

We have reviewed, albeit briefly, how firms increasingly understand the economics of relationship marketing and how technology permits its implementation. The final long-term factor promoting the development of customer-centric businesses is changing customer behaviour and motivation.

Today's customers have growing expectations of suppliers, in terms of depth of advice, product and service quality, price transparency, warranty and post-sales service. We believe that consumers and business customers alike expect a 'joined-up-service' where firms' marketing, sales and service delivers against their expectations and the firm's promise. 'It is not my department' is a less and less acceptable means of handling customer inquiries. As businesses integrate around individual customers, these expectations will grow stronger.

There are many instances of customers wishing to influence a firm's internal management processes. Customers are being conditioned to expect that they are 'in charge' of the customer–supplier relationship through advertising, media and management reports. This leads to the firm's internal processes being held up to public scrutiny. Conditions of workers in factories making shoes and jeans for famous brands have been publicly discussed, as have many individual firm's environmental policies. We believe that this expectation of customer sovereignty is creating a new set of customer behaviours and motivations around dealing with companies which, they feel, share the same values across issues that matter to them.

More demanding customers are also becoming more competent purchasers. Customers demand a say in what they are being offered and expect to be dealing with firms that listen and respond. In business marketing, this trend has been evident for many years. Important customers make an early input to suppliers' product development processes because the costs of misjudging customer needs are too high for both customers and suppliers. Even consumers are beginning to insist on knowing more about the products they consume and are contributing to the product development process. Online marketing and communication may help facilitate this development and 'train' consumers to interact directly with the manufacturers of goods and services they consume. We predict that consumers will be increasingly unwilling to accept being the 'object' of companies' marketing processes, and that companies will need to get better at listening, learning and responding to individuals – the basic tenets of CRM as we have defined it.

Massive investment with questionable return

We have identified the long-term trends among companies, their customers and in technology that are acting as a catalyst for the customer-centric view of business. Business leaders have been sensitive to these trends and are making substantial investments in changing their organizations to allow them to flourish in the new environment.

Forrester Research (Chatham et al. 2001) has produced detailed estimates, based upon companies' experiences and a definition of CRM consistent with the one used in this book, of the investments large firms will need to make when implementing CRM programmes. Using American accounting conventions, Forrester suggests that large firms (i.e. Global 3500 firms) should expect to spend between $60 million (retailers) and $130 million (banks) over three years on the requisite CRM applications, data maintenance and operations. Manufacturing companies will come in at around $75 million.

It is the size of investment companies need to make to move from a product to a customer focus that is fuelling the growth of the CRM IT services market. The European Centre for Customer Strategies (2001) quotes an estimate from Accenture that the global CRM market (software, hardware, training and services) will top $700 billion by 2006. The ECCS also estimates that the European CRM market will top $34 billion by 2004.

At the time of writing this book, it would appear that the downturn in technology spending early in 2001 has not significantly affected CRM. The more customers access services through proliferating media and devices, the more firms seem willing to invest in technologies that will help them integrate this stream of contacts around individual customers, analyse the data and communicate back to customers through an increasingly complex web of inter-related media and channels.

However, despite the level of investment in technology, processes and people to improve customer relationships, there is growing concern that many, if not most, firms fail to realize or measure a sufficient return on these investments. Given the level of investment and sensitivity of the programmes, it is hard to find a definitive and authoritative view on the actual return which CRM programmes are delivering. Clearly, if financial returns were proving hard to measure and achieve, that would make unwelcome news for a massive industry. Nevertheless, from our regular reviews of consulting reports and web sites, the authors find a pattern emerging whereby less than one third of CRM programmes deliver the intended return. Below are some examples of the data from which we draw this conclusion:

- *Internetweek online* reports research results from the renowned CRM consulting firm AMR that only 12 per cent of companies that have implemented CRM software say it has exceeded their expectations (Kemp 2001).
- Insight Technology Group (ITG) reported on the web from a survey of 1000 sales force reengineering projects that only 21 per cent met or exceeded expectations. Of the 38 per cent that met none or only some expectations, two thirds plan major rewrites to the systems and one third will shelve their current systems.
- The OTR group surveyed 1500 companies in six European Union countries and found that only 27 per cent of those which had implemented a data warehouse were able to identify a quantifiable financial benefit.
- KPMG research from 1997 entitled 'The Hidden Advantage' revealed that only 16 per cent of UK companies measure the ROI of data warehouse investment, 30 per cent do not use it regularly once it is built and 87 per cent fail to attribute value to the information generated.

Barriers to success

We should not be surprised that firms embracing new management thinking through large-scale change programmes find that immediate returns fall below expectations. Many of the benefits of change programmes take longer to realize than was initially predicted and entail more fundamental organizational and cultural change than was planned. In this sense, CRM is similar to other change programmes that have preceded it. This section looks at barriers to success across each of the three letters in the CRM acronym – customer, relationship and management:

- lack of a sufficiently robust customer strategy;
- relationships that are managed in the interests of the firm and not the customer;
- management that lacks sufficient ambition and information for the programme to succeed.

Lack of customer strategy

At the heart of any CRM programme must lie a profound understanding of how customers differ and the creation of a unique and relevant value proposition to address and exploit these differences. However, unfortunately, many organizations fail to get these two basic building blocks right.

Firms seem to spend more time trying to understand customers' different profitability (or potential profitability) than their needs and purchasing styles. We believe that many CRM customer propositions, such as creating a one-stop shop, providing a total solution, offering end-to-end service, and disintermediation, reflect a firm's desire to sell more rather than a customer's desire to buy more. The business case for CRM often begins with the assumptions about cross-selling and up-selling, that the business needs to justify an investment, rather than from a profound understanding of customers. In some industries, this homogenizes the CRM strategies of major competitors. Customer strategies move in the same direction, with firms making similar claims to the others and using similar technologies to implement their strategic choices. This is unlikely to lead to the kind of differentiated proposition necessary to generate a strong return on investment. Naive market research may point to customers' desire to buy the 'total end-to-end solution from a one-stop shop', but a more sophisticated analysis of actual behaviour and purchasing styles may suggest otherwise.

CRM-based value propositions require firms to have exceptional insight into how their customers use their goods and services, derived from customer behaviour models as well as data. But firms seem to have more data about their customers than insight. The KPMG report into the UK experience of data warehousing, mentioned above, suggests that IT and Marketing do not fully leverage each other's skills to extract value from the investment, and that Marketing lacks some of the technical and modelling skills needed to generate valuable customer insight from data warehouses.

Relationships, but in whose interest?

At the heart of the problem with CRM implementation lies the view that customer relationships can be managed, and managed by one partner in the relationship.

Purveyors of new technology encourage managers to think that they can predict and manipulate customer behaviour for their own benefit. For example, data mining allows firms to analyse a limited set of customer behaviours and create procedures and rules among customer-facing staff in their new integrated front offices that encourage 'desirable' behaviour. Where these procedures and rules are blatantly in the interests of the firm rather than the consumer, they risk alienating both customers and the front line staff that serve them.

Anecdotal evidence from industry suggests that consumers are increasingly reluctant to provide firms with the extensive information that they desire for their CRM systems. Consumers are ultimately rational and will understand both the value of their data and the likely benefit they will get from sharing it.

Advances in data management, data mining, consumer profiling, content management systems and online personalization require highly sophisticated, rule-based systems that risk marginalizing both the customer and the firm's customer-facing employees. For example, call centre employees are driven to reduce the average time spent with customers in an effort to increase productivity. It is obvious that this can frustrate both customers and the people employed to service them. Another example of 'rules before customers' can be found in a newspaper article about Marks & Spencer's direct mail campaign to husbands of 'husband and wife' cardholders, suggesting lingerie as a gift and 'helpfully' providing the wives' sizes. The article suggested that many cardholders felt this to be too intrusive and, in a number of instances, the sizes were wrong: women often buy underwear for other women.

Intuitively, using customer data in this fashion does not sound like the basis of a trusting customer–retailer relationship. UK journalist Alan Mitchell likens the modern CRM marketer to a stalker who 'gathers ever more information about his target and tries to get close entirely for his own purposes, regardless of the feelings and wishes of the person he is targeting' (Mitchell 2001).

For customers to enter into a relationship with firms, and provide them with invaluable, non-public, data about their needs and motivations, there must be some perceived value for the customer. Firms need a differentiated customer strategy, grounded in the different needs, behaviours and motivations of different customers, to persuade customers to part with this information. Firms need to understand the potential value they can create for customers, as well as for themselves, in order to create powerful relationships with customers.

Management lacks the required vision and ambition

The success of large change programmes, such as moving from a product- to customer-focus, depends on management. Early published research on CRM effectiveness suggested that firms are not embracing a wide, customer-centric vision and pushing changes throughout the organization (Ryals and Payne 2001). Despite the tremendous financial investment in CRM programmes illustrated earlier in this chapter, Hewson Consulting found that only 18 per cent of firms surveyed met its criteria for implementing CRM (European Centre for Customer Strategies 2001). Recently, Bain Consulting reported that as many as one-fifth of CRM investments have actually destroyed customer relationships. You can, of course, challenge the definition of CRM, but the conclusions of much research generally do suggest that CRM change programmes often lack the scope and depth needed to succeed.

A major study by Computer Sciences Corporation Index (1994) found a correlation between the level of ambition and the success of reengineering change programmes. CSC's research found that reengineering programmes with 'breakthrough' ambitions were more likely to succeed than those with more modest objectives. It would appear that modest ambitions provide insufficient incentive to management to make the necessary changes in organization, processes, technology, training and reward systems that change requires. If CRM is managed as a separate campaign initiative, the firm is unlikely to become truly customer-centric – which explains Gartner's conclusion that few companies have implemented 'real' CRM.

The fact that so few companies set themselves high aims for CRM may be explained by the challenges of creating a business case: companies need to justify what is a major investment in CRM by identifying 'hard' business benefits in a short time frame. The intuitively obvious response is to promise specific achievements in cross-selling, up-selling and reduced service costs. However, 'real' CRM involves ongoing learning, where the customer receives incentives to teach firms what they want to know by the firm's continual response to the information provided. Cross-selling and up-selling may be good outcomes of effective customer relationships, but they are perhaps not the right objectives: at the point of creating a business case, companies risk 'objectifying' the customer, so hindering the chances of a mutually beneficial relationship.

The problem of insufficient ambition is compounded by the lack of any generally accepted measures of customer value. Value risks becoming an overused word in management circles: firms should create more customer value, but measuring it is problematic. Most of the published management literature focuses on measuring customer behaviour and the value of that behaviour to the firm. For example, the lifetime value of the customer, segment profitability, campaign profitability, consumer response rates and repurchase rates illustrate this. But the value of CRM programmes to the customer is merely assumed: people think that customers want a one-stop shop, a total solution and targeted offers, but there is scant evidence to either support or measure these assumptions. Certainly, high-profile dot.com failures should cause marketers to re-examine their assumptions about the components of customer value. A CRM programme geared towards learning, as much as selling, should help firms measure better what customers value.

However, as well as being ambitious and having the right measurement systems in place, to be successful CRM implementations need to work across all points of customer contact. Creating a consistent experience for each customer has long been a mantra for marketers. In the 1990s, consumer services marketers began focusing on customers' 'moments of truth', managing what they communicate to the customer through each experience or touchpoint the customer has with the organization. The challenge of empowering every employee to be able to create a moment of truth for a customer at any given point of contact, has compounded with the explosion of new media.

The moments of truth must now extend to the experiences created through call centres, internet sites (accessed via PCs and mobile phones), iTV and PDAs. Internet-based media also allow customers to direct their experiences, their 'moments of truth', and organizations must strike an appropriate balance between controlling the experience for the customer and the customer managing their experiences for themselves. The opportunity to integrate the business across media and across channels represents a major management challenge for most firms in terms of cost, complexity and change to their business practices. Many of the dot.com start-ups launched their businesses with such integration already in place. But few traditional businesses with substantial investment in existing media have developed a truly integrated approach to managing customers' moments of truth. As we write, this level of integration is leading-edge management and technology practice.

Ryals and Payne (2001) identified further management issues which inhibit successful implementation of CRM in financial services companies. They found that many financial services firms had skill shortages, particularly in technology, and inadequate funding which, inevitably, curtailed their ambitions. Financial services companies were not convinced of the value of investing to create an integrated view of the customer through data warehousing. Additionally, as they came to appreciate the scope of the change effort, firms realized that their initial budget provisions were inadequate. Business unit managers were not always willing to cooperate, a failing which compromises one of the fundamental tenets of CRM – the entire firm must integrate its efforts around customers' needs. Finally, the authors found that many organizations lacked the measurement and reward systems needed to support the change from product- to customer-focus.

Conclusions

We have defined CRM as a far-reaching management process and demonstrated that most large businesses are making very significant investments to implement these relationship marketing practices. There are sustainable long-term customer, business and technical trends spurring these investments forward, and we predict that truly customer-centric organizations will continue to develop into the foreseeable future. However, early returns on investment are elusive for many firms, and more programmes are likely to fail to achieve their targeted returns than those which succeed.

There is perhaps no one company that has 'done it all', whose model we can slavishly follow. The authors believe that there probably is no 'one right way' in CRM, as relationships are so different and heavily dependent on individual contexts. Each firm will need to find its own right way, depending on the customers it wishes to serve, its competencies and the environment in which it operates.

In the next chapter, we identify five processes that we suggest managers focus on to maximize the potential of their CRM initiatives. These processes – strategy development, value creation, channel and media integration, information management and performance assessment – are explored individually in subsequent chapters through best practice case histories.

References

Callinan, P., Weisman, D. and Girard, M. (2001) CRM finds repeat customers in the global 3500. In *Business Technogaphics Brief,* Forrester Research Inc.

Chatham, R., Weisman, D., Orlov, V., Nakashimaru, V. and Howard, F. F. (2001) *CRM: At What Cost?* Cambridge, MA: Forrester Research Inc.

Computer Science Corporation Index (1994) CSC Index: State of Reengineering Report. Boston, MA.

Drucker, P. F. (1954) *The Practice of Management.* New York: Harper & Row.

European Centre for Customer Strategies (2001) Waiting for the customer management revolution (www.eccs.uk.com/suppliers/newsanalysis/april2001_5.asp).

Hallberg, G. (1995) *All Consumers are Not Created Equal.* John Wiley & Sons.

Kemp, T. (2001) CRM stumbles amid usability shortcomings. Available at: http://www.internetweek.com/newslead01/lead040601.htm.

Mitchell, A. (2001) *Right Side Up.* London: Harper-Collins.

Peppers, D. and Rogers, M. (1994) *The One-to-One Future.* Piatkus, London.

Reichheld, F. F. (1996) *The Loyalty Effect.* Harvard Business School Press, Boston, MA.

Ryals, L. and Payne, A. (2001) Customer management relationship in financial services: towards information-enabled relationship marketing. *Journal of Strategic Marketing*, 9, 3–27.

Ryals, L., Knox, S. D. and Maklan, S. (2000) Customer Relationship Management: the business case for CRM. *Financial Times,* London: Prentice-Hall.

Chapter **2**

A strategic framework for CRM

As we pointed out in Chapter 1, customer relationship management – or CRM – is at the top of most corporate agendas. The huge surge of interest in the concept derives from its potential to harness a raft of new technologies to implement relationship marketing cheaply and effectively. As everyone knows, loyal customers are more profitable, and selling more to existing customers has become the Holy Grail of marketing. The availability of data mining tools and data warehouses, to say nothing of the huge opportunities afforded by the internet, offer unprecedented potential to gather and deploy information on customers that will allow companies to tailor products and services to them.

According to Gartner Group, the worldwide CRM services market was worth $19.9 billion by the end of 2000. Gartner predicts the market will grow at over 26 per cent a year for the next four years, and will be worth $64.3 billion by 2005.

Yet, as we mentioned in Chapter 1, despite the massive investment in CRM, many applications of the technique have failed to live up to its promise. Customer satisfaction is falling, not rising, and the few companies which measure the return on their investment, are disappointed by the results. There are a number of reasons for this, but the overriding problem is that, ironically, many companies have lost sight of the customer in their efforts to implement CRM. Lots of their offerings and approaches are supply-side, product-driven, rather than customer-led. They view CRM as a technology issue, which it isn't.

Technology can certainly help companies to create satisfied and loyal customers, but it is by no means essential to successful customer relationship management. People and processes, however, are essential, and companies espousing CRM have largely ignored these two critical elements.

A further reason why most companies' efforts to implement CRM fail is the widespread confusion about what CRM actually is. This is largely due to the misguided emphasis on the technology aspects, and the close association with specific tools being sold by IT vendors and integrators – normally the big implementation consultancies. As a result, many organizations are adopting CRM on a fragmented basis.

However, CRM is not a product; it is a discipline, a framework, an integrated approach to managing relationships with customers, which requires continuous improvement. It is a strategy, not a tactic, and in most cases involves changing the focus and culture of the organization from a product- to a customer-orientation.

This is a lesson learnt by Equitable Life Assurance Society.

EXAMPLE

Equitable Life Assurance Society was founded in 1762, and has long been at pains to improve services to its customers, especially in the area of new technology. Not long ago it established a 'Client Service Centre' at its Aylesbury head office.

However, as part of its ongoing commitment to improve customer service, Equitable Life undertook a study which concluded that its approach to service was 'grey' and lacked emotional connection with customers. Rules prevailed and there was a tendency towards a 'can't do' mentality. The overriding ethos was to 'get the job done' rather than to 'please the customer'.

While offering customers the opportunity to deal with Equitable Life through its website potentially enhanced its efficiency, the technology actually reinforced the sense of remoteness that customers felt.

The management team realized that they needed to rethink their approach to customer service, and implemented a programme to improve the way staff in the Centre relate to customers, whether by telephone or in writing, in order to deliver 'incredible customer service'.

Among the improvements made were:

- responding to written customer requests by telephone whenever possible;
- giving customer work priority;
- injecting emotional warmth into letters;
- reorienting customer satisfaction measures;

- changing reward systems;
- improving management style.

If organizations are to implement CRM effectively, and realize its considerable potential benefits, they need to understand clearly what it is, how it fits with relationship marketing and customer management, and how it behaves within the organization's structure and culture.

We define CRM as:

'a strategic approach designed to improve shareholder value through developing appropriate relationships with key customers and customer segments. CRM unites the potential of IT and relationship marketing strategies to deliver profitable, long-term relationships.'

Importantly, CRM provides enhanced opportunities to use data and information to both understand customers and implement relationship marketing strategies better. This requires a cross-functional integration of people, operations and marketing capabilities that is enabled through information, technology and applications.

Good CRM practice involves all business functions in an enterprise, and must be led from the top. The visible backing of the board is as important as the full commitment of the workforce and supply chain partners. The notion that competitive advantage stems from creating value for the customer and the company is key to the success of CRM. Responsibility for delivering that value must be shared across functions and hierarchies. This pervasive and inclusive cross-functional approach to CRM, as shown in Figure 2.1, drives and delivers a customer orientation.

Successful CRM is not achieved overnight. Nor is it easy. It invariably involves a root and branch reappraisal and reorientation of the company's culture and focus.

In this book we aim to demystify CRM by setting out a simple strategic framework, as illustrated in the diagram in Figure 2.2, which represents the key drivers of CRM, and then illustrating current practices across the five processes: strategy development; value creation; channel and media integration; information management; and performance assessment. While we outline the framework, developed by Professor Adrian Payne, here, subsequent chapters examine each of these processes more closely, by reference to case studies of organizations that are implementing them. Companies implementing the framework in a logical, coherent and strategic fashion can unlock the potential of CRM by delivering customer, employee and shareholder value.

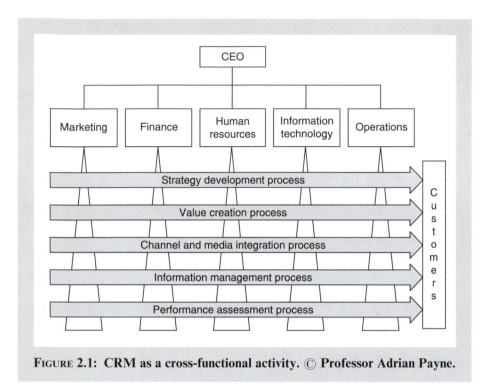

FIGURE 2.1: CRM as a cross-functional activity. © Professor Adrian Payne.

The framework (page 21) is based on the premise that all five processes are critical to the business and need to be closely integrated with each other. If you consider the framework as a progression through each of the processes, approaching them from left to right, then you start by reviewing your organization's strategic context and conclude with improving its shareholder value. However, the process is not linear, but an iterative feedback-driven progression aimed at continually enhancing the benefits of CRM.

We consider each process, which seeks to answer some key questions, in turn.

- Process 1: Strategy development
  Where are we and what do we want to achieve?
  Who are the customers that we want and how should we segment them?

- Process 2: Value creation
  How should we deliver value to our customers?
  How should we maximize the lifetime value of the customers we want?

- Process 3: Channel and media integration
  What are the best ways for us to get to customers and for customers to get to us?

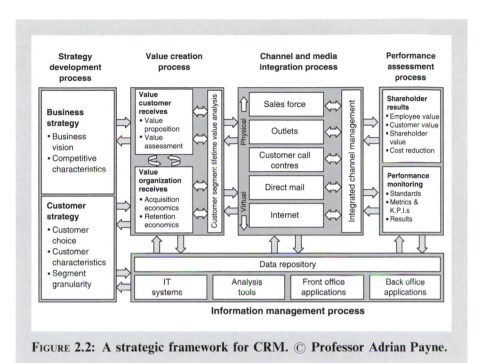

FIGURE 2.2: A strategic framework for CRM. © Professor Adrian Payne.

What does an outstanding customer experience, deliverable at an affordable cost, look like?

- Process 4: Information management
  How should we organize information on customers?
  How can we replicate the mind of the customer?

- Process 5: Performance assessment
  How can we create increased profits and shareholder value?
  How should we set standards, develop metrics, measure our results and improve our performance?

PROCESS 1

Strategy development

Where are we and what do we want to achieve?
Who are the customers that we want and how should we segment them?

The current high profile CRM enjoys is leading some to adopt a quick technology fix. As a result they may invest in the wrong technology or ignore the underlying critical business issues. Before thinking about a technology solution, managers should first consider CRM in the context of their organization's business and customer strategy.

Business strategy

The CRM strategy must be aligned with and support the overall business strategy and take into account the competitive environment. Managers should start by clearly defining the core business and what they would like it to be in the future. This will involve reviewing a number of specific business strategy issues, including: the stage the industry has evolved to; the competition; the company's profile, strategic intent and business scope; media and distribution channels; and, finally, an appropriate technology platform.

This review will provide a realistic base on which to build a CRM strategy. Companies need to understand their own competencies before they can translate them into value for the customer. Everyone within the organization must be clear about its overall purpose and intent, particularly if it is moving from a product- to a customer-orientation, so that they can all pull in the same strategic direction.

Organizations also have to understand the competitive environment in which they operate, and be alert to changes that might signal opportunity or disaster. Additionally, a greater understanding of the external environment helps managers appreciate the opportunities and threats facing their customers.

Customer strategy

The other half of the strategic equation involves deciding which customers to focus on. That involves considering the nature and status of an organization's customer strategy, segmentation, customer service, customer relationships, customers' attitudes and purchasing behaviours, and the value of the customer base.

Organizations have to determine the amount and kind of customer information they need, and how closely and through what channels and media they should interact with customers – today and tomorrow. While satisfying customers' existing needs is paramount, they must also strive to pre-empt their future, often unexpressed, needs.

EXAMPLE

AT & T Universal Card regularly reviews its customers' attitudes and current and future needs through focus groups, one-to-one interviews and customer surveys. It even has a director of customer listening who communicates customers' views to senior management. Some issues are dealt with daily; others are reviewed at the end of the month and then acted on (Ryals et al. 2000).

A key principle of CRM is that customers are different and that relationships with them therefore have to be managed differently. The aim of CRM is to build strategies that refine and increase the value of relationships, and that involves careful segmentation.

Organizations can segment their customer base on a macro, micro or one-to-one level, depending on a number of factors, including their existing and potential profitability, and their current and likely future use of channels and media – not least the internet.

Peppers and Rogers (1993) have highlighted the potential to shift from a mass market to a one-to-one marketing environment by switching from a product- to a customer-focus. What they mean by one-to-one marketing is adjusting the marketing approach to reflect the existing and potential profitability of different customer groups.

EXAMPLE

Australia's St George's Bank raised its mortgage conversion rate from 33 to 51 per cent by tailoring its services to match each customer's level of purchasing sophistication. Using a data warehouse it categorized prospects as Novices, Enthusiasts, Judicious Buyers, Investors and the Indifferent, and the bank staff personalized the way they dealt with these customer groups accordingly. Both company profit and customer service increased (Peppard 2000).

Electronic commerce and the internet allow much tighter segmentation than other media have traditionally afforded. The internet also facilitates closer, cheaper, more immediate, and more interactive relationships with customers. But it is important to remember that the internet is just another medium.

It is possible to move to a one-to-one or one-to-few approach quickly, particularly in an e-commerce environment, where communications can be more easily tailored to individuals. However, in more traditional businesses more macro forms of segmentation will be more relevant.

Adopting the right level of segmentation is a crucial step towards creating value.

PROCESS 2

Value creation

How should we deliver value to our customers?
How should we maximize the lifetime value of the customers we want?

Creating customer value is a major source of competitive advantage and consists of three key elements:

- the value the customer receives;
- the value the company receives from its customers;
- maximizing the life-time value of desirable customer segments.

However, too many companies focus on the second element at the expense of the other two, which is counter-productive.

The value the customer receives

The value the customer receives derives from the total experience they have with both the core product and the product surround. In fact, customers are not buying goods or services, but specific benefits, which solve problems. They value the offer according to their perception of its ability to solve their problem.

EXAMPLE

With a bit of ingenuity, customization can turn a product back into an experience, as an exercise at Levi-Strauss demonstrated. Some stores offered customers the chance to be measured by a body scanner and have jeans cut especially for them. The jeans cost 30–40 per cent more to produce than a standard pair, but the returns were higher. Moreover, Levi's learned from these customers: for example, it noticed that those who designed their own jeans wanted them slung low on the hips months before the average customer stopped buying high-rise jeans. (*Economist* 2000).

Developing a value proposition – defining target customers, the benefits offered to those customers and the price charged relative to the competition – is useful for reviewing the existing offer to customers and identifying how to improve it (Bower and Garda 1985). The value proposition then needs to be assessed to see if it will enhance the customer experience.

The value the organization receives

Fundamental to understanding the value the organization receives is understanding the economics of customer acquisition and retention.

Customer acquisition and its economics

The importance of customer acquisition varies considerably according to a company's specific situation. For example, a new internet entrant will primarily be concerned with acquiring customers, whereas an established manufacturing company operating in a mature market will be more concerned with retaining customers.

The starting point is to determine how much it costs to acquire customers in different segments and micro-segments through the organization's existing channels and media. An organization also needs to consider the expected profitability of the average customer in that segment and the overall profit potential of the segment.

The next step is to consider how acquisition costs may vary across different channels and media. For instance, web sites have enabled companies to acquire customers at a fraction of the cost of other more traditional channels.

Once a company understands how acquisition costs vary by segment, channel and media levels, it can start to look at how to acquire different, and more attractive, customers. Direct mail, advertising and websites have their place, but getting happy, existing customers to act as advocates can be a major and cheap source of new customers. For example, approximately one-third of all HSBC's First Direct customers join the bank as a direct result of recommendation from existing customers.

Customer retention and its economics

It is generally acknowledged that it costs around five times more to win a new customer than it does to keep an existing one. Yet many companies still direct their marketing activity towards acquiring new customers, rather than keeping existing ones.

In the early 1990s, Fred Reichheld, a partner at consulting firm Bain & Co, and Earl Sasser, a professor at Harvard Business School (Reichheld and Sasser 1990), demonstrated that even a small increase in customer retention produced a dramatic and positive effect on profitability. Increasing the customer retention rate from, say, 85 per cent to 90 per cent represented a net present value profit increase from 35 per cent to 95 per cent among the businesses they examined.

Despite these findings, managers don't appear to have changed their approach Research by Payne and Frow (1999) among marketers in 225 UK organizations in mainly mature industries, found that 41 per cent of the typical marketing budget was spent on acquiring customers and only 23 per cent on retaining them.

Companies shouldn't necessarily seek to retain all their customers, of course. Some may cost too much to service. To calculate a customer's real value you should look at the projected profit over the life of the account. The key metric used here is customer lifetime value (CLV), which is defined as the net present value of the future profit flow over a customer's lifetime. But few organizations even understand their existing acquisition and retention economics.

Future profit potential may be significantly enhanced through creatively exploiting alternative channel structures.

PROCESS 3

Channel and media integration

What are the best ways for us to get to customers and for customers to get to us?
What does the perfect customer experience, deliverable at an affordable cost, look like?

Creating an attractive value proposition is not simply a matter of designing a product or service. It also involves the way customers get hold of that product or service, the way it is presented to them, and the support they receive once they have bought it.

Developing both traditional and new distribution channels and media is a priority for companies that are seeking to meet, or even exceed, the expectations of ever more demanding customers. But many companies fail to provide consistently high standards of service across these different channels and media. The quality of a company's service is only as good as the weakest link in its multi-channel, multi-media service mix, and one bad experience at any of these transaction points could scupper the whole relationship. (See Chapter 5, p. 143 for a definition of channel and media).

The multi-channel and multi-media integration process involves:

- choosing the most appropriate combination of channels and media through which to interact with customers;
- ensuring customers experience positive interactions within those media and channels;
- where customers interact with more than one channel or medium, creating a single unified view of the customer experience.

Selecting the best market access involves considering a number of issues, which fall under the two broad headings of channel and media suitability, and channel and media structure.

Channel and media suitability

When developing channel and media strategies, organizations must take into account the benefits the end-consumer seeks at the different stages of the buying process, from their initial enquiry through to owning and using the product or service.

Among the benefits the customer might value, are, for example, being able to obtain information quickly, access the channel or medium easily, or communicate with the supplier effectively. Customers may also wish to physically inspect the product before buying it, have the product customized, and get service and support after they've bought it.

By identifying which benefits are most important for which customer segment, companies can assess which channels and media would deliver them for the lowest cost.

Channel and media structure

Over the past decade, many industries have dismantled and reconfigured their traditional channel and media structures in response to new technologies that have opened up new paths to market. Managers responsible for channel and media strategy need to understand both the nature of their industry distribution structure now and how it is likely to alter in the future.

Technology, particularly the internet, has revolutionized both channel and media strategies. But while it has afforded companies a raft of new media through which to interact with their customers, the internet has transformed channel strategy through two major structural changes:

- *Disintermediation*, where changes in the current business model or advances in technology mean that a company no longer needs to use intermediaries to create value for end-consumers. Call centre technology, for example, allows companies such as Direct Line insurance to create value for customers by dealing with them directly. Expensive broker networks are cut out, premiums are lower, the company understands its customers better and can create superior products and services as a result.
- *Reintermediation*, where changes in the current business model or advances in technology result in new types of intermediary that can create more value than was possible in the previous channel structure. For example, web-enabled information agents, or infomediaries, research alternatives for customers looking to make a purchase. Autobytel, a web-based car sales intermediary, provides information about car prices and availability, and even facilitates the purchase.

When considering its channel strategy, an organization needs to consider two key factors:

- Different channels offer different competencies and abilities. For example, independent financial advisers may be better at helping clients with complex financial planning than direct channels, whereas direct channels may be faster and cheaper.
- Different customers have different purchasing styles. Some prefer dealing with travel agents, for example, while others prefer dealing with the travel company direct – whether by internet, call centre or some other medium.

When it comes to media, companies have five main options:

- sales force and personal representation;
- outlets (including retail branches and kiosks);
- customer call centres;
- direct mail; and
- internet

Multi-channel and multi-media integration

Because customers like to buy in different ways, most businesses will benefit from a strategy based on the integration of multiple channels and media. For example, firms trading on the internet have found that exploiting other routes to market too, such as in-store and catalogue sales, boosts their sales significantly. Many consumers may browse the web, but prefer to buy through different media. The companies in the two examples below have recognized this.

> **EXAMPLE**
>
> A Massachusetts bank, which uses a lot of voice response to answer calls, is building a new call centre as well as developing the internet in recognition of the fact that some customers simply want to talk to someone. However, the more scarce the support staff become, and the longer telephone enquirers have to hang on, the easier it is to encourage customers to look up the answer to their problem online (*Economist* 2000).
>
> At the low-cost airline Go, customers can start the process of booking a flight online, but can request a call back at any point in the process. They can also choose when they would like the call back. However, Go gives a discount of £2 for all return trips booked over the internet.

Four key points to bear in mind when designing an integrated channel and media strategy are:

- Integrating channels and media should create value for the customer and remove barriers to doing business with the company.
- The channel and media strategy should reflect the cost of doing business and be cost effective.
- It should take advantage of the different capabilities characteristic of each.
- The chosen channels and media should contribute to a coherent brand experience for the customer.

Those involved in making the sale usually dominate discussions on channels and media. But for strategic CRM to work, the channels and media need to be considered in the context of the life cycle of the customer relationship, not just the specific sales activity. The customer relationship can be broken down into three main stages: acquisition, consolidation and enhancement. Within these typical stages, a myriad of interactions occur between the customer and the organization across different channels and media (Figure 2.3):

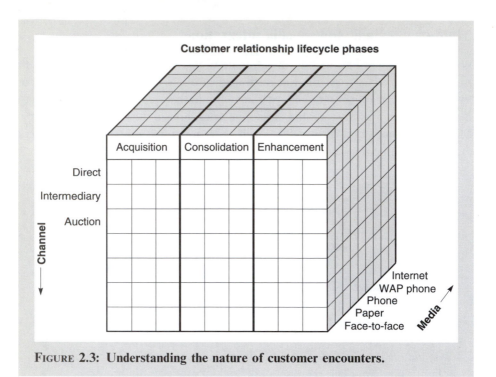

FIGURE 2.3: Understanding the nature of customer encounters.

PROCESS 4

Information management

How should we organize information on customers?
How can we replicate the mind of the customer?

The information management process is concerned with two key activities: collecting and collating customer information from all customer contact points; and using this information to construct complete and current customer profiles which can be used to enhance the quality of the customer experience. As companies grow and interact with more and more customers through increasingly diverse media and channels, having a systematic approach to organizing and employing information becomes critical.

Customer information can be spread across disparate functions and departments, so that interactions with the customer are based on scant knowledge of them, although they may have been with the organization for years. This creates two major problems for the company: the customer is treated impersonally, which may lead them to become dissatisfied and to leave; and there is no single unified view of the customer upon which to act and plan.

The information management process aims to replicate the mind of the customer. That means using information to enhance relationships rather than getting carried away with clever technology. In an effort to keep pace with escalating volumes of data, organizations tend to create more or bigger databases within functions or departments, leading to a wealth of disparate silos of customer information. The result is a fragmented and often unwieldy body of information upon which to base crucial management decisions. Elevating CRM from a specific application, such as a call centre, to a pan-company strategy requires integrating customer interactions across all communication channels, front- and back-office applications, and business functions. An organization then needs a specifically designed process to bring together and manage these data, computers, procedures and people. The key material elements of this information management process are: the data repository; IT systems; analytical processes; and front- and back-office systems.

Data repository

Collecting data about customers, or even generating management information from individual databases, is not enough to make an enterprise customer-focused, because it provides only a partial view of the customer. To understand and manage customers as complete and unique entities, you need a powerful corporate memory of customers – an integrated enterprise-wide data store which can provide the data analysis needed to inform strategic and tactical decision-making. The best approach is to have a data repository together with appropriate analytical tools, along with integration of information from different databases and departments in the organization.

The data repository collects, holds and integrates customer information, allowing the company to develop and manage customer relationships effectively. At its simplest, the data repository is made up of a number of individual databases and a data warehouse, as shown in Figure 2.4.

The data warehouse is a collection of related databases that have been brought together so that the maximum value can be extracted from them. An enterprise data model is then used to manage the conversion of data from databases to data warehouse to minimize data duplication and to resolve inconsistencies.

As well as connecting to internal systems, the data warehouse also often takes feeds from external sources, and is designed to support the kind of analysis

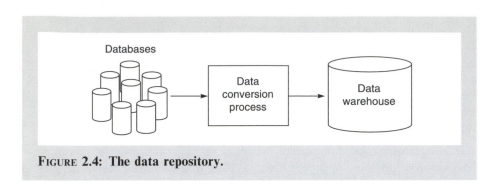

FIGURE 2.4: The data repository.

performed at customer management and strategic planning levels. Analytical tools such as data mining can be used to reveal patterns in customer data, such as buying habits, which form the basis of improved customer understanding and relationship building. End-users can access the data warehouse using online analytical processing (OLAP) tools.

The data warehouse is instrumental to the CRM task of identifying the organization's best customers, ways of retaining them and enhancing their value. It also helps to monitor customers and test and refine customer and product strategy – an increasingly valuable benefit in dynamic markets. In the world of e-business, in particular, where the rules of the game are still being written, effective data analysis is critical.

The retail giant House of Fraser has increased the sophistication of its sales measurement since it set up a data warehouse.

EXAMPLE

House of Fraser has 50 stores under its umbrella, including Army & Navy, Frasers, Kendals and Dickins & Jones. It decided to introduce new sales measurement software to overcome planning problems and improve its sales forecasting.

Historically, management information was held at store and department level, which made it difficult to put together accurate plans. The company knew it had to address the problem at the product level and on a seasonal basis. That meant it had to store product and transaction information to build a history.

It installed a data warehouse to capture sales information, and placed analysis software on top of it. Information about daily sales from different locations is fed into the system from the point of sale, allowing the company to establish which products are actually driving the business and which are not selling.

The new technology allows senior management to see immediately whether or not a promotion is working at the top level, and then drill down to departmental level. They can make comparisons with sales promotions from the previous year, quickly identify non-performing products, and put action plans in place. Rather than just knowing the total number of sales of particular brands at the end of the financial quarter, the company can now establish which brands, in which particular attribute – such as style, colour and size – sell in which stores.

IT systems

Because most organizations' IT structures develop over time, different, and often incompatible, computing systems are used in different parts of the business – particularly where there have been acquisitions. This existing technology needs to be integrated before databases can be integrated into a data warehouse and users across the company given access.

The driving consideration when developing an IT infrastructure should be how it will deliver the customer information an organization needs, now and in the future. An effective CRM strategy relies on integrated data from systems across the entire information management process; from the kind of highly structured data stored in databases to the rich and diverse forms of information shared via intranets and knowledge management technologies, such as multimedia.

Front- and back-office applications

Much of the emphasis on CRM has been directed at front-office applications, including sales force automation, call-centre management and product configuration tools. Front-office applications are used to increase revenues by improving customer retention and raising sales closure rates. Back-office applications support internal administration activities and supplier relationships, including human resources, procurement, warehouse management, logistics software and some financial processes.

However, the growth of enterprise-wide systems and e-business is blurring the distinction between front- and back-office. Goods tracking, for example, has traditionally been a back-office system used by employees who don't interact with customers. Now many companies are giving customers direct access to goods tracking software via the internet so that they can track their own orders.

As such, goods tracking has become a front-office system because its performance affects the customers' perceptions of the organization.

Dell Computer has electronically linked its front-end systems through which customers place orders with its back-end assembly, manufacturing and parts functions. A customer's order automatically sends information down the supply chain and Dell automatically sends e-mails to suppliers every two hours, for instance. By integrating its customer management system with its supply chain, Dell receives shipments from suppliers every two hours and maintains just eight days' worth of inventory (Brown 2000).

Communication and information functions need to be integrated seamlessly, or they can represent a fault-line in the company's ability to provide consistent customer value. For instance, dozens of applications may be spread throughout an organization; or departments may be organized around products and services or business functions, rather than processes, which support the customer relationship. So it is important to review existing applications from the perspective of customer interaction, in order that customer needs drive technology solutions, rather than the other way around.

The data analysis tools described above allow the business to assess whether new ways of managing customer relationships will increase shareholder value. Such analysis provides the basis for the performance assessment process.

PROCESS 5

Performance assessment

How can we create increased profits and shareholder value?
How should we set standards, develop metrics, measure our results and improve our performance?

It is crucial to evaluate the success of CRM to see whether it is helping the organization meet its strategic aims and whether it will continue to deliver looked for improvements. The key actions involve understanding the drivers of shareholder value, identifying the appropriate metrics to measure the various CRM activities against, and establishing an effective performance monitoring system.

Shareholder results

The ultimate objective of CRM is to increase shareholder value. Building value for employees and customers and cutting costs to improve profit margins all contribute to shareholder value.

Employees, customers and shareholders are an organization's key stakeholders. It is widely acknowledged that good leadership and management behaviour lead to positive employee attitudes, customer satisfaction and increased sales, profits and shareholder results. Recent research (Heskett et al. 1997; Hallowell and Schlesinger 2000) has explored these relationships more closely, by developing linkage models which demonstrate how improvement in one variable leads to a measurable increase in another. Such models help companies evaluate the effectiveness of CRM at a strategic level before going on to determine standards, metrics and key performance indicators.

Sears, Roebuck and Company, the large US department store chain, is highly innovative in the area of performance measurement. Not only has it addressed the more common elements of CRM, such as streamlining its information systems from 18 separate legacy databases into a single, integrated data warehouse, it has also developed a linkage model to help manage shareholder results. We go on to look at Sears' experience in greater detail later in this book (see Chapter 7).

Cost reduction

Reducing costs is the time-honoured way of growing short-term profits. In the context of CRM, there are two major opportunities to cut costs: reducing staff and overheads by using electronic systems, such as automated telephony services; and using new channels, such as online self-service facilities, to reduce the costs of acquiring and servicing customers. For instance, it costs GE Capital about $5 to accept a simple order on the phone. An online order, meanwhile, costs just 20 cents (*Economist* 2000). In retail banking, customer transaction costs can also be reduced by broadening the channel options (Figure 2.5).

However, businesses shouldn't take their cost reduction drive too far or they will destroy rather than enhance customer value. For example, many bank customers feel disenfranchised by no longer being able to telephone their branch and have personal contact with employees they know, and banks are losing many of their best customers as a result. Significantly, the Prudential's online bank Egg, now promoted as a telephone bank as well as an internet bank, is also

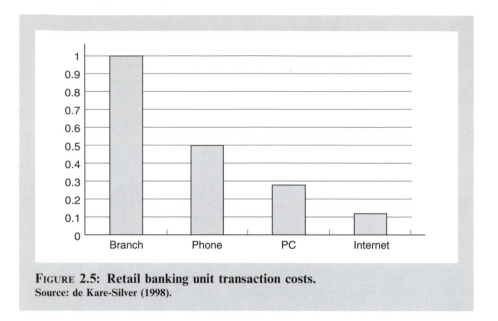

FIGURE 2.5: Retail banking unit transaction costs.
Source: de Kare-Silver (1998).

considering opening a network of branches in recognition that many customers want to deal with a physical presence.

Performance monitoring

The metrics available to companies wanting to monitor their CRM activities are largely unsophisticated. For example, there is no internationally recognized set of standards for CRM against which best practice can be measured. Historically, most companies' performance measurement systems have been functionally driven. The balanced scorecard, developed by Kaplan and Norton (1996), is a popular attempt to provide cross-functional measures, but doesn't address the linkages between the measures, which is crucial to understanding how to improve performance.

Companies should ask themselves two key questions if they are to successfully measure and monitor their CRM performance:

1. What metrics and key performance indicators (KPIs) should we use that adequately reflect the performance standards across the five major CRM processes?

2. How are these metrics and KPIs linked, and what opportunity do these linkages provide for improved results through better management of CRM across the organization?

We advocate that companies consider the following four main categories:

Strategic metrics measure the success of the organization's strategic approach to CRM. They measure, for example, the extent to which marketing information is used when developing the business strategy; the role of CRM in positioning the organization in the market place; and whether the vision and objectives of the company focus sufficiently on the customer.

Customer metrics measure the value delivered by the organization to the customer and the value the customer provides to the organization. These set KPIs to measure, for example, levels of customer satisfaction and customer retention, customer acquisition costs, and customer lifetime value.

Operational metrics measure both people and process performance. People measures include the appraisal, compensation, recognition, training and career progression of staff; measures include employee retention, productivity, employee satisfaction and performance targets; process measures include customer service levels, supplier performance targets, and product and service development targets.

Output metrics measure the effectiveness of the CRM strategy on organizational performance by calculating the value delivered to each of the three main stakeholders: shareholders, employees and customers. Value is determined in terms of customer satisfaction, increased key segment profitability, reduction in operational costs, and employee retention and productivity.

Overall, the test of an organization's performance assessment lies in its ability to respond confidently to the following fundamental questions:

1. Have we selected the most appropriate CRM performance standards? Do we benchmark our standards against best in class?
2. Have we determined appropriate metrics and KPIs? Do we understand where these performance metrics are linked?
3. Can we determine the impact of each metric, individually and cumulatively, on our results?
4. Do we have appropriate feedback built into our CRM monitoring process so that there is continual improvement?

The Yorkshire Building Society has been using automated sales measurement at a basic level for the past few years.

EXAMPLE

The Yorkshire Building Society introduced automated sales measurement after the board decided to deliver all statistical information electronically in order to make it accessible via a common user interface.

The building society set up four main measurement segments: security, a traditional financial measure; competitive products; service, through tracking customer complaints; and staff measures such as training and knowledge, staff turnover and absence. Within the competitive products section there are 20 sub-divisions, such as: the average interest rate compared with competitors; how much is being sold against objectives; which products are selling well; measurement of relative growth compared with the market; and the number of customers leaving. Green, amber and red lights indicate whether targets were being met.

The system now allows the company to know what it is selling, when it is selling it and what each individual salesperson is selling.

Developing a strategic approach to CRM

The strategic framework outlined above is designed to help companies which are confused and frustrated in their efforts to adopt CRM. It should be approached with an open mind, applied with an element of flexibility and modified where appropriate, as no two organizations will share the same circumstances. Because it is meant to be applied iteratively, it is likely to be refined as organizations learn from using it.

To recap, companies embarking on a CRM strategy should remember:

- It has to be led from the top.
- It requires the full commitment of the workforce and supply chain partners.
- As a strategic activity, it requires coordination, collaboration and integration.
- The aim is to provide a continually enhanced customer experience.
- No amount of IT can compensate for the need for investment in customer-facing employees.

It's a truism, but worth remembering, that customers are people, not simply stacks of transactions, as Thomas Davenport and his colleagues pointed out in the Winter 2001 edition of the MIT *Sloan Management Review* (Davenport et al. 2001). So, any serious effort to manage relationships with them must go beyond transaction data analysis. Ironically, in a climate of considerable enthusiasm for knowledge management, the most human forms of customer knowledge – customer comments and negative customer feedback – are the least likely to be captured and shared.

The following examples demonstrate the all-important human element of good CRM.

EXAMPLE

Companies like Harley-Davidson and Procter & Gamble succeed because they consider the person behind the transaction – recording what customers do during sales and service interactions, for example. By examining this human data, they can better understand and predict customers' behaviours and they can rely less on technologies to collect, distribute and use transaction-driven knowledge.

For example, Harley-Davidson executives regularly ride their bikes cross country to join their customers. Not only do they learn from the customers they meet, they also experience first hand how it feels to ride their product over long distances. Harley-Davidson enjoys a very high level of customer loyalty (Davenport et al. 2001).

EXAMPLE

Hewlett Packard recently switched from an organizational culture based on product types, such as midsize laser printers, to a culture centred on the full customer experience. HP development engineers now think more broadly about their products. For example, surveys suggested that customers would be more satisfied if the Low Toner message indicated how many pages could be printed before the toner ran out. This design change, which will appear in HP's future products, required adding sensors to predict how long the toner would last. Such attention to customer detail contributes to market leadership (Davenport et al. 2001).

EXAMPLE

3M's Telecoms Systems Division holds regular fairs at customer sites to see how that site is using 3M products and to expose customers to products they may not be using. 3M finds the insights useful in approaching other sites and customers and in helping customers learn about the range of its products and services (Davenport et al. 2001).

It is this knowledge of the customer, gained from close observation of them, which sets the good companies apart. Trying to guess what will entice customers rather than actually finding out is a dangerous strategy in today's cut-throat competitive climate. However, it is equally important to remember that companies are far more likely to lose customers because of an indifferent attitude or an inappropriate response by a single employee than because they have failed to anticipate some future need.

Perhaps the final word in this scene-setting chapter should go to Allied Irish Bank, voted the best British business bank for the past eight years by 8000 UK members of the Forum of Private Business.

EXAMPLE

At the heart of AIB's approach is what it calls 'relationship banking' – a dedicated local banking team of experienced branch managers who understand their local markets and businesses and are empowered with a great deal of autonomy. Managers and staff stay in one branch longer than those in other banks, and decisions are made locally and fast.

Customer loyalty is extremely high, as is the rate of acquisition from other banks. AIB receives fewer customer complaints and experiences far fewer defections than other banks.

AIB has always recognized business customers as being an important sector, but it focused on them more closely as a potentially highly profitable business segment five years ago. It invests heavily in recruiting, training and retaining quality people, and can afford to offer the level of personal service it does because it enjoys such high returns from this sector.

The bank is investing in technology as an added value service for customers rather than as an end in itself. For example, it now offers pc banking and is exploring internet opportunities.

Business customers who join Allied Irish from other banks speak of the difficulty they had in sustaining relationships through remote call centres where they never got to speak to the same person twice. So successful is Allied Irish's approach that some of the bigger banks are starting to look at emulating it.

To recap, this chapter outlines a strategic framework for successfully implementing CRM within organizations. In subsequent chapters we go on to outline each of the five key drivers in turn, with case studies illustrating current best practice across each of the processes. As we have explained, CRM is a strategic approach, and the processes need to be closely integrated with each other. While technology is an enabler, it is people and processes which remain crucial to successful CRM.

References

This chapter is based on a paper by Payne, A. (2001) *A Strategic Approach to CRM*, copyright Professor Adrian Payne, and is used with his permission.

Bower, M. and Garda R. A. (1985) The role of marketing in management. In *Handbook of Modern Marketing* (V. P. Buell, ed.). McGraw-Hill.

Brown, S. A. (2000) *Customer Relationship Management*. Canada: John Wiley & Sons.

Davenport, T. H., Harris, J. G. and Kohli, A. K. (2001) How do they know their customers so well? MIT *Sloan Management Review*, pp. 63–73.

Economist (2000) E-management survey, November 18 2000.

Hallowell, R. and Schlesinger, L. A. (2000) The service profit chain: intellectual roots, current realities and future prospects. In *Handbook of Services Marketing and Management* (D. Iacobucci and T. Swartz, eds). Thousand Oaks: Sage.

Heskett, J. L., Sasser, W. E. Jr and Schlesinger, L. A. (1997) *The Service Profit Chain*. The Free Press.

Kaplan, R. S. and Norton, D. P. (1996) *The Balanced Scorecard*. Harvard Business School Press.

de Kare-Silver, M. (1998) *E-shock*. London: Macmillan Business.

Payne, A. F. T. and Frow, P. (1999) Developing a segmented service strategy: improving measurement in relationship marketing. *Journal of Marketing Management*, **15**, 797–818.

Peppard, J. (2000) Customer relationship management (CRM) in financial services. *European Management Journal*, **18**, 312–327.

Peppers, D. and Rogers, M. (1993) *The One to One future: Building Business Relationships One Customer at a Time*. Piatkus Books.

Reichheld, F. F. and Sasser, W. E. Jr (1990) Zero defections: quality comes to services. *Harvard Business Review*, September–October 1990, pp 105–111.

Ryals, L., Knox, S. D. and Maklan, S. (2000) *Customer Relationship Management: The business case for CRM. Financial Times*/Prentice-Hall.

Chapter **3**

The strategy development process

As we have seen, there are two aspects to the strategy development process: business strategy and customer strategy. Business strategy concerns the type of organization, its vision, style and corporate brand; customer strategy is about the type of customers that the organization wants to attract and how to segment them.

Development of business strategy

The business strategy often originates in the vision of a charismatic founder or business leader, such as that of Hans Snook, the former chief executive of Orange, and the subject of the first case study in this chapter. A business vision is a view of how the future might look and the role the organization might play in that future. Sometimes the vision seems unreasonable or far-fetched to outsiders. For example, Microsoft's vision of 'a computer on every desk' seemed extraordinary in an industry accustomed to thinking about computers as room-sized machines that needed an army of technicians to tend them. Yet these 'unreasonable' visions can often be the most powerful of drivers, stimulating organizations to achieve remarkable successes.

Orange's vision – that mobile telephony is the technology of the future – has been successfully translated into advertising campaigns, 'The Future's Bright,

The Future's Orange', and into product and service leadership through leading-edge offerings such as its mobile video phone, the first such product outside Japan.

From business strategy to competitive strategy

The next step in the strategy development process is to translate the business vision into competitive strategy. Competitive strategy is about matching internal competencies to the external environment – understanding the business landscape in which the organization operates and the core skills and competencies it has or can develop, and then matching the two. Important features in the CRM business landscape are existing competitors, potential competitors, customer needs and wants, and technology. Organizations often become involved in CRM because they understand that existing customer service levels throughout their industry fall far short of the ideal. This has particularly been the case in financial services, where banks, building societies and insurance companies have persistently sold products rather than build customer relationships. These organizations have grown into product-based structures in which information about customers is contained within silos that are impenetrable by other parts of the business. As a result some customers are offered unsuitable products or products that they already own, while other customers are neglected. Mortgage customers who move house find that the very organization that lends them money to buy a new house continues to send correspondence and bank statements to their old address. Customers who are overdrawn receive loan offers, while retired customers are inundated with offers of school fees insurance.

In the longer term, these low levels of knowledge about the customer can have a serious impact on the company. Customers become disillusioned about the service and are more likely to defect, particularly if a new competitor enters the market with a completely new style of doing business, backed up by new technologies and the absence of existing information silos. Alternatively, disheartened customers come to believe that the experience will be just as bad anywhere else, and buy increasingly on price rather than on the service promises that they have begun to distrust. Both trends increase competitive pressures.

A few organizations have managed to break out of this vicious spiral and develop a new business model. One, Britannia Building Society, is the subject of the second case study in this chapter. Britannia experienced considerable competitive pressures in its traditional investment and mortgage business. However, rather than compete on price, the Society took a fresh look at its market and opted for a different approach to business, based on knowing its customers better and serving them well and with a personal touch. The case study describes how Britannia gathered information about its customers and turned this information into a real competitive advantage by emphasizing its friendly and approachable style.

Implementation and the importance of customer strategies

To implement the business strategy in a targeted way, companies need a customer strategy. The customer strategy outlines the kinds of customers that the organization wants to target, together with their key characteristics. The customer strategy must also address the issue of segment granularity – how small the customer segments can be before there are too many for the organization to handle. Organizations sometimes implement CRM in the belief that it will help them achieve 'one-to-one marketing', but fail to consider issues of organization structure and marketing effectiveness.

The third case study in this chapter, Homebase.co.uk, charts the development of customer strategies on line. Homebase, an out-of-town retailer of do-it-yourself home improvement products, mapped its market place on two dimensions – competitor and customer. Homebase found that its customers were interested in both the technical aspects of home improvements (the quality of the finished results) and the creative aspects. Competitively, Homebase was seen as being at the lower end of the market place and not a particularly good source of creative ideas. It wanted to move out of the lower, very price-competitive end of the market, where it would struggle to compete with large and powerful rivals, and to reach more of the creative customers who would look for quality, service and advice.

Looking at home improvements from the customer's perspective, Homebase organized its stores so that goods were placed together in project groups, with accompanying ideas, examples and advice. A natural development was a 'virtual store' offering products and advice online. Working against the clock, Homebase.co.uk created a virtual store in which, room by room, customers could both explore creative ideas and purchase the products they needed. Advice was available through e-mail and a call centre as well as by post and fax.

No CRM project is perfect, and Homebase certainly made some mistakes along the way, but it has achieved an industry first. Homebase.co.uk has enabled it both to improve service to existing customers and to attract new, high-spending customers. Moreover, Homebase is learning about its customers and their needs and aspirations from its online operation. In turn, this information informs the development of its overall marketing strategies, creating a virtuous spiral.

CASE STUDY 3.1

A fruitful passion for Orange[1]

OVERVIEW

'Man's passion to communicate and to receive communications seems as central to his success as a species as the fin was to the fish or the feather to the birds.'

David Attenborough

How does 'The Best' get better to protect its dominant market position? The answer lies in strategy development. In this case study CRM presents both difficulties and opportunities for a highly successful enterprise operating in a vibrant (and vicious) industry.

Competition in the mobile telecommunications industry is increasingly fierce, with tremendous market growth being driven by the entry of new competitors, falling tariffs and handset prices, and improved network and service provision. The convergence of communications and computing, and the pace of technological development has made for very little customer loyalty and high rates of customer churn for even the most successful market players. Orange, one of the leading brands, faces a range of threats, including those posed by computing and phone manufacturers, and network operators.

The Orange UK case study illustrates how competitive and market pressures led Orange to reappraise its strategy and change its focus from customer acquisition to customer retention. To forge stronger customer relationships, the newly created Customer Relations department developed a new strategy based on CRM principles, which capitalizes on the company's low churn rates and outstanding customer service. The case study focuses on Orange's decision to use CRM as a strategic vision and the organizational changes it requires.

Key learning points

Orange is an example of a company that is strategically advanced in CRM, but in the early stages of implementation. Its experience

---

[1] This case study was developed and agreed with the management of Orange in October 2000.

demonstrates how CRM can be used to combat churn and enhance customer service. For example, the company offers greater choice, control and connectivity to customers by way of WAP and videophone technology, customized billing, and self-service facilities.

The case examines the supporting role of IT in delivering the strategy. Orange realized that it needed to make a major investment in information systems infrastructure to facilitate the two-way communication with customers that is so critical in identifying, satisfying and anticipating their needs. The case also looks at the appropriateness of some key performance metrics, including churn, loyalty value, and cost to serve.

CRM issues

- Building CRM takes time.

Orange's shift in organizational emphasis from customer acquisition to customer retention coincides with its migration from a short- to a long-term view of customer relationships. This longer-term customer view alters the focus for Customer Relations, the way it works with other parts of Orange and the way it measures performance.

- CRM often requires changes to the organizational culture and structure.

Establishing Customer Relations is an internal declaration of the company's desire for stronger customer focus, and demonstrates senior management's recognition that better customer relationships can improve the company's performance.

- CRM strategies emphasize two-way communication with customers, which can make the design and delivery of messages more appropriate and effective.

Orange has successfully targeted the expanding younger (under-35s) domestic market with an innovative but not overly technical product, and works constantly to reinforce messages of user-friendliness, simplicity, reliability and best value. It seeks to increase customer value, trust and affinity through capturing and exploiting customer data better.

Strategy Development Process issues

An organization may embrace CRM for a number of reasons. Drivers include: the need to respond to escalating competitive pressures and market change; to satisfy increasingly complex customer requirements and expectations; to manage corporate growth and an expanding customer base without detriment to either; and to attract and retain a greater share of an empowered consumer audience.

Orange's CRM strategy embraced all these drivers.

CRM is an integrated approach, aligned with and supportive of 'integration' as a wider business objective

At Orange, responsibility for CRM is shared across the company. This is evident in the strategic direction of Customer Relations being weighted towards IT (data warehouse, communication centres, website), and in IT, investment decisions being made at board level. The new strategy is disseminated through presentations to everyone in the company to try to combat reluctance or resistance to change by employees from disparate departments.

CRM involves changing from reactive to proactive customer service, giving priority to growing customer value rather than growing customer volume

Orange's relationship marketing initiatives, which recognize that customer segments are dynamic entities, signal a change in business approach from increasing the volume of customers to increasing their value. The use of priority routing and queuing systems, and increasingly sophisticated onscreen prompts, are consistent with the move towards creating value rather than simply handling volume.

Introduction: The context for change at Orange

In its six years as a mobile phone network, Orange has acquired over five million customers and expects to double that number within a year. The momentum of its growth rate is staggering: one million customers in July 1997, two million in December 1998, three million in July 1999, four million in December 1999 and a further million in the following two months. At the end of February 2000, some 45 per cent of the UK population owned a mobile phone and one in ten people were Orange customers. Market penetration of Orange mobile phones hit 40 per cent just after Christmas 1999, spurred on by the popularity of Orange Just Talk, which was considered the ideal Christmas gift (*What Mobile* magazine, February 2000). Orange UK moved into profit for the first time in May 1999 and, with an annual turnover of £1.2 billion, is a formidable UK network.

Since its inception, Orange, like most other aggressive growth businesses, has focused on acquisitions, pursuing the notion that more customers mean more business. The context within which businesses operate, however, has been changing rapidly and radically, and nowhere more so than in the telecommunications industry. Most significantly, mobile telephony has had an impact on every aspect of life and work, and the internet has opened up previously unimaginable opportunities for communicating and exchanging information and ideas. Lightning speeds of voice and data transfer are possible – third generation UTMS[2] technology offers data rates of up to 384 Kilobytes per second (Kbps) on the move compared with 9.6 Kbps using today's mobile phones, or 56 Kbps using a modem (*What Mobile* magazine, February 2000).

For Orange, the unprecedented rate of technological innovation has created new opportunities and new threats. The convergence of communications and computing has strengthened the hand of close competitors, and accelerated the entry of new competitors onto the market. Orange competes not only with other network operators (Vodafone, Cellnet, and One2One in the UK), but also with phone, handset and computer terminal manufacturers. The boundaries between sectors of the technology and telecommunications markets have blurred so that telecommunications is no longer simply about transporting information, but is concerned with content, transport and software integration. Virtual network operators (VNOs) are emerging; for example, One2One is the network for Virgin Mobile which has the direct relationship with customers. Distinguishing between a telecommunications company, an independent service provider (ISP) and a portal is becoming increasingly difficult – as is maintaining a market niche, even for a strong, modern brand like Orange.

The challenge of churn

With the telecommunications industry being totally redefined, the pressure is mounting to retain as well as attract customers. Orange boasts the lowest overall churn rate in the industry at 15.8 per cent per annum, compared with the

---

[2] Universal Mobile Telecommunications System is designed to handle the bandwidth requirements of multimedia communications. It is expected to be commercially available in the UK in 2003.

industry average of 28 per cent. Contract churn is 20.7 per cent and pre-pay churn 8.8 per cent (Orange Press Release, 5 January 2000, www.orange.co.uk). This is in large part due to the company's excellent service ratings. 'Orange was easily the best all round. It consistently came first, or very near the top, for both the quality of its network and customer service (*Which?* magazine, November 1999). But the need to combat churn has become even more critical in the face of heightened competition and the fact that loyal customers are more profitable – the longer customers stay with Orange, the more heavily they use their phones. Orange understands that resolving the problem of churn depends on both understanding what motivates customers to leave the market or to switch providers, and on using this knowledge proactively.

The call for CRM

In April 1998 Michael Cascade, then a relationship marketing manager at Orange, was brought in to the brand management department to help push forward relationship marketing (RM) initiatives. Today, his business card reads 'Head of Customer Relations Strategy' and he focuses full-time on getting CRM on the Orange agenda. It was an 'odd journey', he reflects. What he initially accepted as a reasonable challenge, he quickly found a daunting task: there were no foundations upon which to build RM, let alone CRM, into the company's policies and practices. 'There was no access to data, no understanding of the value of our customers, and no front end systems to select segments or subsets of groups', he says. 'We didn't have access to a data warehouse and had only a manual way of using control and test groups.'

It was time to start digging – into the company's archives of information, into the company's pockets of project funding, and into the company's collective ability to undergo fundamental change.

The apparent lack of resource and willingness to accept a new business approach based on marketing rather than sales took its toll. The department suffered a two-year bout of high staff turnover, culminating in the departure of the Head of Brand Management. The constituent parts of the department, Customer Communications, Relationship Marketing, and Retention & Development, were relocated, the latter two being subsumed into customer services operations in order to create a team responsible for end-to-end customer management. With the removal of the Customer Services Director and the decision not to re-recruit a marketing director, Cascade now reports to the newly established UK Group Director of Customer Relations.

It was success that prompted Orange to embrace CRM and subsequently restructure the organization and change its focus. Establishing 'Customer Relations' at Orange as a 'main menu' item was a significant occasion, marking the company's transition into corporate strategic maturity.

The CRM mission

What drives Orange's phenomenal growth and excellence in customer service, and how long it will endure, are questions that concern Cascade and his customer relationship management team. Yet despite Orange's exceptional performance in customer relations, it needs to exploit opportunities to build stronger, sustainable relationships with customers. 'Orange has always had a retention team, but one that functioned as "end of pipe"', says Cascade. It was there to 'stop customers from leaving', not to encourage them to stay, an approach reinforced by a host of largely futile attempts to win back defecting customers, 'who were simply taking advantage of a "buyer's market"'.

Following an appraisal of existing operations and, unusually, extensive consultation with colleagues of all departments, and reflecting the overall business aim 'to be first',[3] the team developed a formal CRM strategy for Orange in August 1999.

> **'Our mission is to build strong enduring relationships with our customers, thereby increasing customer lifetime value and company profitability and building sustainable competitive advantage. We will achieve this through the application of Customer Relationship Management (CRM) strategies.'**

> **'CRM is about building relationships to turn customers into advocates, so that their decision to stay with you becomes more "automatic", they buy more and spend more, and they tell their friends and colleagues about your products and services too.' (See Figure CS 3.1.1.)**

The consensus was that the complete CRM strategy would take five years to deliver, although significant benefits would be realized along the way. The department responsible for pursuing this new strategic direction, both operationally and culturally, would be Customer Relations.

---

[3] Orange plc: 'Our mission is to become the first global wire-free telecommunications brand. Wherever we operate, or our brand is licensed, we aim to be first: first for service, first for quality, first for innovation – first choice.'

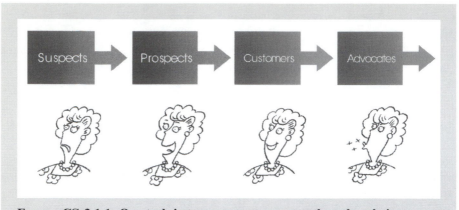

FIGURE CS 3.1.1: Our task is to move customers up the value chain.
Source: Orange plc.

'Customer relations will develop in-depth understanding of customer needs, wants, desires, attitudes and behaviours to deliver a cost-effective and efficient customer service experience, appropriate to different customers' needs and their actual and potential value to Orange.'

Orange believes that delivery of both rational and emotional needs, in a way that exceeds customers' expectations, will make it difficult for competitors to emulate Orange, and help prevent it being seen as a commodity. Orange's new-found commitment to creating and delivering value through CRM strategies involves it managing and treating customers and data as business assets. Orange's capacity to utilize IT and its main customer interface, the call centre, is therefore crucial to CRM implementation.

The role of IT

In today's diverse marketplace, increasingly complex customer segments makes getting the right propositions to the right customers at the right time no easy task. Deciding who are the 'right' customers requires understanding who makes up the customer base and apportioning them a relative value. Changes in customer lifestyle and behaviour have meant that customers can no longer be characterized by a single profile: segmentation has become a bit like trying to colour-code chameleons. For Orange, the problem of dealing with fragmenting segments, ranging from consumer to small, medium and large businesses, is exacerbated by the emergence of new market sectors, such as corporate solutions, telemetry[4] and airtime wholesale.[5] Further, notes Cascade, 'the gap between the "early adopter" customers (those experienced with the new technologies like high-speed data[6]) and the "basic service" customers is widening. Segmentation has filtered into branding, propositions and service, with, for example, pre-pay customers receiving a very different service to contract customers.'

IT has been instrumental in Orange's quest to accurately identify and appropriately manage the differing requirements and expectations of customers. Refining segments to provide a more customized customer experience requires automated and intelligent systems. An internal audit of Orange's current capability has shown that major investment is needed to develop Customer Relations' information systems (IS) and infrastructure. The company's data warehouse, which forms a core element of IS capability, is a major target for development.

Orange's data warehouse originated as a management information system to support financial reporting and analysis functions, and is based on usage data. It continues to be owned and managed by Finance and IS. Customers are categorized according to the company's perception of them as one of two account types: account holders and end users. Account holders are those who generally pay the bill, while end users or subscribers (most commonly referred to as customers by Orange) are the 6 million people that use the handsets. The end user may not be the account holder. For instance, a wife may hold the account but her husband has everyday use of the phone.

With its focus on revenue and cost, the data warehouse helps financial understanding but is less useful when it comes to monitoring customers. It has enabled Orange to offer a flexible Talk Plan scheme, but it doesn't allow it to deliver benefits based on a unified customer contact history. For example, it can't respond to expressed customer contact preferences deduced from customers opting out of receiving mailings and callings, or opting in to receive automated communications like text messaging and e-mail. Carrie Leadbetter, Head of Customer Contact Management at Orange and a member of the CRM team, describes it 'more as a revenue data mart than a data warehouse, as it does not necessarily retain all the key behavioural bits of data, only a sub-set of contact history'.

Architecturally, the data warehouse takes feeds from various different systems. It houses vast volumes of data that allow some segmentation according

---

[4] Telemetry is the automatic transmission and measurement of data from remote sources by wire or radio or other means.
[5] The requirement to provide wholesale airtime to independent service providers (ISPs) is a license condition of mobile virtual networkers (MVNs). It enables the competitive supply of mobile services to customers by ensuring they can purchase services from competing service providers.
[6] High-speed data refers to data that are compressed to enable rapid speed of transmission. They are then decompressed to access.

to value, churn, loyalty (restricted to loyalty scheme registration), and customer type (consumer versus business: small, medium or large). When the data warehouse is refined, it will allow further segmentation according to life stage, loyalty in a broader sense and customer contact preference, for example. Orange believes its customer segmentation is relatively accurate, as it has validated the quality of its own data against external data. However, it acknowledges that most of its data is consumer-oriented and that it needs to do more to address its business customer base.

Orange has built a predictive modelling system that calculates the value of every subscriber and account on a monthly basis. It uses some 200 variables, which take into account the customer's payment behaviour, propensity to churn, and usage. The system is currently being redeveloped under Cascade's stewardship to indicate what a customer would be worth over a 12-month period. Meanwhile, plans are in place to further refine the system to measure customer lifetime value (CLV), so that Customer Service Representatives (CSRs) can use predictive value in making decisions about customer management. By gaining a more holistic and longer-term view of individual customers, Orange can not only personalize offers better, but also trace the dynamic movement of segments to reveal signals and patterns of change. For example, 53 per cent of acquired customers are known to be previous mobile users, which represent a significant replacement market.

Orange also wants to develop its data mining capability. The company's data warehouse is built from the best bits of hardware and software on offer, which means it is a composite of different providers' products. Although the end result is a mix of superlative technologies, the lack of common origin among the component parts is a potential weakness. In the process of evaluating alternative mining tools to help reduce the data warehouse's hybrid nature, Cascade has identified a surprising gap in the basic functionality of sophisticated mining tools. Although they excel at complex tasks such as cluster analysis, he has discovered that they neither profile the segments they derive nor do cross-tabs. Cascade believes that this shortfall needs to be addressed if CRM strategies are to be practically feasible.

Carrie Leadbetter has also identified a shortcoming in campaign management tools used to manage customer communications. 'There is a need to profile and prioritize customers real time, and this is complex to do in a live environment', she says. 'The difficulty is finding one package that can manage the huge volumes of data, and on the predictive modelling side, do everything in one tool.' Available tools tend not to have, as Leadbetter puts it, 'a nice reporting GUI[7] front end, which means you have to employ a statistician to interpret the

---

[7] Graphical User Interface (GUI) is pronounced 'gooey'.

information and then plug on a visual tool to be able to report back to the company' – an expensive and laborious process. In the absence of the ideal 'all-in-one' tool that can simultaneously handle wave campaign management, campaign tracking and response analysis, different tools must be integrated, and this has serious drawbacks and difficulties.

It is vital both to generate accurate, comprehensive customer profiles, and to make them easily accessible throughout the organization. Presenting a unified view of the customer reduces the chances of misunderstanding and missed opportunities for relationship development, such as cross-selling and up-selling. A variety of users access Orange's data warehouse, including Customer Relations, Marketing, Sales, Finance, and technical departments. (See Figure CS 3.1.2.) The data warehouse, with its reporting and analysis tools, supports a range of information needs. (See Figure CS 3.1.3.) But the more sophisticated 'expert users' are the only ones who currently enjoy desktop access and do not have to consult IS to produce data output such as selective lists. Without the front end tools to easily access and manipulate the data warehouse, it is not possible to exploit its full potential, and consequently return on investment is limited.

In an effort to gain a fuller and truer picture of Orange's customers, the CRM team has spearheaded a project to develop in-house a customer-centric database as a foundation for its operational systems as well as modelling and reporting tools. The integration of disparate data and systems, across increasingly diverse distribution channels, will promote a shared, 'collective memory' of the customer, and provide seamless handling of a wide range of products and services. A key challenge for IS, as highlighted in the CRM strategy, will be:

> 'to operate and maintain reliable and efficient systems whilst developing new capabilities, managing growth in data, and supporting increased demand for capacity and 100 per cent service levels for continuous 24 × 7 service.'

The role of communication centres

Orange is acutely aware of the imperative to facilitate two-way communication, not only *for* its customers but also *with* its customers, and is investing heavily to that end. For example, it recently renamed its call centres 'communication centres'. As Cascade says: 'Call centres were always reactive service centres, and they can and should become more proactive. Call centres should help manage positive *and* negative experiences.' He believes call operators should not only be expected to resolve problems and answer queries, but be encouraged to suggest

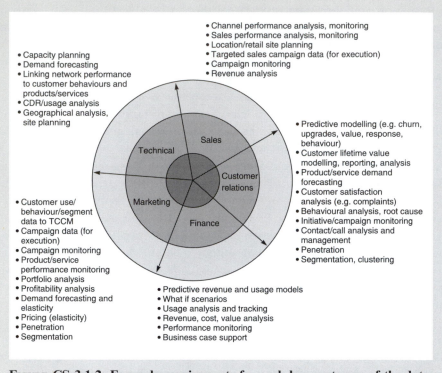

- Channel performance analysis, monitoring
- Sales performance analysis, monitoring
- Location/retail site planning
- Targeted sales campaign data (for execution)
- Campaign monitoring
- Revenue analysis

- Capacity planning
- Demand forecasting
- Linking network performance to customer behaviours and products/services
- CDR/usage analysis
- Geographical analysis, site planning

- Predictive modelling (e.g. churn, upgrades, value, response, behaviour)
- Customer lifetime value modelling, reporting, analysis
- Product/service demand forecasting
- Customer satisfaction analysis (e.g. complaints)
- Behavioural analysis, root cause
- Initiative/campaign monitoring
- Contact/call analysis and management
- Penetration
- Segmentation, clustering

- Customer use/ behaviour/segment data to TCCM
- Campaign data (for execution)
- Campaign monitoring
- Product/service performance monitoring
- Portfolio analysis
- Profitability analysis
- Demand forecasting and elasticity
- Pricing (elasticity)
- Penetration
- Segmentation

- Predictive revenue and usage models
- What if scenarios
- Usage analysis and tracking
- Revenue, cost, value analysis
- Performance monitoring
- Business case support

FIGURE CS 3.1.2: Example requirements for each key customer of the data warehouse.
Source: Orange plc.

relevant new products to customers at the right time. Planned developments in IS capability, particularly the incorporation of behavioural and preference data, and projects to build contact capacity, will enhance the role of the communication centres in gathering valuable information and improving service.

Orange operates seven communication centres in Plymouth, Bristol, North Tyneside, Peterlee and Darlington (where there are three). The £8 million state-of-the-art customer communication centre in Plymouth handles calls exclusively from Orange's escalating number of Just Talk customers. Customers aren't aware that Orange operates a number of communication centres, because of advanced call routing technology which automatically directs those who wish to speak with a customer service representative (CSR) to someone with pertinent skills and training, regardless of their physical location. In this way, Orange's various centres operate essentially as a single 'virtual call centre'. This efficient and effective system will help grow the customer base, and, consequently,

Analytical and reporting requirements can be represented as follows:

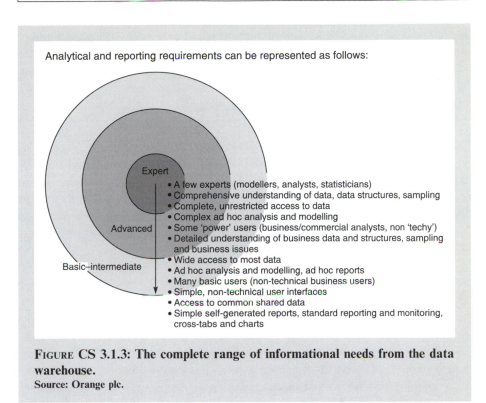

- • A few experts (modellers, analysts, statisticians)
- • Comprehensive understanding of data, data structures, sampling
- • Complete, unrestricted access to data
- • Complex ad hoc analysis and modelling
- • Some 'power' users (business/commercial analysts, non 'techy')
- • Detailed understanding of business data and structures, sampling and business issues
- • Wide access to most data
- • Ad hoc analysis and modelling, ad hoc reports
- • Many basic users (non-technical business users)
- • Simple, non-technical user interfaces
- • Access to common shared data
- • Simple self-generated reports, standard reporting and monitoring, cross-tabs and charts

FIGURE CS 3.1.3: The complete range of informational needs from the data warehouse.
Source: Orange plc.

increase Customer Services' ability to handle ever more complex customer requirements and product/service offerings.

The use of priority routing and queuing is further testimony to Orange's endeavour to actively confer and convey customer value. The top 10 per cent of customers, rated by value of calls, are put through to pre-dedicated CSRs, while the remainder are matched by call type (registration, handsets, billing queries and so on) to appropriately skilled operators. Certain communication centres handle certain call types. A specialist team deals with more complex queries about products or services.

Call operators are clued in to customers' details by onscreen prompts, via a front-end system called Merlin – essentially a contact management and process flow system. Building on this early attempt to overcome the 'facelessness' of telephone communication, the new CRM strategy is designed to provide more intelligent customer databases and systems to support CSRs in decision-making and process management, and also to reduce the knowledge and 'intelligence' demand on them. Orange offers some 35 different handsets and a multitude of service plans, and, even though network operations employees are continually trained, expecting individuals to retain and recall every detail of every product and service is unrealistic.

The need for meaningful metrics

Performance measures are key to the delivery of 'an integrated, clear, consistent and relevant service experience', Orange's expressed goal for its CRM strategy. The benchmarks it uses to measure and monitor organizational performance are predominantly those imposed by the industry, including regulatory body OFTEL and independent consumer protection agencies like Which. Key measures include churn, average revenue per customer, and gross and net connections. These benchmarks are expected to change as market competition continues to diversify.

Loyalty

Loyalty continues to be a major indicator of both perceived and delivered value. The drive to adopt CRM is highlighting weaknesses in Orange's ability to measure and manage propensity to churn across increasingly complex segments. It is also stimulating debate about more fundamental business metrics. As Leadbetter notes: 'The impact of the pre-pay market has dramatically changed how you even measure churn. For example, how do you measure customer attrition when a customer doesn't have to tell you that they're not a customer any more? Two years ago Orange's customers were primarily "contract", but now a substantial number are "pre-pay" and have no contract, so loyalty must be measured in terms of "dormancy". But how do you define a dormant customer?' asks Leadbetter. Normally this means that the customer has no outbound calls for between one and 30 days. However, if the customer is purchasing a certain amount of vouchers a month as a way of controlling their costs, they may be an active customer but 'invisible' to the dormancy measurement.

Orange established its current loyalty programme, Equity,[8] after earlier moves to get closer to customers and to value them better. It launched a glossy customer magazine (still untargeted), for example, in the mistaken belief that this constituted 'one-to-one' communication, as one copy was sent to each customer. Then came the data warehouse with its well-intentioned but inadequate approach to understanding customer lifetime value, as it lacked the capacity to provide a 'total customer view'. Like these predecessors, the Equity loyalty programme was launched with some fundamental flaws. Based on a points collection

---

[8] Orange launched the industry's first standalone loyalty scheme, Equity, in 1997 as a means of combating customer defection using relationship marketing.

scheme, it rewards people for having a phone on a talk plan, regardless of whether they are using minutes on that talk plan. It therefore does not stimulate usage or encourage relationship longevity. 'The rewards themselves are mediocre, comprising prizes such as bungee jumping, Orange accessories, or redemption against more minutes of free talk time', says Cascade. He is adamant that loyalty should not be a 'programme' but 'built into everything we do'.

Cost

Orange is also debating the whole issue of service costs. Leadbetter throws open the debate: 'If a customer calls us, is that a cost?' she asks. 'Should we penalize the customer for calling us, when their call may have been driven by a problem generated by Orange, such as an unresolved complaint, or by a response to a company advertisement such as a product promotion or customer survey?'

Orange hopes that the improved data warehouse and a reappraisal of customers will help it define and identify costs, as well as reduce them. Understanding what drives customer preferences and assimilating this knowledge into day-to-day practices can lead to substantial cost savings. For instance, one of the aims of the CRM strategy is to create competitive advantage by cutting the number of contacts that Orange needs to handle. Analysis of repeat calls has shown that customers primarily call the company for four reasons: a problem has not been properly sorted; they do not understand how to use a product or service; something has not been explained fully or clearly; or they are the type of customer who simply calls frequently and will always be expensive. Incorporating such information into customer lifetime value (CLV) modelling can help to minimize the number of routine calls and cost-to-service.

Service

Orange is also scrutinizing how it measures service. Customer Relations is proud of the quality of service it provides, but it wants to raise the number of customer calls it answers within ten seconds from 70 per cent to 90 per cent. However, its ultimate goal is 'first call resolution' – resolving the caller's issue first time. Answering calls quickly on a consistent basis is not the right metric for measuring service dedicated to first call resolution, and it could also be masking other problems. So the company needs to make changes to ensure that the right services are measured and the right measures are used.

The impact of CRM

Aligning and refining processes and systems to deliver both increased operational efficiency and pervasive customer centricity in a way which is consistent with the Orange brand values, is a major thrust of the strategic plan.

'We will use intelligent systems to build customer understanding and provide the tools and resources to deploy this understanding to influence strategies and tactics for building customized propositions and relationships.'

Although still in the early stages of adoption, the CRM strategy is already having an impact on the way customer data are gathered and performance monitored. For instance, quarterly upgrade and churn research programmes, monthly internal CSR meetings and periodic focus groups, are replacing the rather ad hoc mailing campaigns traditionally used to measure customer satisfaction.

A deeper understanding of customers is leading to product and service developments which improve performance, enhance customer benefits, empower customers and increase their choice.

Leveraged loyalty

Applying improved intelligence has allowed Orange to change its upgrade pricing strategy to incorporate loyalty value. If a customer wants to upgrade their handset, they are charged a price based on their length of service and value to the company. Statistics show that 30 per cent of customers change their handset every year, and most want to switch at the hint of any superior model coming onto the market.

Greater connectivity

Responding to and pre-empting customers' needs also means improving the interconnectivity between customers, providing a swift and smooth service over a greater distance. New base stations have boosted the network's coverage to more than 98 per cent of the UK population and over 80 per cent of the UK's geography. Orange has 25 per cent more base stations (over 6000) than its nearest competitor and 75 per cent more than the weakest (Orange Press Release, 3 December 1999, www.orange.co.uk). This investment has led to a very low call drop rate, and to the introduction of the Network Performance Promise, a UK first for its Talk Plan customers, whereby if a call is dropped by the network and remade within five minutes, Orange will credit up to one minute of free talk time.

'Remote' possibilities are fast being realized to meet customers' demands for greater mobility across the globe. Customers' ability to use Orange outside the UK depends on roaming agreements, or arrangements with overseas networks. Roaming with Orange is now offered on 151 networks across 82 countries, including the US, India and China. Orange offers more EU networks than any other operator and is aggressively pursuing further expansion.

Orange was also the first to sign a text messaging internetwork agreement, enabling its customers to exchange text messages with customers of other UK mobile networks. Chief Operating Officer Bob Fuller elaborates: 'The ability to text message users of other UK mobile networks will be particularly beneficial for those customers who have moved across to Orange as a result of number portability, but want to continue to message friends on their old network.' Connecting with customers' desire for continuity and freedom of choice recognizes their growing appetite to take ownership of their communication needs. Features such as extended text messaging and number portability not only provide consistency, but also reduce the hassle factor for customers and enhance customer control.

Customized billing

Orange has customized its billing procedures. Through Talk Plan a customer can receive one bill that can be itemized to give greater budgetary control and simplify account administration. Customers can also consolidate usage to gain better value for money through a kind of 'phone pooling' on Talkshare service plans. These are designed to meet the specific needs of groups of personal users, small businesses, and medium to large businesses. The data about customers that such services will generate in terms of demographics, psychographics and so on, will prove invaluable in helping the company to identify and develop more profitable long-term relationships with customers.

Self-service facilities

By providing self-selection and self-service facilities, Orange is acting on the willingness of customers to have certain services automated if the option to speak to a service representative directly is kept open. Orange has enhanced its IVR (Interactive Voice Response) system to make it easier for customers to use, especially for services such as checking the balance of minutes remaining on a Talk Plan. The IVR handles over 1.4 million calls a month on this task alone.

The customer self-service section of the Orange web site (www.uk.orange.net), launched in November 1999 as an ISP and portal, offers an alternative to using IVR or speaking to a CSR. Here, customers can update their profiles and access value added services (such as sending text messages to Orange phones, receiving press updates and finding the latest product and service information). The site receives over 25 000 visits every month. As well being an attractive personalized service, it represents:

'A move to drive down costs-to-serve through encouraging customer self-fulfilment (especially) for low value-added customer contacts.'

The immediate popularity of the site as a management, communication and information tool stems from an extended pre-trial with a sample of real customers drawn at random from a public response to an online advertisement. The fact that it differs greatly from the original concept illustrates the success of the trial and the value of customer involvement in service development. Through facilities such as online discussion groups and the Usenet News Group, the web site expands customer research activity, which has traditionally been confined to consumer surveys and focus groups, and promotes intercommunication and inter-identification between supplier and customer.

Personalized service

Wildfire, a wire free personal assistant that uses voice recognition technology, is a good example of the way technology allows companies to deliver personalized services on a mass-market basis. Wildfire takes messages, collects the phone numbers of callers and places calls in response to spoken commands. With Wildfire, Orange has handed the controls to the customer.

Augmented choice

As well as working to further penetrate the market, Orange is trying to move deeper into customers' consciousness, providing a complementary portfolio of attractive products and services. The CRM strategy states:

'Proactive customer relationships will position Orange as an integral part of customers' lifestyles and business, ensuring that Orange becomes the supplier-of-choice for a wider array of customers' communication, information and entertainment needs.'

The company's growing range of multimedia services includes the WAP (Wireless Application Protocol) phone, whose global open standard enables Orange customers to access a variety of multimedia services including news, travel, entertainment and business information. Orange has also pioneered the world's first GSM[9] videophone. By no means an attempt to compete with fixed line videoconferencing, this significant tool enters new realms of functional diversity, serving simultaneously as a PDA (Personal Digital Assistant), digital camera, video player and phone.

Competitive pricing

With around 23 million people in the UK now using mobile phones (*What Cellphone* magazine, February 2000), there is far greater scope to provide a range of price plans which are increasingly tailored to individual market and customer requirements. For the 'pay as you go' market, Orange has designed its talk time vouchers and distribution to appeal to higher usage customers, such as through discounts for higher amounts of talk time. On a more global front, Orange supports choice and competitiveness by providing its customers and suppliers in Europe with pricing and billing in euros. (See Figure CS3.1.4.) The unique Orange Value Promise underpins the company's belief that it offers the best value: if a customer thinks another popular digital tariff would better suit their needs, Orange will give them the equivalent on its own network. Such an offer requires tremendous billing flexibility, which Orange has secured by developing its billing systems in-house.

Expanded presence

Orange is trying to accommodate different customer lifestyles, and to enhance product/service exposure and ease of access, by expanding the range of options customers can choose from in terms of where and how to buy Orange products. In addition to a rapidly growing high street presence, Orange makes it easy for customers to gather information and make purchases over the phone and internet. (See Figure CS3.1.5.) Orange is also embracing new concepts, such as The Studio in Birmingham. Geared to user enthusiasts and small businesses, this high-tech hub is an Orange shop, internet café, and conference centre with full video conferencing and editing facilities.

---

[9] The Global System for Mobile communications. There are three frequency bands used by digital mobile phones: 900 MHz, 1800 MHz and 1900 MHz. Orange uses GSM 1800 in the UK.

Orange EMU policy statement

Orange is a global communications provider with a significant European presence and major European customers and suppliers. European Monetary Union (EMU) and the euro are important to us, and we have therefore adopted a proactive stance. Orange's euro policy is to anticipate and be responsive to customers' and suppliers' needs and to be able to transact in the euro in any of its operations.

To this end our businesses in the Euro zone are now fully euro compliant and are able to offer euro pricing and billing to customers for all products and services. Orange plc's Euroland operations will also be able to pay their suppliers in the euro when appropriate. Over the next two years these businesses will continue to move toward adopting the euro as their accounting currency and prior to the end of the euro transition period all staff will be paid in the euro.

Orange plc's other businesses outside the Euro zone have also undertaken a number of initiatives to prepare for EMU and the euro. In line with the desire to meet expected customer demand, the UK in particular, will be able to offer corporate and business customers a euro billing service for their airtime bills and will be able to pay suppliers in the euro.

FIGURE CS 3.1.4: Orange EMU policy statement.
Source: www.orange.co.uk

Revolution and revelation

The battle to broaden thinking within Orange, from a so-far-successful, short-term service orientation, to a guaranteed-future, long-term market orientation, is revolutionary and will not be won in a day. But progress has been made through the focus on internal collaboration. This case study was written in the first year of shared objectives across the directorates. Historically, Sales focused on acquisition, Marketing on revenue and Customer Services on churn. The three directors now have joint objectives to deliver on all three, demonstrating the interdependence of these performance measures.

Eliminating competing objectives is a crucial step towards becoming customer focused. In the past Orange had a counterproductive practice of offering inappropriately priced handset upgrades. Orange paid a subsidy on each handset upgrade (a not insubstantial sum) and this cost to the company was reflected in the upgrade's price, often making an upgrade more expensive for existing customers than the model of choice would be for a new customer. If a customer left Orange and rejoined to get a better deal, Sales were rewarded for winning a new customer and Customer Services were penalized for losing a customer; although the customer was, in truth, neither won nor lost.

how to buy

buy online
buy Just Talk, Boxed & Ready or Talk Plans
online now, in a secure payment environment

Orange shops
find out the details of your nearest Orange shop

telesales
speak to the experts over the phone, call 0500
80 20 80

Orange dealers
search for your specialist dealer by a postcode
or name

high street retailers
find out which high street shops stock Orange

switch to Orange
join Orange and enjoy more benefits without
having to change your number

Orange Business Team
the Orange Business Team can take care of
your company's telecom needs

FIGURE CS 3.1.5: Online advice of the options on how to buy from Orange.
Source: www.orange.co.uk

The newly established Orange Business Team is another manifestation of Orange's progress towards CRM. This cross-functional group, comprising business, sales, technical and customer service experts, works to attract new corporate clients and to deliver appropriately tailored product/service packages. Such moves to collaborative organization and working practices also help different functions understand each other and consolidate their goals.

The drive to push CRM out into the organization is extremely challenging. Cascade and Leadbetter are still in the process of presenting the CRM strategy to company members. They started with their own directorate. Customer Relations accounts for a large portion of Orange UK's 9000 strong workforce, and the pair still have some way to go to reach these employees, and win their commitment to new attitudes and approaches. Seventy per cent of the audience at a recent presentation were from Customer Services, and 'it was a huge step for them [Customer Services]' says Leadbetter. A customer relations focus means proactively offering added value in every customer contact – a radical departure from the conventional 'reactive' customer service focus.

On the sales side, there is no real buy-in yet. 'CRM is not on their radar screen', notes Cascade – probably, he believes, because the sales force are incentivized to close sales rather than to serve the developing needs of existing customers. Orange shops, for example, are rewarded for acquiring customers, not for resolving their problems. However, the reconfiguration and customization of service plans does reveal a shift from product-focused to proposition-focused marketing. This is a critical transition as the market reaches maturity, and there are signs that product developers are also beginning to think about retention and to reflect this in their activities.

Cascade notes 'a lack of detailed understanding at all levels of segmentation'. The pervasive view is that segments are fixed, rather than dynamic, entities.

Overcoming such preconceptions will require patience and perseverance, not least because the pace of change is merely reinforcing the barriers to CRM. Because the market is expanding so rapidly, the race to acquire customers is frantic, catapulting the development and launch of products and services into 'fast forward' while relegating any real benefits analysis to the back burner. It is crucial to assess the appropriateness of the products and services on offer in order to understand the market and to continue to improve and innovate. But that requires taking frequent 'snapshots' of activities to glean insights into customer usage (or non-usage) patterns. On the premise that meaningful research produces meaningful insights and meaningful action, more needs be done at Orange if the company is to achieve its aim of being customer driven by being data driven.

Achieving harmony between proliferation and performance is one of Leadbetter's prime concerns: 'There needs to be a balance between how much technology you can do and just getting the basics right', she says, 'and the basics are down to data'. She cites the fact that Orange has provided answering machines for the past six years, but has little idea what parts of the machine – the forward option, time delivery, messaging and so forth – customers use. Knowledge of product usage and user grouping underpins penetration and, as Leadbetter points out, 'little features can add significant benefits to customers' lives'.

Connecting with the future

As in any enterprise, the quality of output relies on the quality of input. But selecting and integrating the best ingredients can be a challenge:

> The proliferation of choice and complexity makes it more difficult to understand customers, to collect the right data and to respond with the right strategies and tactics.

Orange has developed its CRM strategy to provide a practical framework for tackling these difficulties. The strategy takes into account the need to facilitate a step change in the company's CRM capability through creating internal synergies, competencies and efficiencies, while at the same time embracing and exploiting market growth. Business expansion creates a mixed blessing of opportunities and responsibilities. With its focus on using 'intelligence' to build retention, CRM offers a practical means of reconciling commercial pressures with overall business strategy. In the words of former Orange Chairman, Canning Fok: 'With a view to maximizing shareholder value, our strategy continues to focus on the attraction and retention of high value subscribers. To this end, we have further invested in network and service quality and pioneered value for money tariffs' (Interim Report 1999). Orange recognizes that subscriber numbers, while a useful measure, do not tell the whole story, and that success is more meaningfully measured in terms of value: the value of the customer to the business, and the value of the business to the customer.

Effective customer relationships have always been the lifeblood of business, but now increasingly they are also the life-support. With heightened expectations and breakthrough technologies, the competition to serve and supply is fierce. A company's ability to differentiate both itself from competitors, and high value customers from less promising prospects has become a test of intelligence, technology and vision. It needs the capacity to see and capitalize on the interconnectivity between systems, networks, communities and the individual. Success is no longer about survival of the fittest, but survival of those with the strongest relationships.

As penetration of communication products and services increases, developing customer relationships that delight and retain customers becomes increasingly important for optimizing acquisition investment, enhancing revenue streams and providing Orange with entry points into other market sectors. The resultant share of wallet and reduced churn will bring significant bottom-line benefits.

Orange's expansion into multimedia services will increase the opportunities to receive customer communications as well as to initiate and transmit them, offering further scope for developing more mutually rewarding relationships. At the same time, the requirement to address issues of resource, relevancy, access, security and brand elasticity will become even more acute.

As service becomes more 'distributed' through remote channels, the need for contact management, process management and performance management increases. A key aim is to achieve balance between efficient processes

that maximize consistency and control, and providing flexibility and empowerment to exceed customer expectations.

Customers are helping to drive change and are demanding greater participation in shaping that change; they are the emerging powerbroker of future competitive advantage. With multiple customer interfaces, a 'talkative' market, and now an agreed strategy for managing and maximizing relationships, Orange has a sound basis on which to build its capacity to 'connect' with customers.

Forward-looking and optimistic, like their company, Cascade, Leadbetter and their team have embarked on a mission to relate to and influence both employees and customers. Their passion to communicate to each stakeholder group the benefits of adopting CRM will no doubt bear fruits in ensuring a bright future for Orange.

CASE STUDY 3.2

Britannia Building Society: Turning information into insight

OVERVIEW

When it was clear that merger and conversion had become the chosen route for most of the large building societies, The Britannia had to move fast to sustain its independent position in the industry. Research amongst their members showed that a majority were against a merger or conversion, feeling that they risked losing service quality and convenience. Desk research conducted by The Britannia at the time also suggested that their ability to continue to provide competitive investment and mortgage rates would be best served as a mutual society. Alongside this, The Britannia also sought to express their difference through sharing their success with their members. What emerged was a concept of 'modern mutuality' that provided the Society with the opportunity to differentiate themselves in the financial services marketplace.

The Britannia uses the power of information to express its mutuality status as well as provide a quality service to customers. It understands customers through customer segmentation, propensity to purchase modelling and customer profitability analysis. They are rapidly turning information into insight and opening up new possibilities for the management of their business. Using both operational and analytical CRM software the Society has seen significant benefits being delivered.

More recently, its legacy IT systems have been replaced because they impacted the organizations ability to respond to marketplace changes. In particular, the emergence of flexible mortgage products placed the Society at a considerable disadvantage because it was unable to offer these products to customers as its back-office IT systems could not cope with the vagaries of these offerings, particularly daily interest rate calculations.

This case study also illustrates how The Britannia is currently undertaking a core system renewal programme to replace its entire legacy IT infrastructure. This 'Really Big Programme', as it is known internally, also involves significant re-engineering of core business processes.

Key learning points

This is a very rich case study addressing many aspects of the CRM framework. The Society has a very clear customer strategy, a strategy that pervades all of its activities. In addition, it has a clear understanding that if it is to be successful it is not just about value extraction from the customer but also about returning value back to the customer.

CRM issues

- Legacy IT infrastructure can impact product offerings.

Back-office legacy systems can severely impinge on the implementation of a CRM strategy. Despite the fact that customers were seeking flexible mortgage products, the Society had been unable to provide these due to the inability of its systems to support such offerings.

- Organizations must develop an F2B (Front-to-Back) strategy for integrating the front-office and back-office components.

The integrated customer initiative (ICI) project had seen The Britannia successfully capture customer information and provided an integrated view of the customer across all channels (a front-office strategy). However, the Really Big Programme is about developing a total front-to-back strategy, enabling the Society to deal with the constraining aspects of the back-office technical infrastructure and providing a platform for the future.

- Information technology supports a multi-channel integration strategy.

From analysis of its customer information, The Britannia knows the channels favoured by customers. Technology also supports the operationalization of the integration strategy.

- Successful CRM is not solely about value extraction from the customer but also about providing value to the customer.

The Britannia has a clear view on providing value to the customer and is the cornerstone of it concept of 'modern mutuality'.

Strategy Development Process issues

- Understanding the value of information precedes the development of a CRM solution.

The CRM technology is just a means to an end and that end must have a clear understanding of how information will support the process of value creation.

- Customer information must be turned into customer insight.

Gathering customer information is fruitless unless it provides insight into their behaviour and preference and is then acted upon.

- CRM should be at the centre of all business activity.

For The Britannia, CRM drives everything it does. It pervades business strategies and drives all planning activity.

Introduction: Changing information requirements

Many businesses today realize how important CRM is and the potential it has to help them achieve and sustain a competitive edge. These organizations are already changing their business processes and building technology solutions in order to acquire new customers, retain existing ones and maximize their lifetime value.

There is compelling evidence that superior customer relationships make for better businesses:

- relationship marketing increases retention;
- relationships are more easily built through two-way communication – and organizations can learn from their customers when they set up feedback loops;
- relationship behaviour anticipates customer demands;
- retained customers are inevitably more profitable.

The effective management of information plays a crucial role in CRM. Information is critical to tailor products, to create service innovations (for example, tailored websites), to provide a single consolidated view of the customer, to calculate customer lifetime value and to establish integrated multi-channel capability. But CRM is not just about having better customer information to offer new services, for example, prompting customers to transfer money if they build up a large balance on a non-interest bearing account. It is about personalizing the transaction with a customer. The company should know the customer at every point of contact, whether the phone, ATM, the internet or any one of their outlets or branches. The need for consistent service across channels is prompting growing numbers of organizations to adopt an integrated channel management strategy.

In essence, CRM is about making it easier for the customer to deal with an organization. Customers shouldn't have to deal with an organization's complexity, which is often brought about by outdated structures, legacy systems and technologies. Equally, CRM is about analysing customer information for business decisions. It can help organizations understand customer needs; differentiate between customers via market segmentation; predict the likelihood of customer churn, and analyse customer loyalty and customer profitability; and channel effectiveness and the performance of sales campaigns.

The Britannia Building Society understands how important information is in effective CRM. Indeed, as a mutual society,[10] it uses the power of information to express that mutuality, to return value back to members as well as provide a tailored service to every customer. It focuses on the way staff deliver service supported by effective information and systems.

Britannia Building Society remains a mutual

The Britannia Group is a market leader in financial services in the UK. It comprises a building society, life and pensions company, investment company and a general insurance arm. It began life in 1856 as the Leek & Moorland Benefit Building Society and after its first year of trading had 203 members and total assets of £3000. Today The Britannia Building Society is the second biggest mutually-owned building society in the UK, with 2.6 million customers. It has over 200 branches stretching from Torquay in Devon to Aberdeen in North East Scotland and it employs more than 4000 staff, including 76 in its call centre. In 2001 its total asset base was £17.4 billion.

---

[10] A mutual society is an organization set up and owned by its members and run for their benefit. Building societies, friendly societies and some life insurers are examples of mutual societies. These societies trace their roots back to the end of the eighteenth century. Typically a group of people would get together and between them save up to buy their own homes. Every so often, there would be a ballot and the winner would be lent funds from the kitty to make their purchase – in other words, they would be given a mortgage. The savings process would continue and in due course all of the members would be lent funds and on repayment the societies would be wound up.

From the Mid-1850s there was a change – permanent societies began to emerge. They had the same functions as the older societies but they didn't wind themselves up when their members had been satisfied. Today, these societies vary from being small regional groupings to national personal financial retailers. They have boards of directors which can look and behave much like those running a public company with shareholders.

In recent years building societies have seen a great deal of change. Since the market was deregulated in the mid-1980s, competition has been fierce and the shape of the industry has altered radically. The Abbey National was the first building society to convert to a bank in 1989 and the Halifax, Alliance & Leicester, Woolwich and Northern Rock all followed suit. In the process, The Leeds Permanent Building Society and National & Provincial were swallowed up.

As the large building societies started to become public limited companies (plc's), Britannia had to move fast to sustain its position in the industry. However, it wanted to be sure that whatever it did was in the best long-term interests of its members. Research among members showed that most were against merger or conversion to a plc because they feared they might lose service quality and convenience. In addition Britannia's desk research also suggested that it was best able to continue to provide competitive investment and mortgage rates as a mutual society. It was clear to the board that just getting bigger was no guarantee of future success. In the financial services industry cost efficiency does not correlate with size, and some relatively small institutions are very efficient while many of the larger ones are not.

Britannia saw the way forward in retaining its strengths in providing competitive products in a friendly and approachable way, and it based its CRM strategy around these objectives. But Britannia also sought to express the fact that it was different from its competitors by sharing its success with members. It created a concept of 'modern mutuality' that allowed it to differentiate itself in the financial services market while maintaining its independence without rapid growth.

Its decision to remain mutual has enabled The Britannia to refocus on the loyalty of its core member base and to build a strategy around it that has strong customer and staff support. Britannia chairman Barrie Bernstein recently noted: 'With no outside shareholders to satisfy, our sole task is to provide value and service to our members.'

Expressing mutuality

An organization might express the mutual concept in terms of the 'hard' benefits to customers in a number of ways, any or all of which might be appropriate depending on the organization's corporate requirements. After much research The Britannia chose to instigate a Members' Loyalty Bonus Scheme (MLBS) as a mechanism for giving additional value back to members.

The scheme pays members a bonus by distributing a proportion of profits based on each member's financial holding and the length of time they have been a customer. For some customers this can mean a cash bonus of up to £500, paid directly into their account or sent to them by cheque each year. They continue to receive a bonus as long as they remain a member.

The basic details of the scheme are:

- A scheme member is someone who has an investment share account and/or has a mortgage and/or holds Permanent Interest Bearing Shares and who has registered for the scheme.
- Products earn points. For example, investment accounts earn one point per £100 of average balance (up to £20 000).
- Points can be increased according to the length of time the individual has been a Britannia customer (their 'tenure'). So a customer who has been with the company for at least five years sees their points value increase by a multiplier of 1.5. This increases to a multiplier of 2 for customers who have been with the company for at least ten years.
- Each year the directors decide how much will be paid out as a bonus pool and distribute that bonus pool to members in proportion to the number of points they have earned.
- The bonus pool divided by the total number of points will produce a point value and the individual customer bonus is calculated as follows:
  points × tenure × value = bonus.

The scheme operates as well as, not instead of, discounts awarded as a result of normal competitiveness and Britannia clearly positions it as 'an extra' rather than a 'replacement' for a discount. In 2001 loyal Britannia members shared a record £53 million through this scheme, bringing the total amount shared since the bonus scheme was introduced to £250 million. Britannia's deputy chief executive Neville Richardson notes: 'Our unique loyalty bonus scheme provides real proof of the benefits of belonging to a mutually owned building society. It directly rewards loyalty: the more you put into the Society, the more you get back.'

The mutuality strategy and the customer base

While the MLBS is a clear expression of The Britannia's mutual stance, sustaining that stance requires more than a regular reward. Britannia also needs to understand its customers, their behaviour, their preferences and their attitudes.

Like most financial institutions, and probably most other commercial organizations, the quality of Britannia's customer data was good enough for account administration and general marketing purposes but inadequate to the task of accurately calculating and paying bonuses based on a customer's total product holdings. So when the company announced the MLBS in 1996 it had no idea how it was going to make the payments. Neither was the quality of its customer data good enough to allow it to do meaningful customer analysis such as customer segmentation and propensity modelling.

However, Britannia saw the poor quality of its data as an opportunity. It knew that customers would be unlikely to upgrade the data it held on them without an incentive. So they made members' eligibility for an annual bonus conditional on their updating the data the Society held on them, achieving a response rate of over 75 per cent.

Nevertheless, Britannia faced a daunting task. It needed to build a customer registration database from scratch, keep it updated from its legacy systems and provide a helpdesk to advise customers and to sort out discrepancies in the information provided. What is more, it had to do all this within a few short months.

The Integrated Customer Initiative

In 1996 the Society embarked on its Integrated Customer Initiative (ICI) project to build this customer database and establish a telephone helpdesk. Customer-facing staff in branches and, over the phone, at head offices can all access the new customer database.

In partnership with Fineos Corporation, Britannia also developed a Customer Information System (CIS) to distribute information to customer-facing staff in an operational CRM environment. Alison Thompson, business project manager for ICI, says: 'The project started with a vision to provide a single view of the customer at every point of customer contact. Like many other organizations we had a number of account-based systems that did not tie up.' Once customers had purchased products, Britannia segregated customer enquiries unnecessarily. 'If you had a query on the life policy you had to talk to the life company, if you had a mortgage you had to talk to the mortgage people, and so on. So we are working on pulling the whole thing together and making it a far more customer-focused process', explains Thompson.

Britannia devoted three months, from March to June 1995, to setting out the business case and determining what to focus on for the first two years of the project. 'We also knew that it was going to be a fundamental part of our business on a long-term basis and that we should look to exploit it as much as possible', says Thompson. 'But we knew we also had to have some fixed objectives to focus on and to deliver, to make sure we just didn't just go round in circles.'

Once the business case was approved, Britannia set up two pilots where the emphasis would be to cross-sell – one in the head office of the life company in Glasgow and the other in the building society's head office in Leek. Each used the CIS applications (the operational CRM solution) developed by Fineos. Britannia chose to use head offices as pilots because the technical infrastructure was more straightforward than using branch systems and distributed networks.

The pilot in Leek was a telesales operation based around a mortgage promotion. Keeping within the rules about compliance, Britannia selected a segment of its customer base who had signed up to become group customers and carried out some basic cleaning of data held on those customers on different systems. 'We had five operators who were using ICI and CIS applications and five who were not', explains Thompson. In line with usual business procedure, the Society mailed existing investors with details of a special mortgage offer and followed up with a phone call. 'We found that those operators using ICI, who had more knowledge of the customers' relationship, achieved a 66 per cent improvement over those who did not, in terms of taking an offer through to a quote', says Thompson. The pilot ran from March to June 1996, and also yielded feedback outlining how the CIS application could be further enhanced.

The other pilot was based at the life company's help desk in Glasgow and focused on incoming calls. In this case Britannia used the CIS application to make sure all relevant information was to hand when customers called in with queries after receiving their annual bonus notices on life policies. Thompson says that over 50 per cent of calls resulted in 'a positive outcome' such as wanting to do more business with the group or requesting more information about products.

In tandem with improving its data and establishing a distributed operational customer information system, Britannia took the first steps towards understanding customers through customer segmentation, propensity to purchase modelling and customer profitability modelling. It rapidly turned these data into useful decision-making information and opened up new possibilities for the way the business was controlled.

Figure CS 3.2.1 below illustrates the relationship between the ICI project and the data warehouse and customer information system. It also shows the back-office account administration systems – mortgages, loans, life and pensions, general insurance and so on – that were subsequently replaced.

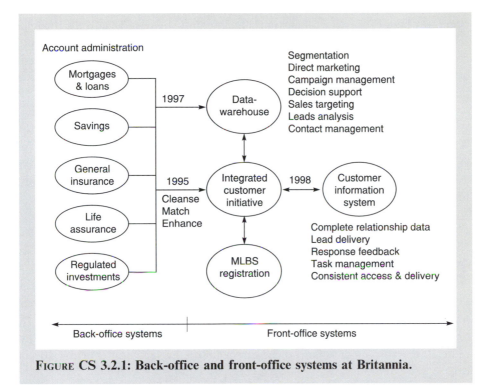

Account administration

Segmentation
Direct marketing
Campaign management
Decision support
Sales targeting
Leads analysis
Contact management

Mortgages & loans

1997

Data-warehouse

Savings

General insurance

1995
Cleanse
Match
Enhance

Integrated customer initiative

1998

Customer information system

Life assurance

Complete relationship data
Lead delivery
Response feedback
Task management
Consistent access & delivery

Regulated investments

MLBS registration

Back-office systems   Front-office systems

FIGURE CS 3.2.1: Back-office and front-office systems at Britannia.

Customer segmentation

The segmentation work has identified groups of customers in terms both of their worth to the Society 'now' and 'in the future', and of their 'loyalty' or the strength of the relationship they have with the Society. Britannia has identified just ten customer segments that it believes captures the profile of its entire customer base.

For example, one segment includes customers from affluent, dual income households, who are generally married and either childless or have young children. This segment tends to consist of big spending customers. Another segment comprises customers who are unemployed or on low incomes, who tend to be financially unsophisticated.

The segmentation work is now having a direct impact in almost every part of Britannia's business. One of the major benefits of customer segmentation and the associated propensity modelling is more targeted direct marketing. This in turn generates better leads for all customer-facing staff, delivered via the Customer Information System, and creates direct mail lists. To effectively organize and control such a broad span of customer communication, the organization needs a centrally-driven, customer contact strategy and for leads to be delivered via a dedicated campaign management system.

According to director of operations, John Suffolk: 'You're doing pretty well if you get a two per cent response rate (with direct marketing). Now we're into the 40–60 per cent response rate. And all of that is because we only send letters to people who we think are going to buy something, and buy our products that we know they don't have and we think they don't have from other organizations, based on the data that we hold.'

Britannia meets individual customer needs

Once it had built its customer database, the Society began using it for direct marketing. In the past it had to spend about 90 pence to make £1 profit. By analysing its customer information to work out exactly who it should mail, it reduced the cost–income ratio of its direct marketing activity to below 20 per cent.

Gerald Gregory, director of sales and marketing, says Britannia can now rank its two million customers in terms of profitability, from the most profitable customer to the least profitable customer in rank order. 'There are very few organizations that I believe can do that. And we can do that both as a snap-shot profitability view and also in terms of lifetime profitability. All of this stuff has enabled us to behave in a completely different way from the vast majority of financial services companies', he says.

Before the ICI project, Britannia was a classic case of the 80/20 rule: 80 per cent of its profits came from 20 per cent of its customers. 'The big difference for us now though is that I know who the customers are' says Gregory, 'I know where that 80 per cent of our profits are coming from. I know who that 20 per cent of the customer base is. Not by segment – we know who they are by name. We know where they live. We know which products they hold. We know which products we'd like to sell to them next. And our business planning actually starts with a view of growing our target segments. So we try to grow the target segments by selling products to them. We don't start with a product target; we start with a customer target.'

He continues: 'The same thing applies with our cross-selling activity. The prompts that we give to our sales staff are geared towards trying to improve the profitability of the customers that we already hold and we sell to customers' needs. We know these individuals need these particular products and we encourage our sales staff to meet that customer need by having a product conversation with them on a one-to-one basis. We don't run on a campaign basis – that is, "Today is Tuesday, today we will talk to every-body about personal loans". That's how it used to be. The way that we work now is that we will talk to one individual about this product because it's relevant to them, and we'll talk to the next person in the queue about something completely different because that product is relevant to them. So it's about focus. We approach each customer segment differently because they have a different likelihood of buying products, they have different product needs and they actually wish to be spoken to in a different tone of voice.'

'Then there is the issue of retention. Clearly there are certain parts of our customer base where we do not want to lose that customer relationship. By putting things like customer profitability in the hands of your retention staff, you know exactly how to behave in terms of trying to retain a customer relation-ship. You know how far you can go.'

Britannia knows its customers intimately

Britannia knows exactly what relationship it has with any customer who comes into one of its branches. It also knows what products they hold. It knows how long they've been a customer, their relationships with other people at the same address, whether it has sent them a direct mail shot recently, whether they responded to the mail shot, whether they have recently visited this or another branch and where that branch is.

So, for example, if a customer goes into the Aberdeen branch one day and appears in Exeter branch the next day, the teller in Exeter knows that they were in Aberdeen the day before and what they talked about, because all that infor-mation has been captured. Gregory says: 'It does enable us to know the full extent of the relationship between us and the customer and we behave as though we know the customer. That has significantly enhanced our service proposition to the customer.'

What's more, tellers' screens carry prompts suggesting they talk to the cus-tomer about a specific product offer. John Suffolk notes: 'Our CRM system allows tellers to know that someone they are dealing with is, for example, the sort of person who doesn't want a relationship, who's very price driven, who buys and sells all the time. There's not much point in us trying to keep a con-versation going for a long time at a counter because it's not what that customer is looking for. We either know what sort of products they have, because they've told us via data collected through the members' loyalty bonus scheme, or we know from our propensity models what they're likely to have. Therefore, we will have a conversation with them that's specific to their particular needs.'

Suffolk continues: 'So, for example, the CRM system will prompt the teller: "When you speak to John Suffolk, he's the sort of guy that should have an ISA. He doesn't have an ISA with us, so pose the question." We've free format triggers that we pop up on the teller's screen that gives them the confidence to have that conversation.'

The approach in telesales is similar. Call centre staff know the extent of the relationship with the customer, including whether or not they have been into a branch recently, because they use the same system as branch staff. All interaction data are captured and fed back into the data warehouse, allowing the Society to refine and enhance its propensity models.

As a result of this analysis, Britannia can now start to look at customers and their activities with an eye to their value in a mutual relationship. This has had a significant impact, particularly on cross-selling and retention strategies. Since the CRM project began The Britannia has seen the average number of products per customer rise from 1.3 to over 2.

From information to insight

The Britannia turns information in its CRM database into customer insight in a number of ways.

- Distribution and channel strategy. An important aspect of Britannia's distribution strategy is understanding what it can sell to whom and how. Its segmentation work indicates what type of customers use particular branches and highlights the sales channels that are acceptable to them. Already this is helping Britannia to understand customers who have high levels of branch transactions and how it might serve these people more profitably, and it plans to apply this concept to its direct telephone operations.
- Corporate communication. In order to communicate its mutuality strategy effectively Britannia must understand who its key customers are, what they read and what they watch. It also needs to develop the most appropriate message for those customers. The customer segments give this work a clear framework and direction.
- Sales targeting. The more the Society understands the types of customers who use branches or live within particular catchment areas, the better it should be able to set branch sales targets. The customer make-up of a branch can have

a major effect on cross-sales targets, for instance. Britannia now develops the sales and marketing plan around an understanding of sales potential rather than basing it purely on acquiring market share. Sales targets are based on what the Society believes members will buy next year based on their needs today.

- Product design. The segmentation work and the related propensity modelling allow The Britannia to identify gaps in its product portfolio and determine potential market sizes for them. Since new products can broadly be targeted at particular segments the Society can fine-tune the products to further attract these customers and design communications more appropriately. Developing innovative products underlines Britannia's commitment to support members in all aspects of home ownership.

- Sales training. Although customers should not be overtly aware of it, the Society's strategy requires that different segments are treated in different ways. For instance, the extent to which it wants to retain a customer's business, the amount of contact it has with a customer and the products it offers a customer may all vary according to the type of customer it is dealing with. This variation is driven by segmentation and customer facing staff need to be trained to do it properly.

- Mutuality strategy. The mutuality strategy requires the Society to carefully control the number of members it has in relation to its profits. It manages two distinct sets of customers: members and non-members. Segmentation helps it determine, for example, which customers it wants as members and which it would like to migrate from non-membership to membership.

Supporting IT systems

Britannia's database built from the loyalty scheme registration information overlaid its legacy systems data to create an integrated customer information system. This system not only affords staff access to customer data, it also permits data to be delivered to customer-facing points, whether branches, postal or telesales units, and eventually directly to customers via interactive units and internet technology. The Society used middleware technologies to integrate the legacy systems with the CRM systems.

The employees' ability to see everything the Society knows about its customers while they are interacting with them makes it much easier for those employees to talk to those customers in a manner which makes them feel that The Britannia understands them. This automatically enhances the customer's perception of service. The system also allows enhanced information to be fed to customer-facing staff, highlighting a customer's likely next purchase or helping the staff respond correctly to changes in customer buying behaviour.

According to Suffolk: 'Technology plays a relatively small part in terms of what we're trying to do. It is about brand and external perception. It is about the processes. It is about the product. It is about the way the people deliver the service – all supported by very good CRM-type technology. Technology that gives the people dealing with the customer excellent knowledge about their customers in terms of their products, their holdings, their relationships, the times they contact us, whether they like leaflets or don't like leaflets. We've also got all the tools and the techniques, and the confidence to execute the information that we are presenting.'

'So Britannia had a clear strategy in terms of what it wanted to achieve. It wanted to attract a great number of customers. That's not just about CRM. It wanted to make sure that it retained more of the customers that it had, and it wanted to maximize the relationship. And the only way it could do that was to have this full knowledge, and to make it available to its customer service staff.'

Britannia's operational CRM system delivers the information that provides this 'full knowledge' directly to customer-facing staff. In addition Britannia believes that to benefit from the era of the information warehouse, it must use the information well. Keenly aware that it must not flood customers with relevant but unwanted offers delivered through numerous media, it is currently engaged in creating and managing an all-embracing customer contact strategy and controlling customer contact through it.

The Core Systems Renewal Programme

The ICI project has been the first step in Britannia's drive to become customer focused. It had developed most of its back-office legacy systems in-house over many years and these were becoming increasingly expensive to maintain. According to Suffolk: 'If we colour-coded the types of technologies that were in operation we'd have more colours than the colours of the rainbow. It's a very complex system to maintain and is prone to errors.'

More critically, and strategically, the legacy technology hampered the Society's efforts to adapt to an ever changing business environment. Despite its very good IT people, its old technology constrained its ability to build an internet channel, deal with the Euro or introduce new products. It had to change its systems.

The 'Core Systems Renewal Programme' or the 'Really Big Programme' as it is known within the Society, is replacing all legacy systems. Suffolk explains: 'We're replacing all the teller-based systems and all the investment account administration systems. We're replacing all the mortgage systems from application, processing, and point of sale to administration. We're replacing all our CRM environments. We are integrating all the environments to get a straight-through process whether it be from the web or the call centre right through to the accounting systems. We are re-training all the people in terms of process and the value to the business. Overall, it's about a 220 person-year programme. That's spread over three years.'

One of the first systems to be replaced was the mortgage processing system. Members were looking for products that the Society just couldn't provide because of the constraints of the legacy systems. The Society tried for many months to work out whether they could introduce a flexible mortgage. However, the amount of man effort required to change the existing system to be able to calculate daily interest was prohibitive. The systems just couldn't cope with such a structural change.

Suffolk continues: 'One of the first projects out of the Really Big Programme was what we called the fast-track project. And the fast-track project started before full board approval, before the final design was completed. It was about putting a flexible mortgage onto the new system.'

The project took nine months from conception to going live – far less time than it would have taken to upgrade the old systems. Today, 20 per cent of new mortgages Britannia sells are flexible. Suffolk notes: 'To me this is a good example of how the newer systems have proved their capability and added business value.'

Measurable business results

A key metric for the Society is the cost–income ratio of its business activities. Gregory stresses: 'With direct marketing, for example, we started off this process with a cost–income ratio of about 90p; it's now down to about 20p, which is a huge improvement. That has been achieved both by increasing the sales rates of direct marketing and also by reducing the wastage by not writing to people who clearly have no interest in our product offer.

We look at things like the cross-sale ratios which we achieve, and over the past three years the rate of sale into our customer base has actually doubled. One in four of the customer interactions in our branch network actually lead to a sale.

We do a mailing. Is the response rate greater? Yes it is. That's wonderful! And have we sold any more and can we prove we have sold more? The answer is yes. Because we only mail segments of our membership based on the customer segmentation and we track the purchases made by people in that segment or that mailing versus others, we can measure the difference.'

The average number of products a member holds has risen dramatically since the Integrated Customer Initiative was launched. From a level of about 1.3 products per customer it has increased to over 2, and is rising year on year. A shift like that takes some time to achieve when a company is dealing with over two million customers.

Gregory continues: 'We are in a very, very competitive marketplace and if we had continued to operate in the way that we used to where 80 per cent of our profits came from 20 per cent of our customers, this rule would still apply. In fact, it would get more and more difficult for us because everybody is after that 20 per cent who make all the money.'

'Because we have been able to acquire more profitable customers, we are increasing our proportion of profitable customers. And we will be able to sustain that strategy in a highly competitive and complicated marketplace.'

Britannia uses international benchmarking firm QCi to benchmark its CRM strategy and implementation. QCi conducts an intensive audit by exploring what lies behind the statements The Britannia makes regarding CRM. The firm interviews all the key players in the organization, talks with branch staff, looks at the Society's direct marketing and examines how its systems are structured. QCi's most recent audit ranked the Society's CRM framework among the top five per cent in the world.

In the year ended 31 December 2001, Britannia Group assets grew to £17.4 billion, net lending more than doubled to £1.8 billion and operating profits rose five per cent to £138.3 million. Costs have remained in real terms unchanged since 1997.

The ingredients of success

Pondering on the success of Britannia's CRM strategy and implementation, Gerald Gregory asserts: 'I think there has been a lot of rot spoken about CRM across the industry in the recent past, with the perception being that CRM starts and stops with buying a system. That's not the case. There is no point buying a CRM system if you don't change the organization to use it effectively. CRM is a combination of having the appropriate systems in place, having the appropriate data in place and being prepared to stick with it.'

Suffolk continues: 'It's important to have clear objectives and to measure the benefits clearly. Where it's working, stick with it, as we did, and be prepared to cut out the things that don't work. We balanced the objectives, the people issues, the process issues and the technology issues, and we are continuing to do that with our new programme, the "Really Big Programme".'

CRM drives everything The Britannia does. Gregory stresses: 'We start with a customer view. It drives all our planning. It's what we think about. It really pervades all our business strategies. And unless you are prepared to make that change then I don't think you will ever achieve a true CRM approach.'

CASE STUDY 3.3

Time to remodel at Homebase.co.uk[11]

OVERVIEW

Homebase's core activity had long been the provision to local communities of products and services for carrying out do-it-yourself (DIY) home repair and redecoration. As the home improvement market grew, however, so too did the level of competition, threatening Homebase with potential relegation to the commodity league. In autumn 1999, Homebase realized that to protect its established market position and positive differentiation, it needed to refurbish its offering and modernize its strategy.

As a result Homebase added a 'virtual' store to its well-established retail estate, as a way of increasing the market share by providing a complementary alternative to the traditional Homebase shopping experience. It developed online product and service strategies to capture customers' imagination as well as their custom, and further distinguish Homebase from its chief rival B&Q. Online customer and business strategies were aimed at acquiring and retaining a profitable customer base without incurring perpetual excessive investment.

Key learning points

Homebase's rapid entry into the world of e-commerce is a vivid reminder of how competitive urgency can precipitate commercial decisions, which, with hindsight, might have been taken very differently. The problem is that every business situation is unique and, until valuable learning is manifest, what constitutes the 'best' strategy is anyone's guess. To complicate matters, organizations also have to cope with changes beyond their control, such as market trends or, as in the case of Homebase, being bought by another company with a totally different outlook and approach.

---

[11] This case study was developed and agreed with the management of Homebase in November 2001.

Homebase learnt a lot from developing its e-strategy. Recognizing the business potential of an online venture, the company sought to expand its customer base and modus operandi by hiring external expertise and selling online to customers. It extended the nature of the offer to include creative ideas as well as tangible tools. Homebase motivated the e-customer to buy through a combination of necessity and persuasion, reinforced by unprecedented convenience. Having established the industry's first transactional web site with great expectations, the company then had to temper its optimism with realism, and to make the e-business economically viable as well as educationally valuable.

CRM issues

- Simply throwing money at a CRM problem isn't a CRM solution.

Homebase spent a considerable amount of money building a retail web site, which early on showed scant sign of generating the return on investment (ROI) it expected. This was partly due to the unrealistic nature of the founding expectations and partly due to events in the market place. The revised e-strategy seeks to improve ROI and to increase the number and value of customer relationships by incorporating patterns of customer purchasing behaviour into e-strategy development.

Strategy Development Process issues

- E-strategy *must* be integrated with corporate strategy.

Homebase set up its 'virtual' store as a separate business, in isolation from the rest of the company. Without the support and input of other areas of the business, the e-enterprise struggled to meet customer and commercial demands cost-effectively. Subsequent moves to integrate e-commerce issues with overall business concerns have delivered benefits to Homebase, Homebase.co.uk and their customers.

- Resolving the tension between business promise and business delivery is a matter of priorities.

Unless Homebase's e-business can make a profit, or at least break even, it is not a viable proposition. Thus, the revised e-strategy prioritizes economic stability over market share.

- 'Market share' can be a misleading objective.

As Homebase.co.uk found in a number of cases, pursuing market share without fully considering all the implications can be counter-productive.

- The body of internal talent and expertise is a treasure chest too rarely opened.

Homebase.co.uk initially outsourced many of its e-commerce operations. In the ensuing campaign to cut costs and centralize control, it brought all e-business responsibilities in-house and trained internal staff to fulfil them. The consequent benefits of reduced costs, empowered staff, direct relationships with customers, and reinvested learning have strengthened morale, enhanced proficiency and improved the bottom line.

Homebase.co.uk: entry strategy and ownership

For the past 20 years Homebase Limited has been a leading UK supplier of home improvement and garden products. Since its first store opened in Croydon in 1981, continued growth in the do-it-yourself (DIY) market has seen the company expand to nearly 300 stores nation-wide, serving more than one million customers each week. Homebase employs more than 15 000 people and has an annual turnover of £1.5 billion. As a DIY brand, Homebase is ranked second behind fellow domestic retailer, B&Q.

In July 2000 Homebase entered the e-commerce arena, launching its online store at www.homebase.co.uk. The addition of a web-based retail channel to its network of bricks and mortar stores not only signalled a 'move with the times', but also set in train the company's new strategic direction.

Since introducing the web site, Homebase has experienced a sharp learning curve and a change of ownership, which have combined to transform the company's original e-strategy almost beyond recognition. When Schroder Ventures bought Homebase from Sainsbury's in March 2001, the 'virtual' store was a discrete, standalone proposition aimed at capturing market share. Today, it is an integral part of a business-wide initiative to improve the company's bottom line and secure its commercial viability. This about turn in e-strategy signifies a radical revision of Homebase's initial e-commerce priorities and the assumptions on which they were based.

Context for change

In autumn 1999, while still part of Sainsbury's, Homebase was under mounting pressure to compete more effectively, both to protect its market position and to exploit evident commercial potential.

The company visualized its market niche in the context of two parallel dimensions: the competitive spectrum and the consumer spectrum. In the band of competitors, Homebase saw B&Q residing at one end and more upmarket retail chains, Ikea and Habitat, at the other, with itself somewhere in the middle, overlapping with B&Q. It saw its consumer base ranging from the 'technical' to the 'creative'. The former were keen to ensure a professional result but more interested in hiring someone in to do the project work rather than do it themselves. The latter were less interested in the end product they were creating than in the look and feel of the activity, and the idea and the inspiration behind it. 'Creatives' might be hands-on or not, and were likely to have multiple projects going at the same time (possibly never completing any of them). Again, Homebase fell somewhere in between, but slightly towards the technical end of the market, the extreme of which was represented by B&Q.

To avoid being perceived by customers as sharing the lower end of market with B&Q, and to better promote its growing range of products, Homebase sought to expand towards the creative pole or 'ideation space', as it is called in the industry. The underlying objective was to be responsible for initiating ideas that customers could then use as the basis for their DIY project, so that Homebase shopping was not just about getting the materials for the job but envisaging what one was aiming to achieve. By offering customers the means for inspiration as well as implementation, Homebase believed it could attract the creative as well as technical customer and thus capture a wider band of the consumer spectrum.

There was another business rationale as well: if Homebase were to concentrate on price, it would be more difficult to compete with B&Q. Moreover, customer research had shown that Homebase was perceived as less knowledgeable than B&Q, and the company was determined to reverse this impression and demonstrate a higher level of quality and service than its main competitor.

Catalysts for change

Within this context of revised strategies for growing the business and its customer base, two key drivers took hold and propelled the establishment of the Homebase web site. One was the idea of a new shopping experience that emphasized different kinds of activity, not simply different kinds of products. This concept was being introduced in Homebase's newer 'megastores', where sheer space allowed an alternative approach to product display. Instead of following traditional rules of shelf management, materials and equipment for a particular project – such as laying a laminate floor – were grouped together. Showroom set-ups of rooms of the house or suggested projects within houses, designed to provide decorative ideas and creative inspiration, were conveniently positioned near the relevant lighting fixtures, wall finishings and so on. The new layout was intended to mirror the customer's thought process (shop by project or room), rather than the company's stocktaking register (shop by manufacturer or department/industry), thus creating a more exciting and enticing customer proposition. The construction of a 'virtual' megastore was seen as a natural component of this business development strategy.

At the same time Homebase was in the process of reclassifying the products in all its stores to establish product categories more closely aligned to the way customers undertake a home improvement project – that is, how they move from product to idea to other products which feed into that idea. Identifying and implementing this new product structure, however, involved painstakingly considering every product and systematically re-registering it into a new classification system, ensuring no products were left out, duplicated or overlapped. If Homebase was going to invest in new systems and technology to implement an e-strategy, now was the opportune moment, while other fundamental changes were taking place.

The other and perhaps more powerful catalyst for action was the knowledge that chief rival B&Q was planning to launch a trading web site in January 2001.

E-business rationale

Homebase decided to develop and operate a web-based store alongside its local stores because it believed it would strengthen its customer base and boost sales. Homebase would become a knowledgeable source of information online, visibly distancing itself from B&Q while enhancing customer value. More specifically, a web presence would help Homebase capture customers early in the buying process by providing services for each stage of home improvement, from 'ideation' and planning, through to purchasing, execution, and subsequent purchasing of replacement or complementary items (see Figure CS 3.3.1).

The potential commercial and customer benefits of providing an end-to-end solution for customers online surpassed what the offline stores could achieve. The virtually unlimited space on the electronic medium meant Homebase could

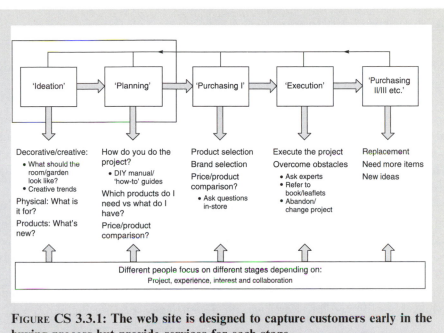

FIGURE CS 3.3.1: The web site is designed to capture customers early in the buying process but provide services for each stage.
Reproduced with the kind permission of Homebase Limited.

offer a broader range of products than any single store could stock. The range of products could be supported by more comprehensive information and speedy search facilities, making it easier for customers to find and compare products, and for the company to confirm availability and monitor stock levels. The provision of information could extend beyond the description of product features and usage instructions to encompass ideas, suggestions, home project stories, 'how to' guidance and buying advice. The ease with which customers could search, browse and buy from the comfort of their own homes offered a degree of personalization unmatched by an in-store experience.

Because costs-to-serve would arguably be much lower on the interactive medium, Homebase could offer better prices and customer value. An integral e-mail facility would make customer communications more cost-effective, which would allow correspondence to be more immediate and relevant, though handled by a smaller team than is necessary to deal with offline communications. Furthermore, giving customers the choice of conducting their interactions and transactions via telephone, the web or in-store would give the company the opportunity to improve its customer service, and demonstrate product knowledge and expertise.

A daunting challenge

Anticipating that B&Q was planning to launch its own web site imminently, time became a critical factor for Homebase. It had to act quickly and smartly in order to design and deliver a quality web site and e-commerce proposition before its chief competitor. The challenge was daunting: how to create a suitable, useable, profitable, manageable and sustainable web-based trading platform in just six months? There were no precedents within the UK DIY retail industry, and Homebase had set itself the objective of becoming the 'signature' home and garden enhancement site.

Outsourcing seemed to be the solution. Homebase engaged leading specialists to develop and operate many of the virtual store's key elements: Boston Consulting Group (BCG) advised on market management strategy; Sapient designed, constructed and managed the web site and call centre operator Brann provided customer service. Homebase's own picker-and-packer team based at its dedicated e-commerce warehouse in Corby undertook fulfilment, while major shipper Parcelforce was the designated carrier (see Figure CS 3.3.2).

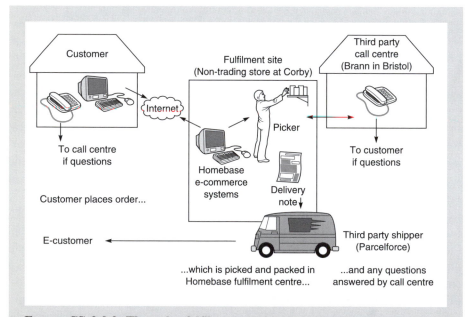

FIGURE CS 3.3.2: The order fulfilment process.
Reproduced with the kind permission of Homebase Limited.

By working closely with these outside experts, Homebase was able to quickly develop the main components of an e-strategy.

E-strategy development

Online product strategy

Given the tight time frame and the complexity of converting an offline catalogue of thousands of products to an online display, directory and delivery system, it was not feasible to offer all Homebase products on the web site. Therefore the company needed to decide which products should feature on the site initially and in the future. As Sapient consultant, Kai Turner explains: 'Homebase realized they couldn't get all their products online for launch and given that, they wanted to find a smart way to scale back and to determine which products would be best online. They also didn't want to abandon this idea of the inspirational space.'

Homebase quickly realized that some products transfer less easily online than others. For example, the pigment tones and textures of paint are difficult to replicate accurately via the internet. Homebase's solution was to offer customers the opportunity to order a traditional set of paint cards on the web site, which they would then receive by post, and to buy their paint online. This would satisfy both 'technical' and 'creative' customers: those who knew what paint they wanted could get it quickly, while those wanting to learn about paint ranges or wanting to search for the paint they had envisaged could still do so.

Compliance with legal restrictions also confined the online product portfolio. DIY items such as white spirit and aerosols, for example, could not be sold online due to safety regulations.

Web site design strategy

Accepting the limitations of the electronic medium, and working within the constraints of time and compatibility, Homebase designed and implemented a web site using three main building blocks: ideas, projects and products. The ideas element allowed customers to browse through the online suggestions and photographs of living room and bedroom options in search of products or ideas room by room. Design articles for each option covered colour trends, tips from designers and seasonal alternatives. The site also featured special offers and promotions. The projects element constituted searchable, step-by-step guides to projects such as undertaking repairs, installations or decorative makeovers. A personal account facility behind Homebase's own firewalls enabled customers to store their personal contact and credit card details, and order history, making repeat and future purchasing a simple and safe exercise. The product range included detailed information covering 75 per cent of the most common household DIY projects. This consisted of an overview of categories, product descriptions and comparisons, buying guides, newly introduced products, plus dynamic visual and editorial content on the home page.

The web site offered a credible range of products from each department (paint, electrical, power tools, ironmongery, etc.) in searchable directories and adopted a 'room theme' promotions strategy to display products online, similar to that which Homebase used in its terrestrial megastores. This provided a way to rationalize promotional content on the site, which was tied to a searchable product database organized in the same manner as the retail databases in the bricks and mortar stores. It also allowed Homebase to bring customers through an 'inspirational' layer where it was less apparent that the company did not have the full product range online. 'It would have been easy to say: "This is 30 per cent of what you might find in one of the bigger Homebase stores", but people would want to know "where is the rest of it?"', says Sapient's Turner. 'At least this way you could build relative completeness within the context of a specific project. It would be a shame if you were able to buy a few items for the job from your home computer but had to go out to a store for the remainder.'

Online service strategy

Outsourcing web site management, customer service and distribution to relevant experts helped to ensure quality control and adherence to Homebase's high performance standards. Working with top technologists ensured that both the design of the web site and the way it worked were innovative. The professional call centre handled customer queries and complaints issued by post, telephone, fax, and e-mail, giving customers the choice to shop either online or offline or both simultaneously. The partnership with a national delivery company enabled Homebase.co.uk to offer customers the simplicity and convenience of being able to buy online 24 hours a day, seven days a week, and have their purchases delivered to their door within a guaranteed 24 or 48 hours, depending on their preference. Customers were thus spared the time and hassle of travelling, parking, queuing, and loading and unloading often heavy or cumbersome purchases. Crucially, using third parties allowed Homebase.co.uk to concentrate on its core competence: selling quality home improvement products at affordable prices to the local community.

Online customer strategy

Besides finding online product and service strategies that were both immediately deliverable and practically scalable, Homebase.co.uk needed to identify an online customer strategy that would attract and retain its target audience. Homebase was geographically concentrated in the South East of England. The company considered its customer base to be demographically biased towards professionals aged 35–45 years, with a female proclivity, presumably because of the retail emphasis on 'cosmetic' home improvement, or 'soft' rather than 'hard' DIY. By ensuring that the online proposition accentuated the value of the tangible products as well as the softer side of what the company was offering (the benefits of inspiration, ideas and support), Homebase.co.uk hoped to further penetrate the DIY market and grow a greater market share.

Acquiring knowledge of its e-customers was obviously key to targeting its online products and services effectively. Homebase.co.uk ran special offers, promotions and competitions on the web site to draw customers in and to highlight products available online which were marked down in price. These 'teasers' also served as a tool to get additional information about customers. Homebase.co.uk's process for building customer relationships and 'intelligence' employed the model of moving customers along a row of swimming lanes, from the slow, or beginner lane through to the fast, or advanced user lane. A first-time visitor to the web site might browse around but would probably leave without disclosing their identity or revealing any personal information. A more serious visitor, when making their initial purchase on the site, would divulge their name and address, and perhaps some basic personal details. If appropriate and authorized, this information might then be used by the company to issue special promotions or product recommendations via e-mail to the new customer. Repeat users of the site, who have grown accustomed to transacting online and formed a bond of trust with the company, would probably willingly offer information about themselves and their experience of the company. Homebase.co.uk's aim was to 'push' prospective customers into the fast lane.

Homebase.co.uk saw this method of gradually obtaining customer data and insight as a more successful way of gaining customer knowledge than asking customers to provide in-depth information up front. The company felt its customers were unlikely to complete online questionnaires and lengthy forms, and knew that the offer of gifts or giveaways to stimulate custom was open to 'joke' responses, or misinformation. The incremental accumulation of data ensured the greatest accuracy of information, enabling the company to align strategic delivery more closely to customers' requirements.

Online business strategy

While the company could have planned the web site as an umbrella layer over all the stores, instead it established it as an independent entity with its own profit and loss account, and treated it as a single store in the branch network. The e-business had its own data warehouse and stock warehouse. Customer information generated online was held separately from that relating to the offline stores, but the Homebase marketers and customer service operatives who viewed the offline stores' data could also access the online store's data, albeit through a different system. This partition between online and offline data and stock was mainly due to time constraints. While it simplified order/purchase/delivery and inventory processes, online customers were initially deprived of some of the benefits offered to in-store customers, such as eligibility to collect 'Spend & Save' points.

Valuable lessons

Developing its web site has provided Homebase with valuable, if expensive, learnings about venturing into the world of e-commerce. The early e-strategy was a mix of success and failure. This is epitomized by the fact that while Homebase launched its web site ahead of B&Q (which launched its site later in January 2001), it failed in its objective of distancing itself from its rival: the B&Q web site was curiously similar to its own.

When Schroder Ventures took over, Homebase.co.uk was in the process of re-evaluating its e-strategy. Fortunately, the changes it was discussing coincided with its new parent's focus on profitability. The web site's design was to remain essentially the same, but the e-commerce priorities would change significantly. This changeover is reflected in the one-word amendment to Homebase's original mission statement, which now reads:

> **To create shareholder value by becoming our customers' favourite home enhancement retailer.**

In the original version, Homebase aspired to being Europe's favourite home enhancement retailer. The alteration denotes the transition in business stance from one of market expansion to one of growth through developing the existing customer base.

In terms of financial outlay and return on investment, 'the initial e-strategy didn't work', concludes Simon Holder, now Head of E-commerce and Customer Relations at Homebase. According to Holder, the original e-strategy and cost base were premised on unattainable figures, 'the Boston Consulting Group strategy, like that of many of the first dot.coms, had sky-high expectations. Their sales revenue forecasts predicted astronomical returns in the immediate to near term. This was clearly never going to happen.' Holder spent six months on a tactical initiative to cut back the cost base to a sustainable level and to move the e-business towards break-even by concentrating on the basics: reducing costs and improving sales.

This drastic redrafting of e-strategy reflects the very different business approaches of the two consecutive parent companies, Sainsbury's and Schroder Ventures, which, ironically, might be characterized as 'Spend' and 'Save' respectively. Under Sainsbury's, Homebase invested substantial sums in prospective development, whereas under Schroder Ventures, the retailer is seeking to minimize costs and maximize returns by pragmatic means. For example, at the start of the new regime, the megastore strategy was deemed a losing proposition (sales income would never exceed rental expenditure) and the vast stores were sold to Kingfisher. Homebase's business development strategy now aims to leverage existing infrastructure and improve sales in the remaining stores. Many of the assumptions underlying the development of the web site were also proved wrong.

The assumption that to be an e-business success means seizing market share and online market leadership was too simplistic. The company's experience of selling garden sheds over the web (which led to shed loads of problems literally as well as figuratively) is one example of the danger of attempting to generate sales and grab market share without considering it might lose money. When Homebase.co.uk advertised garden sheds for the first time and on its standard Terms and Conditions – delivery to anywhere in the UK within 48 hours – it sold hundreds. Customers living in the Orkney Islands were especially impressed. The actual cost of dispatching a shed, dismantled into several pallets, far exceeded the customary delivery charge of £6.99. In effect, the company had created a delivery mechanic that was counter-productive. The revised e-strategy stipulates a volume-related delivery charge, calculated by product size and quantity, and Homebase.co.uk does not deliver heavy goods to the Highlands and Islands. 'All told', asserts Holder, 'the sheds episode was good learning. We now know people want to buy that type of product from us and, subsequently, we have sold other bulky items using a sustainable fulfilment process, with a promising amount of success.'

Delivering online purchases also taught the company a lot about customers' favoured delivery times. Homebase.co.uk chose to partner with Parcelforce at the outset so that it could give customers the option of taking delivery of their purchases in the evening or at the weekend, a service the competition did not offer. But its analysis later showed that few e-customers were taking up the offer.

Had Homebase.co.uk enquired why traditional home shopping businesses did not offer such customer convenience, before trying to exceed customer expectations, it would have learnt what others already knew about customer purchasing behaviour.

The assumption that the clever web site design would bring customers through the 'ideation' space was also unfounded. As Holder observes: 'People come to the site for a number of reasons. They may be a destination shopper looking for the cheapest option, or a "hit and run" buyer. They may arrive by accident, through browsing, or be one of our Spend & Save customers. The site was designed with purely one type of shopper in mind – the customer who comes to the site to be inspired and then buy.' Holder believes the web site development team tried too hard and created a site that was overly complicated. 'They built a Ferrari, when we could have done with a bicycle. We then had to learn not only how to drive this, but how to maintain it while it was moving.'

The original e-strategy was also inflexible. 'Everything happened at the same time', Holder explains. 'There was no room for learning and, if an alteration was proposed, it was too late to change anything. The revised e-strategy is based on pilot projects, which enable us to put new ideas into the business quickly at a low cost and to develop these strategies based on customer behaviour, rather than spending months producing analysis and then rolling out a large project at great expense.'

Since Schroder Ventures bought Homebase, web site management, customer service, technology and development activities have all been brought in-house. Consolidating control has served both to remove the huge expenditure on outside contractors and to build internal expertise and more direct relationships with customers. Excellent service levels have been maintained through concerted training of internal staff. Merging E-commerce and Customer Relations responsibility into one department (under the current direction of Simon Holder) has resulted in greater co-ordination between sales and marketing. For instance, Holder can get detailed reports on what customers' issues are from his Customer Relations managers and can take these to sales meetings where they will be fed directly into commercial decisions. The increasing integration of e-strategy and overall company strategy is helping the business to be more customer focused, and creating a cross-fertilization of ideas and input. 'The integration of the business allows e-commerce to benefit from the experience and resources of the core business divisions such as marketing', says Holder. 'It is important to note that it is a reciprocal relationship. The core business is benefiting from our learning and from the specialist skills e-commerce can offer, such as product photography, stylists and creative writing.'

The present effort to cut costs and enhance service includes simplifying the web offering to provide what online customers wish to buy, rather than mimicking what the other Homebase stores sell. The accumulation of on line customer and purchase data is providing Homebase.co.uk with the means to identify what its customers want and what sells online. 'Not everything in our core range sells on the web', notes Holder. 'With the benefit of learning, we are tailoring our range strategy to serve our online customers better.' The move to scale down the number of products available online is based on the finding that few customers buy across the host of products ranges offered. It is sufficient, for example, to sell only one top of the range, middle range and lower range of paintbrushes. Rationalizing product choice has resulted in savings on both stock, content management and fulfilment. In addition, customers can be certain that their purchases are in stock in the dedicated warehouse and will be delivered to them on time.

In the course of operating the web site, Homebase.co.uk has discovered that its on line customer is typically 'gentrified, multicultural urban'. Internal data analysis suggests that the majority of these customers, like Homebase customers generally, are relatively wealthy and use the site for the sake of convenience. This finding indicates that the web site is reaching a previously elusive customer sector – city residents who use public transport and do not have big cars to carry DIY shopping – and has overcome the access problems of distance and location suffered by the traditional stores. Homebase.co.uk has both web-exclusive customers and customers who employ all of the channels – web site, call centre, and local stores. 'The challenge', summarizes Holder, 'is to give the customer every opportunity to buy from Homebase in whatever way they find most convenient. It is important that they feel comfortable and confident with whatever medium they choose to use.'

Future outlook for Homebase.co.uk

For Homebase, the web site was and is a big element of their new strategy. From the beginning, Homebase understood that its customers were predominantly focused on getting something done, on accomplishing a task, and developed the web site to make it easier for them to do so. The company also appreciated that added value for the customer meant added return for the company. Today, the Homebase products and services online, and the way in which they are offered, reflect the customer's need for inspiration, as well as for the tools and materials to turn ideas into reality.

The evolution of Homebase's e-strategy reflects in part the different business approaches imposed by its parent companies. Whilst it was part of the Sainsbury's group, Homebase's competitive focus was to further differentiate itself from B&Q, and it set up the website to help it achieve this goal. Now, as a subsidiary of Schroder Ventures, Homebase is principally concerned with growing its own business in a more focused manner, and its primary objective for the e-business is profitability.

The 'virtual' store has been transformed from an isolated business to an integrated function. Outsourcing has been replaced by in-house activity, and the drive for more square footage and product offerings supplanted by more prudent use of existing stores and popular product ranges.

Yet despite the modifications to its e-strategy, the basic principles of the e-business operation remain unchanged. Homebase.co.uk continues to believe that providing consistently excellent service and relevant products is what really builds long-lasting and profitable customer relationships.

Chapter 4

The value creation process

The role of value creation in business has grown as the idea has taken hold that successful customer relationship management (CRM) is based on the company and the customer exchanging 'value' rather than money, goods and services. Companies now pay more attention to 'value' and how to create, convey and exploit it better.

Managers and researchers agree that value plays a key role in building and sustaining vital customer relationships, and are increasingly interested in learning how to balance the value organizations give to and receive from customers.

As we outlined in Chapter 2, the value creation process consists of three key elements: determining what value the company can provide to its customers (the 'value customer receives'); determining the value the organization gets from its customers (the 'value organization receives'); and, by successfully managing this value exchange, maximizing the lifetime value of desirable customer segments.

To many companies, customer value means:

- How much money can we extract from customers?
- How can we sell them more of the existing products and services they are buying?
- How can we cross-sell them new products and services?

But in today's competitive arena, where a growing number of businesses vie for a greater share of a finite customer pool, organizations also have to consider customer value in terms of customer benefit, i.e.:

- How can we create and deliver value to our customers?
- How can we ensure the customer proposition is relevant and attractive?

- How can we ensure the customer experience is consistently positive?

The aim of all businesses is to create a value proposition for customers, which, implicitly or explicitly, is better and more profitable than those of competitors.

Building the value proposition for target customers

A 'value proposition' is the offer defined in terms of the target customers, the benefits offered to these customers, and the price charged relative to the competition. Value propositions explain the relationship between the performance of the product, the fulfilment of the customer's needs and the total cost to the customer over the customer relationship life cycle.

Formulating the value proposition involves defining the target customers, the benefits offered to these customers and the price charged relative to the competition. To determine whether the value proposition is likely to result in a superior customer experience, firms must quantify the relative importance customers accord to the various attributes of a product.

The value the supplier receives from the customer is the *outcome* of providing and delivering superior value to the customer; deploying improved acquisition and retention strategies; and utilizing effective channel management. Fundamental to this concept of customer value is understanding the economics of customer acquisition and retention, and the opportunities for cross-selling, up-selling and building customer advocacy.

The importance of customer acquisition varies considerably according to a company's specific situation. For example, a new entrant to the fast-paced world of e-business will focus primarily on acquiring customers, while an established manufacturing company in a mature market may be more concerned with keeping customers.

Despite the fact that it costs much more to get a new customer than it does to keep an existing one, many companies have traditionally focused their marketing activity on acquiring new customers, rather than retaining existing customers. This may be due to the historical convention in many companies that rewards customer acquisition better than customer retention, or it may stem from ignorance of the bottom-line benefits of keeping customers.

Reichheld and Sasser (1990) suggested a number of reasons for which customer retention has such an effect on profitability.

- Acquiring new customers involves significant costs which may take years to turn into profits.

- As customers become more satisfied and confident in their relationship with a supplier, they are more likely to give the supplier a larger proportion of their business, or 'share of wallet'.
- As the relationship with a customer develops, there is greater mutual understanding and collaboration, which produces efficiencies that reduce operating costs. Sometimes customers are willing to integrate their IT systems, including planning, ordering and scheduling, with those of their suppliers, and this further reduces costs.
- Satisfied customers are more likely to refer others, which promotes profit generation as the cost of acquiring these new customers falls dramatically. In some industries, customer advocacy can play a very important role in winning new customers, particularly when choosing a supplier is a high-risk activity.
- Loyal customers can be less price-sensitive and may be less likely to defect due to price increases. This is especially true in business-to-business markets where the relationship with the supplier becomes more valued and switching costs increase.

Our research (Payne and Frow 1999) suggests that although many organizations say they understand the importance of customer retention and its links with profitability, very few measure the economic value of their customer retention strategies. Customer acquisition and customer satisfaction are measured much more often than customer retention and profit per customer.

Enhancing customer retention involves taking action. Key elements include: marshalling top management commitment; ensuring employee satisfaction and dedication to building long-term customer relationships; utilizing best practice techniques to improve performance; and developing a plan to implement a customer retention strategy.

Increasingly, firms are recognizing that enhanced customer satisfaction leads to better customer retention and profitability. Many are reviewing their customer service strategies to find ways to boost retention to boost business performance. This often entails a fundamental shift in business emphasis from customer acquisition to customer retention. Achieving the benefits of long-term customer relationships requires a firm commitment by everyone in the business to understanding and serving the needs of customers.

To calculate a customer's real value a company must look at the projected profit over the life of the account. This represents the expected profit flow over a customer's lifetime. The key metric used here is *customer lifetime value* (CLV), which is defined as the net present value of the future profit flow over a customer's lifetime.

Achieving the ideal equilibrium between giving value to customers and getting value from customers requires skilled understanding of customer needs. To anticipate and satisfy the needs of current and potential customers, the organization must be able to target specific customers, and to demonstrate added value through differentiated propositions and service delivery. This means adopting a focused approach to creating value, supported by dynamic, detailed knowledge of customers, competitors, opportunities, and the company's own performance capabilities.

The cases in this chapter illustrate the significance of 'value' in building, managing and sustaining the profitable, long-term customer relationships that lie at the heart of competitive advantage. The cases are:

1. Friends First. This case describes the new strategic vision of the Irish financial services group to be 'customer centred, trustworthy and easy to do business with'. A central pillar of its value creation process is a customer service centre with the guiding principle: 'If we look after our customers better than the competition then everything else that is important will follow.' The new infrastructure provides a single integrated view of the customer across all the company's businesses.

2. Canada Life (Ireland). Starting with the problems of information spread across three different legacy systems, this case describes how Canada Life creates customer value through a new CRM system called CREST (customer responsive-enhanced service technology).

3. Sun Microsystems. This case explores how the company, which has historically focused on customer acquisition and revenue maximization, is now also emphasizing customer retention and profitability. It describes how a new Relationship Marketing team is building customer value among Sun's 250 industry customers.

CASE STUDY 4.1

Friends First: Building the customer centric organization

OVERVIEW

Friends First launched its new group identity in 1998. It had a clear business objective of growth through becoming a 'broad-based financial services provider', although the company faced a number of critical issues. As with all traditional financial services companies, Friends First staff were used to servicing policies as opposed to brokers and customers. One of its major shifts in focus would be to adopt customer service as a core strategy. Management put it simply: 'If we look after our customers better than the competition then everything else that is important will follow.' However, the organization had been structured to meet the requirements of control rather than the real needs of customers or brokers. In addition, the company's IT platform was a complex myriad of systems with questionable data quality – the result of acquisitions. Indeed, not all of these systems were under the control of the Irish operations as some were based in the UK, with its former parent company Friends Provident.

In response to these challenges, the management team set itself several key objectives. The focus of the company's new infrastructure would have to provide a single, integrated view of the customer across all businesses. It would have to cater for different ways of doing business – whether through direct or broker channels – and in time be capable of accommodating whatever channels might emerge, such as digital TV or personal digital assistant (PDA) access. In addition, it would have to be flexible enough to accommodate changes in future business strategy.

Key learning points

A key emphasis of this case is on the definition of the value propositions that Friends would offer its different broker segments as well as the type of relationship that it wanted to build with brokers.

CRM issues

- The design of the organization can impact any CRM strategy.

Friends First was structured to meet internal organizational demands rather than the requirements of customers/brokers. In addition, processes and systems were built around policies not customers/brokers. This impacted on the quality of the service it could provide to customers.

Value Creation Process issues

- Place customers at the centre of the organization.

The guiding principle at Friends First is 'If we look after our customers better than the competition then everything else that is important will follow.' Staff had traditionally serviced policies not customers/brokers and therefore to achieve this required a 'mindset' shift within the company.

- In creating customer value, different customer segments may want a different type of relationship.

Friends First seeks to provide the type and level of service that is appropriate to the needs of the individual segments. It identified three different broker segments, each having different product and service needs, and sought a different type of relationship.

Introduction

Trust and reputation are critical to the success of financial services institutions as the institution is often managing customers' futures. These core attributes are embodied in the brand name; and where there is no brand there is no customer loyalty. However, establishing a brand identity usually takes considerable time, can be expensive, and is risky, particularly in a mature industry like financial services. Yet, this is what one financial institution has managed to achieve over a short period of time with a customer-focused strategy. This required the creation of a new customer centric organization, supported by a Customer Relationship Management (CRM) solution.

Friends First

Friends First is a leading financial services group in Ireland. It provides a comprehensive range of assurance, insurance, banking and investment products and services to more than 220 000 customers. The group has enjoyed exceptional growth in recent years, with total assets exceeding £4.5 billion and employing over 600 people.

In an international context, Friends First is the Irish Division of the pan-European Eureko Alliance. Eureko is the sixth largest insurance group in Europe, with a total asset base of £143 billion and more than 43 000 employees in 15 countries.

Friends First is, in fact, a very recent manifestation that has emerged from a long established player in the financial services industry. It is essentially a rebranded Friends Provident, a company that was first established in Ireland in 1834. This decision to rebrand was driven by the tremendous changes that were taking place in the industry in the mid-1990s, coupled with changing customer preferences and a changing ethos within the company.

Friends Provident and its associated companies re-evaluated the way they communicated their 'corporate personality' to existing and potential customers, their business partners, distributors, the media and the State. Central to the brand re-evaluation was what the new company would be called. Based on consumer research and internal marketing expertise the company decided to replace the cluster of brands that had evolved over the years (due primarily to acquisitions) with one name and one visual identity to communicate the organization's essential values. In 1998, the new group identity was launched to communicate the strong customer ethos under one brand name – Friends First.

The group began to take on its present form in 1993 when Friends Provident Life Assurance Company Limited, Celtic International, CelticDirect, National Mutual Life (Ireland), Friends Provident Life and Touchline Insurance were brought together to form Eureko Ireland Group.

Today the company comprises three businesses: Friends First Finance, Friends First Life and Friends First International. It uses a variety of channels to distribute a comprehensive range of products – including pensions, permanent health, savings and investment plans, personal lending, and motor finance – to its customers.

Mission 2000

The changes highlighted above began in earnest in 1996 with the appointment of a new managing director who was given a new business mandate to drive the business forward. This called for the company to become a 'broad based financial services provider', to grow, to become customer centric with a strong service culture and to be innovative.

However, the new company would face a number of critical hurdles – not least the fact that it had no recognized brand name. The old Friends Provident had been a mediocre performer financially, was losing market share and depended on broker business. The acquisitions had resulted in a mix of cultures and staff morale was low. Critically, particularly given the nature of the business, there was no customer service ethos.

As with all traditional financial services companies, Friends First staff had always serviced policies not brokers, nor end customers. This created a mindset that was at odds with the type of relationships the organization wanted to foster. It set about adopting a customer service orientation, whether direct to end customers or through superior broker service, as a core strategy. In the past it had used a 'one size fits all' approach in terms of both product range and service, despite customers' different requirements. What's more, operational processes were brittle and there was no end-to-end view of transactions, nor a consolidated view of different customers.

On the technology side, the IT platform was a complex myriad of systems with questionable data quality – again, the result of acquisitions. The Irish operation didn't even control all these systems: some were based in the UK with former parent company Friends Provident. In addition, many of the systems were not year 2000 compliant.

Industry analysis highlighted the trend towards diversified financial groupings (for example, Irish Permanent, Virgin Direct, and M&S Financial Services) and a significant lowering of entry barriers. New distribution channels were also springing up (First Call Direct, Guardian Direct and Premier Direct, for example), channel infrastructure costs were rising, and product development cycles shortening. The market's focus was also shifting from life/savings products to pensions/investment business (such as PIPs, PEPs, Investment Bonds and Equity Bonds) and from 'defined benefit' to 'defined contribution'.

Through extensive research and analysis the company sought answers to four seemingly simple questions:

- Who are our customers?
- What do they want from us?
- Who are our most profitable customers?
- What do we need to do to keep existing customers and attract new ones?

The company surveyed customers and distributor channels for their preferences; it conducted focus groups with customers and brokers; it taped calls to the service centre to analyse the nature of customer and broker interaction; and employed 'mystery shoppers' to establish how the company responded to requests and enquiries.

The outcome of all this activity was a new strategic vision. The implications of this new vision were that Friends First would:

- be customer centred, trustworthy and easy to do business with;
- focus on the growing market of pensions provision;
- focus distribution channels and administrative support systems to ensure that the company meets the unique needs of target customer segments and distributors: retail customers; small, medium-sized and large brokers serving the retail customer; and brokers serving corporate customers.

The new positioning represented a significant shift in the company's proposition and the way it conducted business. This shift is captured in Figure CS 4.1.1 below, which illustrates the situation in 1997 and where the company planned to be by the year 2000.

The challenge the senior management team set itself was to:

- reduce the cost base while increasing the quality of service;
- gain control of distribution channels;
- provide different service offerings to different segments ('differentiated products');
- increase the effectiveness of acquisition, cross-sell, and retention programmes;
- use the power of information to understand customers.

Under its Mission 2000 initiative the company established seven distinct but interdependent programmes (see Figure CS 4.1.2 below). These included the development of direct and broker strategies, a product development strategy, and the establishment of the new brand, which would capture the essence of the new organization and its values. These would be supported by a new customer service centre to provide the infrastructure necessary for the new customer focus. IT would also play a significant role in the implementation of the new vision, not least because many of the core systems would need replacing because of Year 2000 compliance issues and the advent of the Euro. Central to the success of Mission 2000 would be an ongoing cultural revolution to instil a customer service ethos throughout the company.

After Mission 2000 was launched, the traditional direct channel was coming under growing pressure from new sales channels, posing a challenge to the company's profitability. The company carried out further analysis that led them to downgrade the direct channel and today over 95 per cent of business comes from the broker channel. Friends First has 'policy holders' but its relationship is with brokers rather than end customers. Indeed, brokers are very protec-

1997		Target (2000)
• Product focused with emphasis on new sales • Unfocused branding, unclear message • Little/no distinction from the 'rest of the pack'	*Brand positioning*	• Customers need focus • Focused, consistent branding with clear, concise message • Stands behind product offerings and advice given—will 'put things right' and guarantee *not* to sell products people *don't* need
• Poor understanding of customers • Limited customer data, poor quality	*Customer knowledge*	• Ongoing development of a comprehensive understanding of customer needs and values • Expanded use of customer data collected from all sources – holistic view of customer
• Complex products that are difficult to understand • Charging structures buried in the 'fine print' • Products priced on an individual, standalone basis • Limited product guarantees	*Product range* *General principles*	• Simple product propositions that are easy to understand • Transparent, flexible charging structures • Product pricing geared to rewarding loyal customers • Move away from product guarantees
• Dependent on broker channel • Little control over the way business is conducted with customers • Emphasis on sales performance and targets	*Sales and distribution channels*	• Greater emphasis on direct channel in line with customer preferences • Increased control over distribution channels to ensure 'trustworthy' value is met and professionalism rather than sales targets • Emphasis on meeting customer needs with profitable product offerings • Remuneration of channels not based solely on meeting sales targets – balanced scorecard
• Standardized servicing for all customers' distribution channels • No formal, structured service proposition with defined target performance levels • No formal regular information update to policyholders regarding their financial position	*Servicing and sales support*	• Servicing requirements structured to the needs of specific channel segments (e.g. corporate broker versus small/medium sized broker) • Defined service proposition with targeted performance levels • Structured process for regular communication with policyholders regarding their financial position

Figure CS 4.1.1: The company situation in 1997 and the aims by 2000.

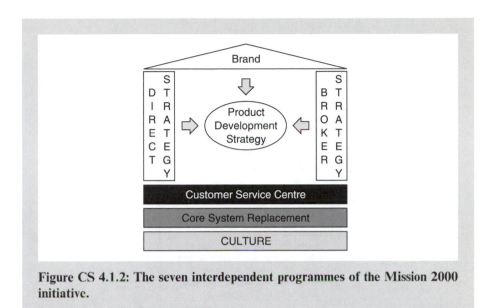

Figure CS 4.1.2: The seven interdependent programmes of the Mission 2000 initiative.

tive about their relationships with customers and the company recognized the folly of encroaching on this terrain.

Group distribution strategy

Friends First reviewed its approach to segmentation (the emphasis is on the distributor) through its 'Group Distribution Strategy' (GDS), a comprehensive project looking at distributors' characteristics and needs. The project also tackled the way the company worked with its distributors, seeking to move from a 'broad brush' to a more targeted approach that matched product and service offering to distributors' particular needs. The GDS also involved a comprehensive review of front- and back-office processes to ensure they provided a fully integrated offering to this 'customer' base.

Traditionally, brokers were segmented on a regional basis. The GDS identified three different broker segments: corporate and large brokers (such as Marsh & McLennan), small and medium retail brokers (from one-person operators to medium-sized players) and retail financial institutions (essentially banks). Each broker segment has a different way of doing business, different processes and wants to be treated differently. Friends now has a different relationship with each segment (see Figure CS 4.1.3 below).

	Product and service needs	Required relationship
Corporate and large brokers	• Good investment performance/price competitive • Good account executives with strong technical expertise and access to technical support (actuarial and fund management) • Product flexibility and participation in product development • Quality service and administrative support	Expert to expert
Small and medium sized retail brokers	• Good investment performance/price competitive • Demonstrated commitment to the broker • Speed and ease of conducting business (especially sales process) • Technical back-up and support • Wide range of standard products suitable for end customers	Strong personal relationship with reliance on 'trusted' suppliers
Retail financial institutions	• Good investment performance/price competitive • Training of branch staff • Streamlined, efficient administration • Support cross-selling to existing customer base • Dedicated provider resource (account team) • Own brand products	Partnership

Figure CS 4.1.3: Segment needs and required relationship.

Friends seeks to provide the type and level of service that is appropriate to the needs of the individual segments. From the information the company has collected it is beginning better to understand their requirements and is now designing products that are tailored to their particular needs – some products may not be offered to all segments.

Friends offers different value propositions to each segment, reflecting their specific requirements, particularly in terms of products and service delivery. It has also established appropriate service levels for each segment.

Corporate and large brokers are looking for efficient service – particularly at renewal time – appropriate risk rates, and to get information early and quickly to their customers. Service is important, but less critical, for retail brokers, whose key need is assistance, particularly technical support, which is generally not available in-house.

Retail financial institutions (RFIs) tend to service their own customers centrally and have different requirement from the other two segments. Staff training about products is critical for them, as is communication – particularly about where different products are in the lifecycle. For example, RFIs want to close the mortgage as quickly and efficiently as possible, so they need to know, say, if Friends hasn't yet received the medical report because they can't put the required policy in place until they've got all the relevant information.

The organization has also been redesigned as a result of Friends' segmentation strategy, in order to meet the requirements of control and reporting rather than the needs of brokers. For example, if a broker was taking out a pension scheme on behalf of a customer, the work required passed through many different departments within Friends – risk assessment, underwriting and protection, asset management and so on. Each department often had its own systems. As far as the broker was concerned it was one piece of work, whereas to Friends it was six different pieces of work. If a broker phoned with a query, the call was often directed to someone working in the underwriting department, for example, who may have known nothing about the status of the application from the other areas of the business as there was no end-to-end view of the transaction.

The fact that processes and IT systems had been built around policies not customers created significant problems. To overcome some of these problems and provide flexibility, Friends created 'manual workarounds'. As a result the IT system and paper files existed side by side, which hampered the ability to provide good service, particularly at policy renewal time.

Today, the company is organized around the different broker segments. Sales and service for each segment have been combined, so there is no disconnect between the two – a common problem in all sorts of organizations. The different segments also have different process designs. Each segment has dedicated service teams, each with the necessary skills and competencies to meet the requirements of that segment, for example underwriting, although the chief underwriter sits outside the teams. Each segment now has its own general manager with total end-to-end responsibility. In making the organization more service focused, Friends First is attempting to get away from the situation where the back-office is seen as just that, a back-office far removed from the broker, rather than an integral part of the value proposition.

All this change had to be carefully managed. According to Friends First director John Murphy, 'breaking up the organization and putting it back together in a different way creates uncertainty'. To reduce uncertainty, Friends put great emphasis on communicating with staff, particularly the rationale behind the change and why the new segmentation strategy was necessary. 'Do not assume that because you have told them they understand. You need to continue to go back and reinforce', Murphy says. The implementation also focused on quick wins in order to demonstrate to staff that it was the right strategy. Service staff now regularly visit brokers in order that they can better understand their servicing requirements and what is important to them.

One of the unlooked for side effects of reorganizing on a segmented basis rather than along regional lines was that a layer of managers needed to be removed, further reducing costs.

The CRM solution

Creating the service centre infrastructure was a central pillar of the strategy to become more customer centric. The guiding principle was 'If we look after our customers better than the competition then everything else that is important will follow.' The objectives of this infrastructure were to:

- provide a single integrated view of the customer/broker across all businesses;
- cater for different ways of doing business, whether through direct or broker channels, but capable of accommodating the internet, digital TV or other channels that may emerge in the future;
- be flexible enough to accommodate changes in business strategy;
- permit easy integration with legacy systems of any acquired company.

A central element of the new services centre was a CRM initiative. This initiative sought to:

- understand customers/brokers;
- put a value on customers/brokers;
- tailor products to service them;
- target customers/brokers appropriately;
- evolve the product and service portfolio through learning.

In seeking to build deeper relationships with customers/brokers, the objective was not only to improve opportunities for cross-selling but to provide customers/brokers with appropriate products.

'Partner not package'

To meet the challenging business requirements as well as implement the technology, the Friends First team wanted a packaged solution rather than to engage in bespoke development. However, while the package would be available 'off-the-shelf', the company wanted a strategic partner rather than a pure vendor.

Friends, advised by Andersen Consulting (now Accenture) started looking for a modern contact management and task management application for their Customer Services Centre in December 1997. A key feature would be the ability to provide a one-stop-shop for customer queries, with efficient hand-off of complex calls and tasks, to specialist middle office professionals. After exhaustive evaluations it chose Fineos and its Front-Office solution in March 1998.

The first customized version of Fineos' Front-Office integrated with document imaging (from Filenet) went live in October 1998 in the Customer Services Centre. This initial implementation was the combined result of Friends First's business expertise, Andersen Consulting's project management and Fineos' software design and implementation proficiency. Later, Friends First and Fineos went on to identify and implement further product enhancements that greatly improved the performance and usability of the CRM system as implemented today. This operational CRM systems and workflow have been rolled out across the life company, in the call centre, customer services and distribution services area. There are plans to implement the CRM application across the branch network.

Friends First can now find and greet existing customers quickly with a sophisticated search engine, or rapidly add new customers with the full range of centralized customer data including names, addresses, contact numbers, profile and so on. As a result, the company is beginning to better understand customers, their needs and changing requirements and consequently to grow. For example, on the life side, it has identified and targeted customers with maturing business. A detailed analysis and segmentation exercise is allowing Friends further to capitalize on business opportunities with existing customers.

A two way interface with back-office administration systems ensures that new or updated customer data can be efficiently transferred to the administration systems, and that key policy data are available in the CRM system to answer customer queries.

The solution provides the full range of contact management support, from the rapid registration of simple contacts to the management of the complex web of contacts and tasks that combine to resolve many customer service requests.

In summary, the CRM solution is being used by Friends First to:

- hold customer/broker information, contacts, tasks;
- manage all customer/broker contacts;
- manage specific new business campaigns;
- generate pipeline reports for the sales channels for individual life business.

Tasks are directly set up by support areas and automatically queued for administrative work. This practice alone has helped to cut out roundabout and time-consuming e-mails and phone calls. As one business manager explains: 'In the call centre, when people ring in, agents now have full visibility of the tasks whereas before they had to do an awful lot of call-backs. Before, they had to check with the admin area and ring the client back. That has definitely led to an improvement in service.'

The benefits include:

- availability of full client contact details, particularly beneficial in the call centre;
- tasks being set up by support areas are fed directly into administrative work queues which has cut out e-mails, phone calls and so on;
- full view of tasks within Customer Services and how each area is performing against service levels.

Workflow

The front-office CRM solution is just one element of a total front-to-back (F2B) implementation. Over the course of the project the business requirements for the workflow system were gathered and honed, to include full integration with imaging, process automation, intelligent routing of work and images and rules for differentiated service level management. Integrating customer interactions with back-office processes has been key to achieving operational efficiencies which improve customer service.

Apart from the obvious operational uses of workflow, CRM has become a key tool for team leaders in monitoring work queues. Benefits include:

- close control of work-loads which allows quick response to peaks and troughs;
- clarity of tasks against service level agreements giving greater focus to teams;
- linking of task to contract allowing reports by sales agent;
- batch assignment of tasks, speeding up processing time.

The imaging systems in particular have resulted in significant time savings. 'In the underwriting department it used to take a day to get an old file. Now they can actually see it straight away on the system', says one team leader. Because there is now full visibility of tasks within Customer Services, information on how each area is performing against service levels is available to management. 'From an MIS point of view, the workflow solution is very strong because you can see exactly how your work queues and where the work is. It's very good at controlling the work and workflow', explains one business manager.

The journey continues

Despite having implemented the CRM solution, the journey continues at Friends First. The company is currently constructing a customer value model. It is also using the information in its customer database to profile customers to identify those who are likely to be interested in life products. Product offerings in each broker segment are also currently being evaluated.

CASE STUDY 4.2

Canada Life (Ireland): Committed to excellence in customer care

OVERVIEW

For Canada Life (Ireland) to meet customer expectations across a growing number of touchpoints and to increase efficiency across related business processes, it had to address a number of issues within its organization. Information was spread across different legacy-based systems so that no one department could access the breadth or depth of information that was needed to respond to customers the way the modern business environment demanded. The ability to service a series of customer issues each with its own timeline and interdependencies as a single case was lacking. Without complete and readily accessible customer information, cross-selling opportunities could not be maximized. In addition, the absence of automated workflow meant that the hand-over or assignment of tasks, the tracking of their progress and the management of workloads were all achieved manually – that in turn, meant inefficiencies and often dissatisfied customers.

Service quality is a key competitive criteria for Canada Life and a CRM and workflow solution was implemented to support its 'Excel in Customer Service' initiative. The company wanted to provide a consistent level of service across all channels and to ensure that customer information would be readily accessible to any staff member. It wanted to simplify the creation of – and appropriately route – business processes, and improve the monitoring of service levels and administration performance. Finally, it wanted to integrate seamlessly with specialist tools such as imaging and CTI (computer telephony integration) systems.

CRM issues

The inability to access relevant information and the lack of information integration can impact on relationship building.

Building relationships with customers is a process that is highly dependent on repeat positive experiences. When customer-contact staff do not have immediate access to information this can severely impact the quality of service that they can provide.

Value creation process issues

- To create customer value you must understand customer value.

For Canada Life, quality of service is a key differentiator and an organization has been designed to ensure that the company consistently delivers on this promise.

- The technology solution is just a means to an end.

Canada Life's CRM and workflow implementation supported an organization redesign and cultural change programme.

Introduction

As a leader in Ireland's life and pensions market, Canada Life (Ireland), is increasingly aware that customer expectations in its industry are rising. Delivering on those expectations had always been one of the company's core values. Now it has become a prerequisite in the competition for customers' hearts, minds and 'share of wallet'. To help achieve this objective the company identified the need for a CRM and workflow system that could underpin its drive to improve its customer service and boost both customer retention and acquisition programmes.

With more than 200 000 policyholders and assets in excess of €1.3 billion, Canada Life (Ireland) is part of one of the most venerable institutions in the life assurance business. In the century and a half since the company was founded in Toronto, one might have expected its market to change. Less predictable though are the extraordinary developments in the financial services sector that it has had to face over the past 20 years. Technology and globalization, deregulation and increased competition have all played their part in transforming the life and pensions marketplace, and, indeed, the financial services industry in general.

These same factors have also helped to create customers who are more discerning, more sophisticated and more financially demanding. Moreover, customers have responded to the industry's marketing efforts and have come to demand a seamless service. They expect the organization of their choice to 'know' them and to be able to respond quickly and efficiently with the information they seek.

For Canada Life, delivering on that level of service meant that a new approach was needed. The company not only had to provide excellent customer care – one of its corporate goals – at the point of contact, but it also had to be able to support it with increased efficiency and effectiveness across related business processes.

Growing the business

The life assurance industry is primarily composed of protection and asset accumulation products. Companies in the industry sell their products through direct sales and broker (Independent Financial Adviser) channels. For Canada Life, 'customers' are both the end customers and the broker channels, with sales roughly split 50/50 between each. The broker channel has become increasingly important and any growth strategy must assume that the company will increase its share of business through this channel. This involves increasing broker penetration (i.e. getting more brokers to conduct business with the company if they have not done so in the past) as well as obtaining a bigger share of business from the brokers who have previously provided business. Indeed, this is an area that Canada Life has specifically targeted, particularly the bigger brokers who tend to control the larger contracts.

In general, a broker (or end customer for that matter) will look for many things from a Life company before they will place business with them. Central among these are its products, the investment 'solution', and the service. Canada Life (Ireland) considers its product portfolio to be in line with the market, and in general few would say that you can gain a competitive advantage solely through product innovation. In terms of the investment solution, Canada Life established its own Asset Management company in 1999 to meet the market and company needs under that heading. It is only through delivering a quality service that life assurance companies can differentiate themselves and this has become the bedrock from which Canada Life strives to grow market share.

Fighting the legacy systems

Yet the systems in place at Canada Life did not support the provision of quality service. Information was spread across a number of different legacy systems so no one department could access the breadth or depth of information that was needed to respond to customers in the way the modern business environment demanded. This problem with information was felt most acutely at the customer interface – at the branch and on the telephone.

Had the customer phoned, written or visited about the same issue previously? What had been the outcome of their most recent contact with the organization? Which products did they hold? If they had already made a service or information request, when would it be completed? Was there a complaint currently outstanding? What was the customer's preferred channel of communication? These were just some of the questions that arose for those in direct contact with customers; as it was, none could be answered efficiently.

Each of the company's computer systems had a facility to provide a customer view of the policy (on that system). In reality this was only ever used if a customer did not know their policy number and even then it was simply used to find the policy number that that customer was enquiring on. The majority of queries were usually policy related and, to a large extent, still are. The biggest problem staff faced was the ability to track a contact and ensuing work processing. In addition, policy files were paper-based and stored off-site. If a query or processing required a file, this was requested using a paper file request sheet which was collected twice a day (early morning and late afternoon) by storage personnel, and the file (if it was in the storage area) was returned in the next delivery. If the requested file was not present, the sheet was returned marked accordingly (e.g. 'no file', or 'out to Joe Bloggs'). If the file was out to another member of staff, by the time you contacted that person for the file, it may have been sent back to storage, and the whole process started again.

There were other issues too. The ability to service a series of customer issues each with its own timeline and interdependencies as a single case was lacking. Without complete and readily accessible customer information, cross-selling opportunities could not be maximized. In addition, the absence of a workflow system meant that the hand-over or assignment of tasks, tracking of their progress and management of the workload were all achieved manually – and that, in turn, meant inefficiencies.

Customer surveys regularly reported feedback that customers had to contact Canada Life on a second occasion (and sometimes more often) to follow up their request. The company had no real mechanism to establish who they had dealt with the first time, or who was handling their request. In many instances, the customer service personnel had to take a note of the customer's phone number and call them back when they had established who was dealing with their request, and what the status of it was.

Excelling in customer care

Many initiatives were started to move the organization towards the goal of 'Excel in Customer Care'. They restructured the service areas into *front-office* and *back-office*. They started to collect customer feedback for all departments and all customer groups. In addition, the company joined an initiative in the Irish Management Institute (IMI), run in association with Trinity College Dublin, focusing on World Class processes and process excellence based on the Business Excellence Model of the European Foundation for Quality Management.

The logic behind the front-office–back-office split was that staff in the processing areas would be left alone to do the processing, and that employees who were good at dealing with customers would fill the positions in the front-office. Each would only need to be trained for their specific role. Because of the lack of technology to support the structure, the processing areas were still receiving a lot of calls, although they were now coming from the front-office as opposed to customers. This, in a way, defeated the object of the exercise, as the customer facing staff could not really answer many of the customers' questions.

To address these issues, the company recognized that it needed to implement a central CRM and workflow solution – one that would deal not only with information gaps, but also with the task management aspects of customer care. It was decided that the new system would be called CREST (customer responsive-enhanced service technology) and, critically, that it should be user-friendly enough to win staff acceptance. Also, it was deemed vital that it have the tools and facilities to deliver 'quick wins' at the user level as well as at the organizational level. This meant that it would have to:

- allow all information about Canada Life customers – from their contact history to full product portfolios – to be readily accessible to any staff member;
- create a single point of entry for the customer – irrespective of the channel he or she chose – to ensure a consistent level of service;
- simplify the creation and initiation of business processes arising from a customer contact with the ability to route them to the most appropriate person;

- enable team leaders or management to monitor service levels and overall administration performance, and also to provide the facility to monitor or track the status of a request;
- integrate seamlessly with specialist tools such as Imaging and CTI (computer telephony integration) systems;
- support all types of direct-to-customer operations, from the customer service centre through to the branch offices and Head Office administration.

While solutions for the two primary areas of concern – excellent customer care and greater efficiency – were needed in the short term, there were also other less urgent, although equally important, requirements that needed to be addressed in the long term. These included the need for an enriched data store and improved identification of cross-selling opportunities.

Implementation

Canada Life adopted a two stage approach in implementing the CRM and workflow solution, supporting its goal of excellence in customer care. The primary requirement was to put the contact management and workflow solutions in place, as this would give the fastest return in terms of improving service. In addition, a phased approach would allow the company to make progress more quickly.

Phase 1 of the project was the implementation of the CRM and workflow solutions and was itself rolled out over a number stages, as the company adopted it, one department at a time. This was to ensure that it was well managed, that specific departmental requirements could be incorporated in the software, and that the necessary training to users could be given in advance of 'go live' in addition to 'hand holding' when it went live. To support the implementation process, the project team also visited several other sites that implemented the same or similar software to learn from their experiences.

Early on it was determined that the project would be driven by the business areas and not run as an IT project. Perhaps the most important factor though in helping successfully to implement the solution was that it had early and consistent sponsorship from senior management in the company. Their focus on communication and training and on the cultural and role change issues involved served to enhance and speed user acceptance, which, of course, was of inestimable value in smoothing resistance and building momentum for the project at every turn.

A development and testing team was established by taking four key users (team supervisors) from the four main business areas. This team developed and tested the workflow processes, trained the teams, and then as each of their departments went live, they returned as the team supervisor to 'champion' the new system – and they fully understood the system because they had developed and tested it. The rest of the implementation team were support to the department that went live for a week or two. These four people were seconded for a six-month period; three returned to their departments and the fourth remained as the manager of a new team, which was established for ongoing testing of enhancements, and phase 2 of the project (like a model office testing environment).

The 'cultural change' was part of a wider strategy for excellence in customer care, but the changes in culture which were expected as part of this project included greater ownership for tasks, a responsibility on the front-office staff to solve the customers problem, or deliver the service requested, seamlessly. In the processing areas the focus was on the management information that the new system provided and the 'Work Queue' that each member now had, and its visibility. Tasks that exceeded their target date showed up with a 'red triangle' and there was a great focus on eliminating these. Other initiatives focusing on 'world class service' came about under the IMI initiative and the implementation of a continuous improvement process.

Phase 2 of the project involved document imaging to reduce the paper trail and help remove the delay in requesting paper files. This is now fully live in the life servicing areas with the exception of New Business. In the New Business area the company is currently undertaking a pilot on 10 per cent of new business to establish the benefits and disadvantages of implementing there. It is examining changes in the processes and systems that would be needed in order that productivity is not adversely affected, because that department is highly sensitive to anything that adds even a few minutes to a transaction.

The result – quick wins and long-term support

Having gone live, CRM backed up by automated workflow has enabled Canada Life to provide first-rate customer care. With full information easily accessible to staff and complete with a workflow tool that supports the level of efficiency needed, the company has already had early payback through increased levels of customer service and satisfaction.

Because customer information is displayed on a single intuitive screen along with contact, sales and service information, each user can instantly access a complete picture of a customer's relationship with the company. This means that customer-facing staff can respond more rapidly and more efficiently to customers' requests, with a higher percentage of these being dealt with on demand.

'We initially experienced a 70 per cent reduction in calls from our front-office to our claims department, which would have been queries about what's happening on a file or what's outstanding, etc. I have no doubt that the quality of service has improved significantly as a result', says Richard Caffrey, Associate Director of Pensions, Canada Life (Ireland).

Users now have the facility to record prompts for follow-up with a client when he or she next contacts the organization – for example, if returned mail indicates a change of address. In addition, assignments or tasks that arise as a result of a customer contact can now be automatically routed to the appropriate person or department, whether that contact has been logged in the system via e-mail, data entry, or scanned from a document.

With the automation and management of work allocation, online information can be accessed in relation to monitoring both service levels and the efficiency of overall administration. The advantages of this are clear. As Karl Nolan, Customer Services Manager at Canada Life (Ireland) states: 'The system unifies customer information from our current systems, providing a single enriched view that enables us to gain a more complete understanding of each customer's business needs. It also enables us to automate and manage task generation and provides us with real-time reports on service levels and overall administration performance.'

Also, because of improved mapping of processes and shared information staff can move more easily from department to department, in accordance with peaks and troughs in demand. Team leaders are free to view the workload by team member, re-allocate as necessary or track the status of a task. Indeed, where necessary the workflow system can escalate or prioritize a task, in order to ensure that agreed service levels are maintained – or exceeded.

Caffrey explains how this process works. 'Canada Life delivers its service using a front-office–back-office model. CRM and workflow support this structure ideally as our call centre takes all calls – the details of which are now on our CRM solution – and sets up workflow tasks where necessary for the back-office to perform processing. Progress of the tasks can be viewed real-time and management reports used to ensure that service meets targets.'

Because the CRM solution allows for the automatic production and composition of standard letters there is less scope for errors and more consistency in the quality and style of those produced, as well as the obvious impact that this automated feature has on efficiency levels. Brokers and associates benefit too from the new system as their queries and requests are captured and sent electronically to the appropriate departments.

Perhaps most significantly of all, the CRM and workflow solutions have won kudos from its most important critics – Canada Life's service staff. 'The product is proving very popular with our service personnel as it conveys a very positive image of the company's commitment to service. And also it's very user-friendly – within a week it was even starting to save time', says Caffrey.

CASE STUDY 4.3

Connecting the dots: Sun Microsystems[1]

OVERVIEW

The value creation process is about creating value for both customers and shareholders (and, implicitly, value chain partners and employees). Organizations that adopt CRM often do so as a result of seriously reconsidering the value they create for their customers as well as the value their customers create for them.

This is very much the case at Sun Microsystems. Sun is one of the big-league providers of network computing solutions, helping thousands of businesses worldwide to implement CRM to improve their customer relationships. In an intriguing twist, this case looks behind the scenes at Sun and holds up a mirror to the way in which Sun itself is buying-in to CRM to build stronger relationships with its own customers.

The company's strategic approach is changing. Formerly focused on customer acquisition, Sun is visibly beginning to capitalize on the link between customer retention and profitability. There is a new emphasis on growing the most value-creating customers and improving customer communication. Like other companies embarking on CRM, Sun recognized that it needed a cultural transformation truly to put customers first, and understand and anticipate their needs. In turn, this triggered a need to build a single view of the customer from the disparate sources of data it held.

Sun Microsystems' experience is particularly interesting as the company works to 'practise what it preaches' through developing a portal network that engages not only Sun customers but also employees and suppliers, forming 'a single electronic value chain'. In this wired world the boundaries between supplier and customer begin to blur, illustrating again the close connection between creating value for customers and for the company.

---

[1] This case study was developed and agreed with the management of Sun Microsystems in 2000. The case study focuses on a single company department, Relationship Marketing, which is primarily concerned with business in the UK. It therefore does not attempt to represent the views or ambitions held by other divisions or the company as a whole.

Key learning points

The Sun Microsystems case shows that, even in business-to-business, personal contact is of paramount importance: CRM is about the people who manage the customer relationship as well as the processes and technology that support them. Sun Microsystems established a dedicated team to implement CRM, which worked actively with the account managers on the 'front line'. For the first time, these account managers were involved in designing and developing the relationship marketing programmes. Even in the early stages of implementation, as the case shows, the new approach has yielded measurable benefits in terms of share of spend among these key customers. One particularly successful example was the Smile campaign with the Co-operative Bank.

The case touches on another crucial issue for CRM: the difficulty of getting – and then using – a single view of the customer. At Sun Microsystems, as at other organizations, the challenge is not only legacy systems but also legacy behaviour. As the Relationship Marketing Manager comments in the case, Sun may identify that a customer contact enjoys golf, but will invite them to the Grand Prix rather than a golfing event because the company happens to be sponsoring the Grand Prix that year. The Sun experience demonstrates that real value creation in CRM is about actively applying the customer's perspective and preferences, not solely the company's.

- CRM can be as much about people as it is about systems and processes. Sun Microsystems found that its account managers created a lot of value for customers and they became an important component in the company's CRM strategy. In fact, the CRM project allowed them to grow from their traditional implementer roles into a more strategic role that created value for Sun.

- Legacy systems are a problem which can hinder an organization from developing a single view of the customer. However, once the company has a single view of the customer it will only create more value for itself or customers if it can examine and change its legacy behaviour – the way it has always done things because it is convenient or simply habitual.

- CRM can lead to far-reaching changes in the way a company manages its supply chain. Sun Microsystems is using the notion of 'committedness' to stakeholders to develop more effective communication with its customers, employees, suppliers and partners.

This more integrated information sharing is enabling Sun to create greater value for its entire electronic value chain.

Introduction

Scott McNealy could be forgiven for seeing dots everywhere he looks. He is Chairman and Chief Executive of Sun Microsystems Inc., the undisputed 'dot' in *dot.com* – the power behind web-enabled businesses. Sun is the number one partner to companies for network computing, having so far enabled more than 500 000 companies across the globe to get on the internet, develop their web sites and adopt electronic commerce. A $15.7 billion company with offices in 170 countries, Sun provides end-to-end solutions for doing business in the network age. It is therefore one of the world's leading enablers of dot.com CRM (see Figure CS 4.3.1).

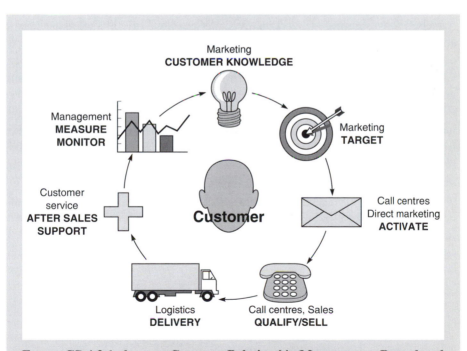

FIGURE CS 4.3.1: dot.com Customer Relationship Management. Reproduced with the kind permission of Sun Microsystems.

Worldwide, Sun supports over one million systems, 80 000 of which are in the UK, and trains more than 100 000 delegates annually. Among an eminent peer group including Hewlett Packard and Compaq, Sun is ranked highest for: customer satisfaction; technical support; UNIX servers, workstations and systems storage; and is the leading platform for key Enterprise Resource Planning (ERP) vendors. With over 50 industry record benchmarks, Sun is conspicuously successful in helping its customers to become proficient and competitive.

Why network?

Sun's secret of success is its innate ability to connect, not just its customers to their customers, but ideas to invention. Sun maintains a clear and simple philosophy: 'IT is all about business benefits, and IT strategy is so fundamental it needs to be aligned with the overall business model.' Sun's systems, software, services, strategic partnerships and alliances enable businesses to establish and expand in the 'networked economy' where the capacity of computers to intercommunicate is paramount.

Network computing delivers many benefits, most notably expedience and accessibility. However, it requires a completely revised set of work practices, competencies and capacities. Sun's portfolio of hardware and software, services and support meets a range of needs, from electronic commerce and intranets to data warehousing and supply chain management.

Sun's credo that 'The Network is the Computer' underscores the company's belief that the network is the most important thing, and what sits on your desk is irrelevant. The arrival of internet access through other devices such as mobile phones has put paid to the notion that advantage comes from possessing the highest-spec PC adorned with all the latest proprietary software. The internet has become the most powerful tool, a fact long predicted by Sun and substantiated by its patent ethos of open systems and standards. Sun's cross-platform Java and Jini technologies,[2] for example, ensure flexibility and competitive pricing, and eliminate single vendor lock-in. They have become the international language of business.

---

[2] Sun Microsystems is the author of Java[tm], the first computer language to provide a platform-independent solution to Internet programming, and Jini[tm] which expands the power of Java to enable spontaneous networking of a wide variety of hardware and software.

Practising what you preach: CRM for the provider

This theme of the importance of the network is prompting new thinking at Sun. Historically, the company has focused on acquiring customers and maximizing revenue. However, while it continues to be revenue oriented, its strategic approach is changing. The link between customer retention and profitability is taking hold. Moreover, within Marketing, the concept of the network is viewed as significant both in terms of enabling customers to do better business, and in making Sun's operations more effective. In essence, what Sun is in the business of delivering to others, it is now beginning to deliver for itself.

Although Sun Microsystems does not yet have a formal CRM strategy, the company is pursuing objectives and initiatives that recognize the value of managing customer relationships strategically. Sun is a good example of how a leading hi-tech solutions provider is exploring the potential of CRM by embracing team-based operations, and open systems and standards. Teamworking and openness are Sun's signature features, and the company is increasingly leveraging them to understand and serve customers better.

Caroline Barcock, a marketing consultant engaged by Sun, is upbeat. 'Sun is starting to draw the big picture and join together the "customer jigsaw pieces" ', she says. 'CRM is not a strategic vision and so the elements are emerging, but not under one umbrella.'

Several company projects demonstrate Sun's increasing recognition of the role of relationship quality as well as quantity in measuring and enhancing business performance. These seek to:

- target the most valuable customers and maximize their value;
- improve communication and 'connect' with customers;
- transform company culture so that it is more conducive to putting customers (rather than profits) first;
- build customer loyalty through gaining and demonstrating a deeper understanding of customer needs and preferences;
- present a more unified view to the customer and acquire a more unified view of the customer;
- build and use a data warehouse which brings together information from core transactional systems;
- adopt and promote eSun strategies throughout Sun including e-commerce and e-communications.

A team for change

1 July 1999 was an especially memorable day for Catherine Raymond, Relationship Marketing Manager at Sun. It marked the launch of Relationship Marketing, a new team set up solely to support Sun's 250 industry customers and placed under Raymond's command (see Figure CS 4.3.2). The Relationship Marketing Team is charged with delivering marketing programmes to these accounts in order to increase their brand awareness and loyalty to Sun, and their revenue-generating ability.

The importance of Sun's 250 industry customers was underlined by an exercise undertaken by the new Sales Director. He found that 20 per cent of the company's customers deliver 87 per cent of total revenue. Industry accounts constitute this high value customer group.

With the exception of a top tier of six corporate accounts, which are not vertically aligned and are served by dedicated Sun teams, the bulk of industry accounts (244) are managed according to industry sector. These industrial markets include wholesale finance, retail finance, retail, telecommunications,

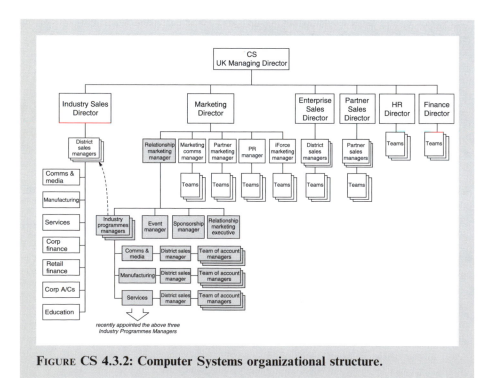

FIGURE CS 4.3.2: Computer Systems organizational structure.

manufacturing, government, utilities, media, and education. The Enterprise Sales Team and the Marketing Communications Team (see Figure CS 4.3.3) handle all other 'enterprise' accounts, comprising some 2000 companies.

Most of Sun's industry customers receive generic treatment, explains Raymond, 'because we haven't had the resources to do it any other way'.

However, she is confident that a more customized approach is gaining currency within the company and that her team of six will be expanded and in a position to deliver vertically targeted marketing programmes. 'Importantly though', she adds, 'we will not dispense with the generic approach, as it does have a value.'

She attributes this value to the ability to connect with senior people in leading organizations. For example, Sun reaches heavyweight audiences by engaging heavyweight speakers for its marketing events. These prominent speakers are attracted by the opportunity to address powerful audiences. Bringing the two together would not be a viable proposition with 'an audience of one'.

Bridges to cross

The Relationship Marketing Team's relationship-building strategy focuses on marketing events and sponsorship activities. The team uses various means for

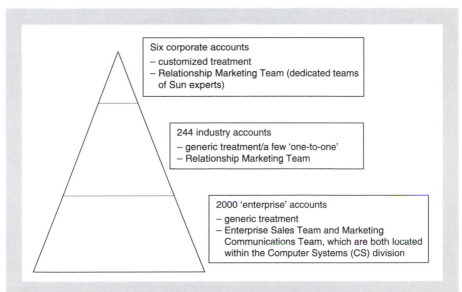

FIGURE CS 4.3.3: Account tiers and management structure.

communicating with customers and conveying the Sun dot.com vision, but has found that channelling the corporate message strongly through account managers is what works best. Raymond observes: 'We have tried targeted direct mail, it doesn't work; we have tried putting information on the web, it doesn't work. Perhaps the person-to-person tradition is ingrained.'

Raymond's team faces a number of challenges in implementing its strategy, and the pivotal role of account managers amplifies the need for change to company culture. Key questions are how to address increasingly diverse decision-making units (DMUs), and how better to exploit the knowledge and positioning of account managers.

The reality of constantly changing DMUs presents the relationship marketers with a moving target. The team knows that to develop these priority accounts means extending the number and level of contacts within them. For example, Sun may currently just deal with the IT director of a client company. As the customer increasingly faces competition from all directions, other departments influence business strategy and it is no longer IT driven. The Sun account manager must therefore broaden the contact base, and understand and appeal to various client interests.

For the Relationship Marketing Team, this raises the issue of extending the use of team-styled operations. The industry account managers need to be given sufficient support, ideally in the form of an Industry Programmes Manager (IPM), for each industry that can update them on relevant developments and advise them of the right Sun visionary pitch to deliver in each unique situation. An IPM could be used to identify trends in the industry, in the account and in Sun, that should be considered when developing each account (not to mention overall Sun strategy). In the technology business the pace of change is rapid, and it is unreasonable to expect a single relationship marketing manager (Raymond) to be able properly to manage 170 account managers with over 200 accounts without additional resource. Significantly, the primary need here is for more staff, not more technology.

Account managers have always been central to Sun's relationship marketing strategy, providing the 'bridge' between company and customer. Curiously, however, they have not been actively included in designing and developing relationship marketing programmes, being regarded more as implementers than innovators. To date, the company hasn't formally sought or integrated into company practice their insights into and experiences of customers. Raymond hopes to redress this situation once more staff are on board, and to make the account managers both more involved and more accountable.

Currently, all company contact and communications with industry customers pass through the designated account manager. Each account manager manages one account (with the exception of corporate accounts, which are managed by teams of Sun experts). As Raymond fully recognizes, the scope to build customer relationships lies first and foremost in maximizing this account manager interface. Tracking the actions and behaviour of account managers as well as that of their customers could liberate valuable information and lead to future improvements in many aspects of the business. Closer monitoring could also help ensure that account managers are appropriately matched to clients, and suitably challenged and rewarded for the performance of their 'linchpin' role.

Any desire to become more customer-driven, rather than solely revenue-driven, will require changes of policy, including appraisal and reward systems. Sun's account managers are incentivized by substantial commissions to sell Sun products and services. This approach obviously reinforces the revenue goal, and distances the objective of attaining a stronger customer focus. The board acknowledges the importance of good relationship management, but this has yet to become embedded in corporate ethos and daily routine.

Signs of promise

Customer loyalty improved during the year after the team was created to manage the company's most valuable accounts. During that first year, the Relationship Marketing Team piloted a few one-to-one marketing programmes with nominated accounts. They consumed extra resources, but the programmes produced justifiable results in terms of account penetration and additional business. This customized activity was later extended in order to reach more contacts within these key accounts and thus secure stronger and more profitable relationships with them. A leading example of the success of one-to-one initiatives is the Smile campaign, as the following example shows.

EXAMPLE

Smile: A one-to-one marketing success

The Co-operative Bank launched the UK's first full-service internet bank, Smile (smile.co.uk), in October 1999. The online bank was designed to be a separate brand from the High Street bank, promoting a new, updated and customer-friendly image.

Smile runs on Sun systems. Keith Girling, Head of Technology, describes the relationship. 'None of this would have been possible without our technology partners', he says. 'We have a growing relationship with Sun, who are one of our key partners in wholesale banking. They enabled us to launch our internet channel 18 months ago, and have continued to partner us in the development and launch of Smile. The core of our system is the UNIX environment. We're using multiple servers in multiple different locations, all on the Sun platform.' He adds: 'Both the systems applications and the firewalls run on Enterprise servers, which were chosen for their reliability, scalability and high-performance' (www.sun.co.uk).

Sun invited a representative of Smile to be a keynote speaker at one of its major marketing events, and ran banner ads with them on the Sun web site and other web sites where they could get discretionary rates. Sun created an ad campaign, 'very Hollywood' adds Raymond, which highlights Smile as one of its customers. The additional marketing externally gave the new brand high-profile exposure and accreditation. It was also great for Sun, which is not as well known as some of its rivals, such as IBM.

The interesting counterside to the campaign was the reaction of Sun's better-established customers, the traditional blue-chip companies. Raymond recalls: 'BP/Amoco said, "We like the idea of doing more marketing with Sun, but you seem to be associating yourselves with these new dot commed companies – which we are not, and do not want to be. We would like to see you working with the FTSE companies."' Reuters expressed the opposite view, enthusiastically wanting to be the next Smile.

While the synergy with Smile was strong, Sun recognizes that such closely integrated marketing is not always appropriate or desirable.

The value of CRM to future performance

Gaining a full and accurate appreciation of what customers want (even when they don't know), and how well the company's activities match market demand, is basically a matter of measurement. Sun measures performance in terms of revenue, customer satisfaction and profit margins. Raymond defends these metrics. 'You can take CRM to a very procedural, detailed level, run a pilot, measure it, evaluate it, in such a formal way that you get a much better measurement', she says. 'But at the end of the day, if your main objective is keeping your customers satisfied and delivering revenue, why are they not the only metrics that should be used?'

She is particularly interested in the power of CRM to deliver customer satisfaction. 'There is a huge area to be covered there', she says.

A separate department is responsible for monitoring customer satisfaction and company performance against customer expectations, and this information is then fed back to director level. However, it is not always passed on to all those who would derive benefit. Raymond is conscious of the need for better knowledge management. 'There's a big disconnect at the moment. We should be linking interdepartmentally much more', she admits.

Giving and getting a unified view

Sun solutions have always been based on open interfaces and industry standards, an approach that promotes competition, innovation and customer choice. Now the advantages of applying a more open approach to internal operations are gaining credence within the company.

Although Sun's overall strategic direction is towards centralized systems via a web-based infrastructure, it has traditionally organized around individual operations. Each geographical unit, division, line of business, and even function was, until recently, responsible for its own relationship. For example, the Computer Systems (CS) division encompasses marketing and sales. The younger Enterprise Services (ES) division, now six years old, has three parts: support services related to customer contracts; education and training (a separate revenue stream); and professional services, in which Sun consultants collaborate on major customer projects (see Figure CS 4.3.4). CS interfaces with customer decision-makers (CDMs), whereas ES deals on a more long-term basis with administrators and technical level contacts that sign and manage contracts, undertake educational courses or manage technical environments and projects. Because they use different kinds of information, CS and ES have different databases, analytical and reporting tools. They also handle call management separately.

Abalon is CS's standalone customer and marketing database, which functions mainly as a prospecting database. Everyone within Marketing has access to the database, which is managed and updated by the Sales Response Group who receive all incoming customer calls. Abalon is a rich repository of customer data, be it product specific, business issue specific, or customer interest specific. Data are contributed by account managers and marketing colleagues, and are input by the Sales Response Group (see Figure CS 4.3.5). The wealth of contact, transactional and behavioural information it holds on client companies and their representatives enables Marketing to produce relatively comprehensive customer profiles, including on all the industry accounts.

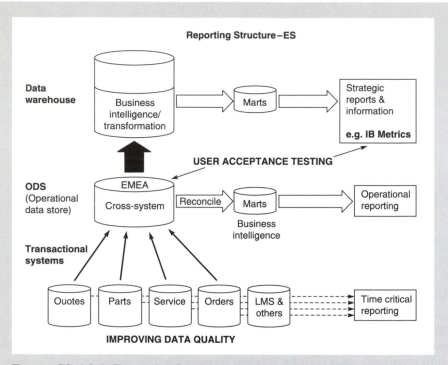

FIGURE CS 4.3.4: Enterprise Services reporting structure. Reproduced with the kind permission of Sun Microsystems, Inc.

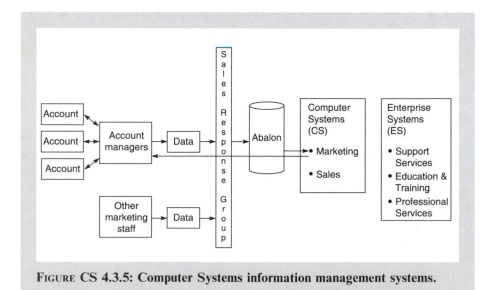

FIGURE CS 4.3.5: Computer Systems information management systems.

Relationship Marketing is developing Abalon further, seeking to control the database more centrally and utilize it more effectively. As Raymond says: 'We can identify that a customer contact enjoys golf, but for budgetary reasons we may tend to take them to Grand Prix motor racing because that's what we sponsor. We need to spend more time evaluating the information we've got and acting on it accordingly.'

With the recent creation of the Global Sales Operation (GSO), which will ultimately encompass both CS and ES sales and marketing resource, it is expected that a new worldwide tool will become the back end database when Sun fully 'dot.coms' itself later in the year. This move will significantly benefit ES, which currently does not have easy access to Abalon. ES's marketing database captures a different level of customer contacts, concentrating on those individuals that sign the service agreements and oversee the various contract details. With access to transactional and behavioural data as well as contractual information, ES will be able to construct more comprehensive and complete views of customers, which can be translated into individually tailored and more mutually beneficial agreements. CS will likewise benefit from a greater understanding of customer logistics, and equipment and skills requirements, knowledge that can be turned into better-targeted and superior selling propositions.

As well as providing a more unified view *of* customers, the integration of information allows Sun to present a more unified view *to* customers. At present there is no way easily to control the uniformity of messages to customers, leading to potentially incoherent, inconsistent and overlapping communications. Obtaining a more complete and comprehensive view of customers by combining data on the multiple customer interfaces reduced that risk and increased the impact of each customer interaction, thereby strengthening the relationship.

Success is 'a seamless experience'

Chief Technology Officer Greg Papadopoulos argues that acquiring and assimilating customer knowledge is crucial. 'The key to success has less to do with ownership of the channel than knowledge of the channel', he says. 'The real challenge then will become bringing everything together to create a seamless experience' (www.sun.co.uk).

Sun is working to turn this notion of a seamless experience into a secure business reality. For the past ten years it has been applying its ethos of open systems and standards to building relationships, supporting employees and customers, partners and channels. The sun.net program originated as a 'portal' for its employees, a means to give staff remote access to their electronic tools (e-mail, calendar, address book and so on.). More recently, the company has extended the concept of 'portal computing' to its customers worldwide through the dot.-com initiative eSun. Sun president Ed Zander says: 'We've been working to get our major customers and all of our suppliers online with us so that we can treat them as part of our environment, give them data, accept input from them, and do all that in a simple, secure fashion to make them part of our electronic value chain' (www.sun.co.uk).

Perfect partners

Sun is definitively network-centric and distinctively partner-centric. In addition to dependable scalable systems, keeping a dot.com going requires teamwork. People, processes and products all have to work together. Sun 'lives and breathes' the partnership leverage model. The company has forged such close relationships with leading software vendors and system integrators that it is sometimes hard to tell who works for whom. This culture of team-working, or channel integration, is reinforced by the growing trend towards outsourcing.

While Sun professes not to be a service provider ('We don't like to compete with our own customers'), the company does work with many of the biggest and best application service providers, internet service providers and network service providers.

Sun's long-term strategic vision is to focus its customer base so that it serves all the leading service providers. The company's future security is based on the confidence that network computing is a permanent fact of life, and Sun will be indispensable to the most indispensable enterprises. Sun is well placed and increasingly well prepared to realize this dream. According to US market research group Forrester Research the volume of electronic commerce in Europe alone exceeded $64 billion in 2001. The Gartner Group predicts that the internet will become the predominant mechanism for conducting business by 2003. Clearly, a radical transformation in business ecology is occurring and bringing with it the evolution of business solutions epitomized by Sun.

Zander says: 'At Sun, we believe the real revolution lies in how the internet is enabling companies to interact more efficiently with suppliers and partners as well as customers – not to mention their employees.'

A measure of Sun's readiness for the impact of this revolution is its recent SunPeak initiative. Three different core environments make up Sun's IT infra-structure: business-to-business, production and users. In one of the five biggest Enterprise Computing/ERP projects ever undertaken, Sun recently dot.commed its own data centres, re-engineering its complex infrastructure in anticipation and preparation for unprecedented demand. As a result, Sun has empowered itself with the scalability and flexibility to double in size over the next three years.

Is Sun CRM-ready?

As a leading provider of computing platforms for CRM, Sun Microsystems is now facing a key decision: should it formally implement CRM in its own business? Would adopting CRM help it achieve its business goals?

As Sun is only 'starting to draw the big picture and join together the "customer jigsaw pieces"', as marketing consultant Caroline Barcock puts it, it is probably wise to hold fire, despite the pressing need to consider CRM. Forming the Relationship Marketing Team to support industry accounts represented a small but significant change to organizational structure and philosophy. The plan to integrate the customer databases promises improvements in the quality and usefulness of Sun's customer information. The managers most closely involved with these relationship-building initiatives are delivering positive results, and the overall response of key customers has been encouraging. While CRM has received the senior level endorsement it requires to progress within Sun, it has yet to clear the hurdles of 'budget' and 'resource'. Sun will clearly have to decide soon whether or not to run with CRM.

Sun is not renowned for deliberation. Its new dot.com/Ready program offers a fast-track methodology for joining the dot.com age. Recently renamed iForce, it now leverages all partner relationships to provide collaborative services for set-up and support (see the following example). But while 'fast' is a governing operational principle, 'fastidious' is a core company attribute. Sun appreciates the issues involved in building a dot.com architecture and deploying networked services on the architecture. In its publication, *How to dot.com Your Business: The Survivor's Guide to the New Net Economy*, Sun outlines three important points to consider when undertaking IT decisions and actions.

1. There is no single dot.com architecture that works for everyone; each one is unique and built to meet specific requirements.
2. You have to build your dot.com architecture starting with your existing systems and leveraging your current applications. No business can afford to reboot the enterprise and start from scratch.
3. Dot.comming is not a one-time event; it's a continuous process.

The same might be said of CRM. What's good for the customer may well be good for the company.

EXAMPLE

iForce offers high levels of expertise in systems integration for e-commerce vendors. Its services include transaction processing, fulfilment, stock management, handling returned goods and CRM. From start to delivery of a turn-key dot.com can take as little as 12 weeks.

iForce's success is linked to that of its customers. Its fees are linked to the number of orders taken by its client's website. For this reason, iForce is very choosy about which companies it will work with and rejects nine in ten approaches. Current customers include: ZXL.com (online auctions); Toyzone.co.uk; and Splendour.com (backed by Marks & Spencer).

Source: Adapted from published sources.

Update

Since this case was written, Sun Microsystems' 'Take it to the nth' campaign has replaced 'the dot in dot.com' slogan, with the purpose of challenging businesses to test the limits of technology and create value in ways beyond the mere 'bricks and clicks' convention. The company has evolved the business model of dot.com to 'dot.can', offering ever more capable products and services aimed at freeing enterprises from external dependency or intermediacy so that they can build and maintain control of their web 'life' and web 'assets' – from sites and strategies to devices and directories. By endeavouring to consolidate ownership of the means of value creation with the businesses themselves, Sun is helping to transcend legacy barriers and produce environments more conducive to effective CRM.

References

Payne, A. F. T. and Frow, P. (1999) Developing a segmented service strategy: improving measurement in relationship marketing. *J. Market. Manag.*, **15**, 797–818.

Reichheld, F. F. and Sasser, W. E. Jr (1990) Zero defections: quality comes to services. *Harvard Business Review*, September–October, 105–111.

Chapter **5**

Channel and media integration process

Product-focused firms have rarely treated channel and media management as a strategic issue, and their relationships with other channel players have often been adversarial. Customer-centric businesses take the opposite view and establish a channel and media framework that manages the customer's experience at each point of contact they have with the company. We will explore this strategic marketing issue under the heading 'channel and media integration' in this chapter. Throughout this book we consider channel and media as separate, but related concepts.

- Media: We define media as the modes of communication between customers and their supplier. At the beginning of the 1990s, customers communicated with companies face-to-face (via sales representatives or in-store), by post and phone. This media choice now includes facsimile, sophisticated call centres and the internet, through devices such as personal computers (PCs), personal digital assistants (PDAs) and internet enabled-mobile phones (WAP (wireless application protocol), for example).
- Channel: We define channel as the legal entity with which the customer contractually engages to provide goods or services. Channels are routes to market and they can be direct or indirect. Indirect channels include distributors, retailers and service providers.

For example, Norwich Union, the UK retail financial services provider, sells financial products directly to consumers and through independent financial advisers (IFAs). The media for its direct sales and service are the internet and call centres, but legal documents are sent by post. IFAs will deal with customers face-to-face but Norwich Union still sends IFA customers legal documents through the post. Norwich Union operates a two channel policy: direct and IFA. The media strategy is to partner with the IFA channel for face-to-face contact, while supporting its direct channel online and through call centres. Post supports both channels.

Business has traditionally had a limited view of channel management, treating it as sales-driven and unworthy of consideration as a strategic marketing initiative. Channel choice has been limited, and the only value channel partners added was restricted to logistics, order processing and credit management. For example, consumer goods makers sold through retailers but sought to control the presentation and pricing of their brands on the shelf. Likewise, computer manufacturers sold their boxes through distribution channels and the customer was left to integrate the boxes with software, networks and other technologies to create a business solution.

New media and new business have transformed channel strategy. Today, grocers add at least as much value to the shopping experience as the branded goods makers, many of whom now produce goods for their distribution partner ('own label') as well as selling their own brands through the channel. Similarly, when the computer industry's business model moved from selling boxes to selling solutions, resale channels became valued business partners responsible for solving customers' problems rather than mere logistics. Distribution channels now create more value, but rely on support from manufacturers. Manufacturers vie for the attention of the best distributors as a way to get to the customer. These mutual dependencies create a complex set of interdependent relationships between manufacturers and channels.

The widespread adoption of the internet adds to this complexity. Manufacturers can now deal directly with large numbers of customers, but channel partners can aggregate solutions from a wide number of manufacturers. In many industries, we are seeing a complex array of alliances dealing with customers at many 'touchpoints', and firms must integrate these touchpoints into a coherent brand experience. Channel and media integration is core both to marketing and customer strategy.

In Chapter 2, we introduced a framework for looking at channel and media integration. In this chapter we illustrate this framework with three cases:

1. Wesleyan Assurance Society is a Life Insurance provider dealing directly with its customers primarily through its sales force. The sales force

represents a major expense for Wesleyan in terms of compensation, travel and support. Slight improvements in its productivity have disproportionate impacts on sales revenue and profitability. Wesleyan enhanced its 'primary medium', i.e. the sales force, through automation. Improved sales presentations and workflow, delivered through laptops, increased turnover and reduced administrative costs and errors.

2. RS Components sells a vast array of office components such as computer cables, modems, lights and connectors to a very wide range of business and home office users. It operated a traditional catalogue and call centre operation serving this diverse customer group. It subsequently expanded its media to go online. The web site has made it much easier for its customers to buy, reducing RS's cost of serving them and allowing it to grow its business faster than would have been possible through its traditional media. This new medium has also attracted new customers for RS Components.

3. asserta home operates an innovative business model in the domestic property market. It launched as a dot.com operation to help potential buyers search for a new home, handing interested customers to traditional (offline) estate agents to close the sale. asserta is interesting for two reasons: it demonstrates a real channel partnership and it offers customers a well-designed, integrated multi-media experience. Instead of trying to disintermediate estate agents by selling online, asserta partners with agents because it understands that homeowners place properties on agents' books. Without an inventory of good property, excellent media add little value. Agents appreciate asserta's ability to qualify leads and reduce their selling and marketing costs. asserta offers an imaginative media mix where each medium is designed to support a specific home search process. For example customers can use their PC and the internet to search rapidly, they can store details of interesting homes and access them by iTV for the family to look at, and they can be notified of breaking news via their mobile phone.

So in this chapter we will demonstrate three aspects of channel and media strategy, namely to:

1. improve media quality within the existing channel structure (Wesleyan);
2. extend media to improve the customer experience, reduce costs and attract new customers (RS Components);
3. design a well-integrated multi-channel, multi-media strategy to innovate in the marketplace and create a new customer value proposition (asserta home).

CASE STUDY 5.1

Wesleyan Assurance Society

OVERVIEW

Wesleyan Assurance Society is a relatively small but highly innovative mutual assurance society based in Birmingham. The case illustrates an aspect of media strategy through automating the sales force, and demonstrates how media strategy has an impact on revenue, cost and quality, even in a traditional business.

Competitive pressures prompted Wesleyan to automate its sales force. The company relied on a large sales force, but the cost of supporting it made it difficult for the society to compete in an increasingly competitive marketplace.

New management appointments and a culture of innovation helped implementation of the Sales Force Automation project (SFA) at Wesleyan. The project involved upgrading sales people into financial advisers, which required new skills and business processes supported by new technology. Each financial adviser was given a laptop loaded with software that tracks sales activity and generates performance data. It also acts as a repository of customer and product information, and enables the financial adviser to demonstrate on the spot to clients the effect that changing their pension contribution levels would have on expected retirement income, for example.

Sales productivity increased as soon as the SFA project was implemented. In the space of three years the number of sales per financial adviser and the average value of each sale tripled. As a result of the project, Wesleyan won a string of awards. The society's SFA software was so highly regarded that Wesleyan was even able to license it to other firms in the financial services industry.

Key learning points

The case demonstrates how Wesleyan smoothly implemented its SFA project, and successfully managed some of the barriers that organizations experience when embarking on such projects. These can include: culture and ingrained practices and behaviour; cross-functional integration; and lack of high-level buy-in.

Wesleyan minimized cultural issues through an inclusive approach which secured the sales force's commitment throughout the project. The sales force also benefited from a new pay structure; the shift to higher fixed salaries allowed them to concentrate on retaining customers rather than acquiring them. Cross-functional integration was not really an issue in this case, because the project was confined to one business area, although it did turn out to have wider implications for the business. High-level buy-in was secured partly through the smooth delivery of the project but mainly because of the immediate and positive business benefits that it secured for Wesleyan. This project exceeded expectations, encouraging Wesleyan to move towards a broader CRM programme the following year.

CRM issues

- Channel and media management are strategic marketing matters. Enhancing the medium through which face-to-face presentations were made improved turnover and the productivity of the sales force.
- Obtaining buy-in from all involved is key successfully to implementing a CRM project.
- Even a relatively small-scale CRM project such as Wesleyan's SFA implementation will have wider organizational implications. In particular, the way staff are remunerated may have to change to encourage them to adopt new ways of working. At Wesleyan this was reinforced through a change in job title: sales people were renamed financial advisers.
- Quick, visible wins from the SFA project were important in winning support for a wider CRM roll-out.

Introduction

CRM at Wesleyan Assurance Society began with a relatively small sales force automation (SFA) project and grew into an organization-wide initiative. The SFA project was so successful, helping to reverse several years of lacklustre performance, that the society is now working towards 'total customer recognition' via a data warehouse, an interactive website and a redesigned organization.

Its various technology initiatives have led Wesleyan to be regarded as one of the UK's most innovative life assurance societies.

About the Wesleyan

Wesleyan is a small mutual assurer, owned by its members. It sells life insurance, pensions, savings and investment, health protection and mortgage products. Financially it is very strong, ranking joint third in a 1999 *Money Management* survey in terms of its free asset ratios.[1] This placed it above some better-known UK brand names such as Standard Life, Scottish Widows, CIS, Pearl Assurance and the Prudential.

Wesleyan Assurance Society began life in 1841, when a few members of the Wesleyan Church set up office in a small room next to their church in Birmingham. The society now has approximately 400 000 customers, and has supplemented its traditional blue-collar bias with growing numbers of professional customers which it has acquired mainly through buying other insurance companies. It bought Provision (a part of Clerical Medical) from Halifax in 1997 and the Medical Sickness Society in 1997. The Medical Sickness Society, which specializes in insurance for Britain's doctors and dentists, has around half the market, with 65 000 customers. The current structure of the Wesleyan group is shown in Figure CS 5.1.1. The Wesleyan's approach is outlined on its website: www.wesleyan.co.uk (see Figure CS 5.1.2)

Wesleyan has been an innovator from the start. It pioneered door-to-door collection of insurance premiums in the late 1800s, and was one of the earliest insurance companies to introduce automatic telephone systems and laptop computers. It was the first insurer to offer loyalty bonuses and policies with guaranteed bonuses. And it was also an early adopter of profit sharing with its customers.[2]

Deteriorating performance – the decision to go for CRM

By the 1980s, however, Wesleyan appeared to have lost its way. A number of other assurers, such as Prudential, Pearl, London and Manchester, Refuge and Britannic, were invading its traditional heartland and Wesleyan was losing customers so fast, its customer retention was in the bottom quartile. The society had a number of weaknesses. For example, although financially very strong it was

---

[1] The free asset ratio is defined as total assets less total liabilities, divided by total liabilities.
[2] The profit sharing scheme was worth £13 million in extra bonuses to Wesleyan customers in 1997 and again in 1998.

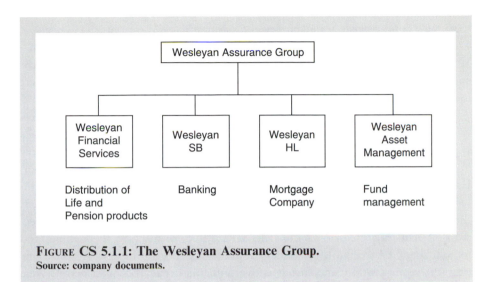

FIGURE CS 5.1.1: The Wesleyan Assurance Group.
Source: company documents.

Sound financial decisions need to be taken on good reliable information. Wesleyan can provide you with such information in the way you want it, and at your convenience.

If you prefer to take your time looking at what is available before making your next move then peruse the site. Or if you know what products you want you may be able to purchase direct from our website select the buy now option above (not all of the Wesleyan products are available direct – but we are working on it). Or we can send you the information you require click here to go to our brochure request form.

Alternatively, you may want to discuss your options, in which case we can offer you a free* no-obligation review with one of our trained financial advisers. Simply click here to fill out our online appointment request. Or call us free on 0800 0 680 680 quoting reference 2054 and we'll arrange it.

What is the Mutual Rewards Scheme?
Because Wesleyan is a mutual society, profits made are used for the benefit of members, and not paid as dividends to shareholders.

The mutual reward scheme was designed to reward members who hold 'with profits' and 'unit linked' policies with an extra bonus, over and above the normal annual bonus. As a result the Wesleyan have already allocated in excess of £50 million as extra bonuses for members. The size of the annual extra bonus depends on the amount invested, and bonuses paid as part of the Mutual Rewards Scheme are not guaranteed to be paid in the future.

Also, Mutual Rewards guarantees to return your money if you are not entirely satisfied with our products. In addition to the statutory 14 day period, Wesleyan give you up to one month to change your mind for regular premium pension policies and three months for regular premium life assurance contracts.

* The cost of advice is met from the charges on the product when sold.

Wesleyan Assurance Society, part of the Wesleyan Financial Services Marketing Group is regulated by the Personal Investment Authority.

FIGURE CS 5.1.2: The Wesleyan website, June 2002.

extremely conservative; it had achieved a strong financial ratio at the expense of growth and expansion. Also, its traditional blue collar customer base meant that Wesleyan wrote a lot of low-ticket business. Moreover, by the early 1990s the society had 90 branches and 900 field sales people at a time when insurers were increasingly questioning the cost of their branch networks and sales forces.

The first signs of change came in 1990 with the appointment of a new Managing Director, Lowry Maclean, who had a retailing background and a strong marketing focus. His appointment was followed by two other key appointments: a new finance director joined from Mars and a new sales director, David Tyrrell, joined from Pearl Insurance. Maclean carried out a major strategic review, which concluded that the role of sales had to change. Accordingly, the society instituted a major change project in the early 1990s with the objectives of reducing the size of the field sales force, re-training the people, and introducing SFA technology to help make sales more efficient. At the same time the remuneration structure was overhauled so that Wesleyan people were rewarded for customer-focused behaviour. Wesleyan rationalized its 900-strong sales force and began the project with 305 professionally qualified financial advisers, each with a laptop.

Customer contact – sales force automation (SFA) and the FAITH system

Wesleyan called its sales force automation system FAITH ('Financial Advice In The Home'). Within FAITH there is a complete sales activity management system. The system tracks everything that the adviser does – how many sales calls he or she makes, what type (sales or fact find), the length of the call and details of any new prospects or referrals they may receive. The system generates weekly, monthly and year-to-date performance statistics.

Each field sales person was given a laptop loaded with the FAITH software. The software helps them carry out a needs analysis for a potential or existing customer, offers help with compliance, and delivers automatic underwriting. A customer can view the impact of making various levels of contributions on their final pension levels instantly as a graph on the screen. Once the data are entered and the customer has indicated his or her satisfaction with the proposal, the sales person can print it off on the spot. This greatly increases customer acceptance of an insurance proposal. Each evening the sales person downloads the information overnight to the Head Office system, where the proposal and compliance documents are printed.

The manager of the project believes that the laptops have helped the sales force obtain higher premiums. He says: 'The laptops drove higher premiums because the discussion moved from "how much can you afford?" to "what income level do you want on retirement?" This was to the customer's benefit; they could see immediately that they needed to save more than they had appreciated to get the income they wanted.'

Results of Stage 1 of the sales force automation

Wesleyan reaped significant benefits from FAITH. Each sales person became more productive, thanks to the laptops, and admin improved too. 'We got tremendous improvements in back-office productivity and far fewer errors', says the project manager.

The most immediate and tangible result of the project was a significant increase in sales force productivity. In 1995 the average business won was 0.8 cases per sales person per week. Wesleyan had estimated that the business needed two cases per sales person per week to be competitive. By 1998, cases won had increased to 2.35 cases per sales person per week. What's more, the average annual premium on new cases increased by more than three times, from £250 in 1995 to £760 in 1998, against a suggested target of £600. Overall, Wesleyan's new business grew by 43 per cent in 1997 and by 37 per cent in 1998.

The FAITH laptop system helped Wesleyan win a number of accolades. The system was awarded Top Point of Sale Technology by *Financial Adviser* magazine in 1997, 1998 and 2000, and the society won the British Life Assurance Sales Force of the Year award in 1998. An independent customer satisfaction survey in January 1999 found that 90 per cent of customers felt that they could recommend Wesleyan to a friend. Moreover, other companies in the industry use Wesleyan's sales force automation software. Initially, Wesleyan received licence payments, but the society subsequently sold its intellectual property rights in the product to the software suppliers.

Implementing the SFA project

Wesleyan's first objective for FAITH was to automate the sales force's regular fact-finds. The project was implemented with two partners, Hoskyns, the IT consultancy that is now part of CAP Gemini, and the software house Crisp. The full-time project team, which took over the fourth floor of the head office in

Colmore Circus[3] for several months during implementation, also included more than 30 people from different areas within Wesleyan.

As well as developing the FAITH system, the project team also trained the sales people, whose titles were changed to financial adviser. The change of title was intended to send a signal about the business's switch in focus from distributing products to a customer orientation. The remuneration policy was also changed to reflect this new focus. Previously, Wesleyan had followed industry norms in paying its field sales force a very low basic salary with high commissions on new business. Now, to reinforce the new drive to serve and retain existing customers, rather than constantly chasing new business, basic salaries were increased almost three-fold and the commission element was drastically reduced.

Barriers to change

There was little resistance within Wesleyan to the FAITH project, partly because it yielded immediate and visible benefits. Improvements in the performance of the sales force made managers quickly aware of the benefits of the project. What's more, because FAITH was a single project within a single department, it was easier to implement than a broader initiative might have been.

FAITH was a significant move for Wesleyan. The implications for the organization were greater than the pure efficiency benefits it achieved; FAITH also focused Wesleyan's attention on customers and demonstrated the financial benefits to be gained from better customer service supported by technology. FAITH was to become an important piece of organizational learning in Wesleyan's changing business environment and a critical catalyst for the next stage of CRM. At this point, Wesleyan would not have said that it had embarked upon CRM. 'We wouldn't have recognized it as CRM while we were doing it – at that stage it was seen as a one-off', says a senior manager.

However, the results of the SFA project were positive enough to interest the senior managers at Wesleyan in a second phase of CRM, which would involve a much larger investment in a data warehouse, website, and developed call centre.

[3] Wesleyan's head office in Birmingham, England.

CASE STUDY 5.2

RS Components: Proactive purchase power[4]

OVERVIEW

Growing recognition of the need for procurement managers to devolve purchasing responsibility to end users has come about as result of the pincer-like pressure to both operate and deliver 'faster, better, cheaper'. By devolution here we mean the *em*powerment of end users, not the *dis*empowerment of procurement managers. How this 'giving to' without 'taking from' purchasing solution can work is embodied in the way RS Components has combined purchasing controls and reporting requirements with the benefits of RS Online.

RS Components is a leading supplier of electronic, mechanical, and Health and Safety products to engineers and maintenance professionals worldwide. The evolution of RS's original mail order catalogue dating from 1937 is indicative of the company's progressive stance: it follows a natural progression from paper format to CD ROM, to a complete, full-colour, online search-and-order facility. Recent integration of the CD ROM catalogue and internet capability has provided a further ordering option. Through CD-WEB orderlink, RS customers who prefer to straddle the technology fence can compile web orders offline and then transfer them online at the click of a button.

RS takes an order somewhere in the world every second. The reason why is linked to the fact that RS offers its business-to-business customers a secure, time- and cost-saving alternative for purchasing frequent, low value orders, or LVOs. LVOs (typically less than £250, and encompassing non-production materials such as office equipment and consumables) often cost a company more to process than the actual cost of the goods themselves, with much of the expense providing no benefit to the company. By empowering end users to access the rich content of the rswww.com site and to place LVOs directly within predefined parameters, RS has developed a successful sales proposition where transacting online represents a powerful and productive use of customers' limited business resources.

[4] This case study was developed and agreed with the management of RS Components in December 2001.

Key learning points

The rapid take-up of RS's e-purchasing solution by engineers and buyers demonstrates the appeal of offering a trading channel that fits well with the corporate culture of the target customer. RS's online customer base is comprised predominantly of companies for whom low value orders are a significant problem, both in terms of generating processing costs that are disproportionately higher than the cost of the goods ordered, and threatening supplier agreements through understandable but unauthorized purchasing.

RS's online ordering system is designed to manage LVOs and is fully integrated into to RS's back-office systems. The customer can implement it without investment in e-procurement software or disruption to existing ERP systems. The e-purchasing solution thus builds on established practice, providing the controls and audit trails that the purchasing function needs while enabling end users to order what they urgently require, with ease and at any hour. Additionally, of course, RS gains a cost-effective and appropriate means for servicing customers across the globe.

CRM issues

- Cost can be a 'saviour' or a 'crucifier'.

Getting the cost–benefit balance right for supplier and customer simultaneously means understanding the value of each to the other within a competitive context. RS recognized the long-term potential return of investing in an online trading channel and developing a customer-specific e-purchasing solution, while its customers saw that immediate cost savings could be made which would also counteract spending tendencies that were currently eroding their profit margins.

Multi-channel integration process issues

- Successful usage of channel/media inspires confidence, control and capability.

By extending its channel/media strategy to an online option which fully integrates with its back-office systems and directly addresses customer needs in a way that customers can easily engage with and depend upon (delivering both cost and non-cost benefits), RS has developed an attractive and suitable route to market.

- A coherent brand experience holds no surprises.

RS's e-purchasing solution delivers the same high levels of quality, service, choice and reliability that its customers have come to expect using telephone, fax and mail ordering, and customers can implement it without incurring any start-up costs.

- Channel/media strategy should consider both the customer and the end user.

By enabling companies to benefit from the speed, ubiquity and cost-effectiveness of online ordering and to delegate LVO purchasing to authorized staff, RS has demonstrated sensitivity to and support for core management, operations, and internal relations.

Figure CS 5.2.1 shows the beneficial impact on the purchasing process through the introduction of internet ordering from RS. The key savings identified were as follows.

- Waiting time (as shown in brackets) was eliminated. This time, up to three days in total, consisted of time awaiting management approval of orders plus the postal delay waiting for the hard copy order to reach the supplier. The delivery lead time of 24 hours from RS was unaffected.

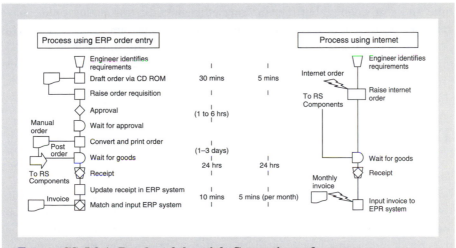

FIGURE CS 5.2.1: Results of the trial. Comparison of processes.
Source: Reproduced with the kind permission of RS Components.

- Actual processing time was reduced from an average of 40 minutes per order to five minutes.
- The time spent by senior management, in approving these low value orders, was eliminated.
- The time required by Finance to manually enter invoices into ERP was reduced from approximately four hours each month to five minutes. Previously, an invoice was received and processed against each order.

Introduction

RS Components, part of Electrocomponents plc, is Europe's leading distributor of electronic and mechanical products. It supports engineers in 160 countries worldwide and has an annual turnover of £761.4 million. From its humble origins in 1937, supplying spare parts to radio repair shops under the name 'Radiospares', RS has grown to a leadership position that encompasses both traditional trading environments and e-commerce.

RS UK provides an unrivalled choice of 124 000 products held in stock for same-day dispatch. In 1998, with the launch of its award-winning, transactional web site (http://rswww.com), the company gave its 150 000+ customers immediate online access to this extensive product portfolio. The advantages of joining search, order and fulfilment capabilities with the ease, convenience and ubiquity of the internet have led to demonstrable returns through the extended supply chain. Not only have RS and its direct customers mutually benefited from time and cost savings, but the resulting efficiencies of transacting online have also served to strengthen RS relationships with their customer's customers. This positive knock-on effect from e-purchasing is a powerful differentiator for RS, giving the company competitive edge in the cut-throat business-to-business arena.

The challenge

The process of purchasing goods and services for the day-to-day running of a business is a growing source of frustration for management. Increasing pressure to improve profit margins and shareholder value has meant a greater focus internally on containing costs and applying controls. Research has shown that the cost of purchasing low value, high frequency items – typically maintenance, repair and operations (MRO) items – often outweighs the actual cost of the goods themselves. The Chartered Institute of Purchasing and Supply has found that orders worth an average £90 can account for processing costs of between £30 and £150 per paper order. This is because much of the inherent workflow is paper based and manual, or only partially automated – and thus slow and laborious. A purchasing professional, for example, may spend much of his or her work day wading through voluminous catalogues for current product information or the best deals, or keeping track of hundreds of paper requisitions and related documentation. (Production purchasing, in contrast, often takes advantage of electronic data interchange [EDI] systems.)

Additionally, in such work environments management control is normally sought through the introduction of institutionalized procedures that ultimately create a bureaucratic barrier to processing small value purchases, which may be urgently required at the last minute. For instance, the time taken by management to approve Low Value Orders (LVOs) and by Finance to respond to queries as well as to record and reconcile invoices prolongs LVO processing and adds to administration costs. Understandably, staff often turn to 'maverick', or unauthorized, buying to shortcut the system and obtain the items they need to proceed in performing their tasks. Consequently, such purchases can go undetected by the purchasing function and can even stray outside contracts negotiated with preferred suppliers, costing the company the full retail price.

In sum, many companies are either unaware of the disproportionate cost involved in LVO purchasing or are unable to quantify the cost and thus justify remedial action. Meanwhile, the key challenges for the purchasing function are becoming ever more clear: optimize cost efficiency, purchase control and use of staff time. In this electronic age, it is no longer necessary or sensible to spend vast sums on routine purchases, and the market response to this situation has been the development of e-purchasing systems and, more comprehensively, e-procurement systems.

RS recognized that a specific customer organization has a variety of purchasing needs and that different channels had specific benefits to offer from a customer's point of view. The challenge for RS was to offer an integrated set of channels for a customer and to enable them to choose that channel most relevant to them at a particular point in time. For example, by going to a 'trade shop' (a branch outlet) the customer can personally inspect the item to ensure it is exactly what they require and take immediate delivery. The call centre is appropriate for placing orders for delivery within 24 hours and it is particularly useful if the items needed and their order numbers are known. These were RS's existing channels.

In 1997 RS saw the opportunity to add the internet as an extra channel. An internet solution would provide an opportunity for customers to undertake their own 'self-service' research and purchase, especially after hours when the call centre and trade shop were closed. This new channel represented an opportunity for RS to not only serve existing customer better but also gain market entry to new customer segments.

RS was faced with a further challenge. On average a given customer only ordered items from 2.1 sections of the 13 sections available in the RS catalogue. Further, every individual customer within a company chooses from a different 2.1 sections of the catalogue. With more than 150 000 line items and in excess of 75 000 companies, most of which had multiple 'user choosers' within them, RS Components wanted to personalize the offer so each individual received offers of fewer items but offers of ones that were more relevant to them.

The solution

To address these challenges RS needed not only an internet technology solution but one with a 'personalization engine'. After extensive research RS Components chose Broadvision as its technology solution. Working with Broadvision and their other technology partners including Cambridge Technology Partners and Sun Microsystems, RS developed a personalized internet solution for its customers.

When RS launched rswww.com, it was the first UK plc in its market place with a transactional web site integrated with its back end systems. Integration not only means that the full range of RS products are available online, but that any purchasing controls already set up between RS and a client company are acknowledged and observed. Existing-customer staff could order items within the pre-agreed parameters by simply entering their automatically-recognized, individual DPC (delivery point code). Customers – current and prospective – wishing to move to ordering RS products online were, therefore, spared any integration costs, and were able to bypass the need for investment in e-procurement software or in integrating e-commerce within their own ERP systems. They could also elect to receive a consolidated monthly summary of invoices generated, complete with a breakdown of individual users' spend for management information purposes.

The major benefits of transacting online are a simplified order process and greatly reduced costs. Ordering online from RS also maintains the high service levels customers have come to expect from traditional telephone ordering and extends to immediate, on-site confirmation of stock availability. RS Components' use of technology to support customers' purchasing policies and processes is a tactical way of exploiting the e-commerce selling model (one supplier to many customers) to secure cost efficiencies and enhance service provision. At a broader, strategic level, it is a means of getting closer to customers by converting customer transactions into longer-term, mutually-beneficial customer relationships.

The results

RS recognized there were two communities of customer within the organization. The first was the traditional purchasing departments and the second was the 'user chooser'. Traditionally the main relationship was with the company's purchasing department and it was based primarily on commercial terms and service level agreements (SLAs). RS's internet channel allowed deeper relationships to be built around the 'user chooser'. These individuals were technical staff such as R & D staff. This group was interested in speed and efficiency, unlike the purchasing department which was principally interested in reducing cost.

Through the functionality of the internet channel the user chooser can be empowered to make direct purchases under the controls of the business rules set by the purchasing department. This enables such staff to initiate purchase and receive goods within 24 hours, whereas, if they had raised purchase orders in the traditional way through the purchasing department, it could be several weeks before they received the item ordered. Also, if this group order the goods themselves the level of accuracy in getting the correct order is much higher. This is also a considerable benefit to RS Components because of the high cost of returned goods.

Evidence of RS's success in encouraging its end users to place orders on rswww.com, and thus to share the benefits of an e-purchasing solution that is fully integrated into RS systems, can be demonstrated through its customer case studies. The following four cases illustrate the wide application of the RS purchasing solution and how it has strengthened the supplier–customer relationship from the customer's perspective. All four companies utilize the RS web site for LVOs as an approved supplier.

Amersham Health

Amersham Health, a leading pharmaceutical company, implemented an e-procurement pilot project to combat maverick buying in order to protect and grow key supplier relationships and to define clear internal spending controls for cost-saving purposes. RS Components was chosen as one of ten vendors for the pilot. Amersham was already successfully using its e-purchasing solution (rswww.com) which enabled both its immediate participation and long-term support for the project. David Cook, Amersham's Purchasing Systems & Process Manager, stresses that limiting vendor selection is important: 'E-procurement in isolation will not bring about significant, tangible savings. Strategic sourcing, by concentrating the spend on a reduced number of preferred suppliers, is fundamental to the overall systems' cost savings.'

Amersham clearly made a wise choice. RS has worked closely with Amersham to meet their auditors' requirement that all reporting and purchasing controls (then held with RS) should be totally integrated into Amersham's ERP system. As a consequence, RS developed a system called 'punch-out'. This enables the user, via an e-procurement package, to punch-out through the firewall to the nominated supplier's web site and to build a shopping basket that is automatically returned to its e-procurement system as a purchase requisition for authorization and the generation of an electronic purchase order. By implementing the punch-out model, Amersham's internal users are empowered to view the full RS catalogue online and place their orders. These orders are then automatically fed back to Amersham's pilot so that Oracle's SSP4 and the relevant controls are validated.

The new system gives Amersham's users, which include engineers, secretarial staff and operational employees, the authority and facility to place LVOs directly with RS without the need for purchase approval. Relieved of daily involvement in maintaining the product catalogue, resolving pricing issues and processing LVOs, Amersham's buying teams are able to concentrate their expertise on strategic negotiations with suppliers. The resultant boost to internal morale and operational efficiency has delivered improvements to Amersham's bottom line.

NPL

In time-sensitive, industry-critical organizations such as the National Physical Laboratory (NPL), accuracy in purchasing processes is paramount. NPL is the UK's national standards laboratory for mass, length, time, temperature, luminous intensity and electrical current. Much of its work requires the use of electrical components and RS Components has long been its official supplier.

NPL employs more than 500 scientists who request LVO items, generating over 200 000 paper orders each year. Errors can occur when detailed product information (e.g. stock numbers, unit volumes, prices, etc.) is taken from a paper catalogue and ordered over the telephone.

The switch from using paper processes to ordering from RS online diminishes NPL's need for retyping order details and for approving every requisition. Placing a ceiling of £100 on each order, controls have been established with the purchasing department that involve adding a password for user recognition and the setting of overall spending limits and contract pricing. An in-built error detection-and-correction facility on the web site ensures that the entry of order information is appropriate to the data field and in line with the product catalogue, the user's profile and their purchase limits. Consolidated job number invoicing is possible, further reducing the scope for error and the time spent processing payments.

The resultant decrease in incomplete or incorrect purchase requests and wrong deliveries, together with a streamlined administration has created significant cost savings. Balgit Sidhu, Buyer for NPL, is very enthusiastic about the e-purchasing system: 'Errors have been reduced substantially. Web-based ordering has removed the need to read out or type in part numbers. There are now virtually no wrong items received, cutting out handling and postage costs of returns.'

Eurotherm Drives

Eurotherm Drives is the UK's best-known supplier of the drives (switches and electronic circuitry) that power the electric motors used in modern manufacturing and process industries. In 1992, the company abandoned its 'make for stock' strategy and adopted 'build to order' manufacturing. Just-in-time ordering of materials became a strategic priority, elevating the purchasing function from a transactional to a strategic role. Ann Craven, Eurotherm Drives' Global Commodities Manager, comments: 'Our job is to establish contracts and relationships with suppliers. The shop floor managers now handle day-to-day purchasing.'

When RS Components extended its channel options with the introduction of online ordering, Eurotherm Drives was quick to take up the opportunity. Through the company's hot link to rswww.com, individuals within production areas can now make purchases direct from RS at any time, day or night, confident in the knowledge that deliveries will be timely and correct. If the authority limits set by Eurotherm Drives are exceeded, RS issues immediate notification to the company's purchasing department so that the problem can be resolved expeditiously.

In this customer's experience, purchasing online from RS provides two highly relevant benefits. First, online product information is always up to date, whereas the RS paper catalogue was often out of date even before it was printed. The second benefit is the time-saving element of no longer having to deal with invoice enquiries, a costly non-value adding activity. 'Internet ordering gives us the correct price each time', explains Craven.

When Eurotherm Drives rationalized its supplier base from 1200 in 1992 to fewer than 200 in 2001, RS was one of the first to be retained as a preferred supplier.

Arjo Wiggins

Arjo Wiggins Fine & Drawing Papers is a division of Arjo Wiggins Appleton plc, one of the largest paper manufacturing and merchanting companies in the world. Arjo Wiggins specializes in supplying high quality paper and board products to the PR, advertising and promotion industries. In 1998, the company introduced a basic SAP Procurement system at all its manufacturing and logistics sites in the UK and France. A separate cost/benefits study in the purchasing function was run in parallel to this ERP implementation. This analysis identified both scope for improvement and the requirement for change in their purchasing systems, which included reducing the time and costs of administrating LVOs. This resulted in the company trialling internet ordering for the first time to see if e-purchasing could: (i) simplify and reduce the costs of the purchasing process without compromising purchasing controls; and (ii) eliminate the need for uncontrolled ordering without reducing the required speed of response. The trial was conducted with RS Components.

Since ERP systems do not differentiate by order value, it was necessary to test the advantage of purchasing LVOs electronically outside the normal ERP route. For one month, seven senior engineers at their Aberdeen site were authorized to self-approve and purchase LVO items from the RS web site within their own designated order value limit. At the end of the month the company received a consolidated invoice summary from RS, which was then fed into the SAP invoice processing system. To the satisfaction of the company's engineering departments and purchasing function, the trial confirmed that internet ordering substantially cut the time and costs associated with obtaining low value engineering parts (see Figure CS 5.2.1), reducing average order costs by some 70 per cent.

John McCormack, mill buyer at the trial site, comments: 'The e-purchasing system provided by RS Components requires changes in attitudes because it operates outside the formal system. However, this trial has proved that the gains far outweigh any perceived disadvantages, and the system is ideally suited to operate in parallel with ERP order processing, but for low value orders only. The quality of the internet service provided by RS has been instrumental in making this trial successful.' Following minor adjustments, Arjo Wiggins now uses the RS e-purchasing solution on an extensive basis.

The conclusion

As a result of its integrated channel offer of trade shop, call centre and the internet, RS has been able to build stronger relationships within its customer base. It has also gained a significant increase in volume from new customers who are inherently more responsive to a self-service internet channel. In particular, the internet enables a level of empowerment not easily replicated through traditional channels.

The move by RS Components to offer its customers enhanced value through e-purchasing has strengthened its business relationships, making it both more valuable as a supplier and more able to withstand the threats posed by competitors and adverse market trends.

As these four cases demonstrate, e-purchasing allows for significant cost savings and added customer value through: empowering its users; reducing errors; expediting orders; removing non-value-added activity; enhancing information supply; increasing convenience; and improving the control of purchasing processes. RS and its online customers have found that devolving purchase power proactively can simultaneously drive down costs as well as speed up delivery – a primary goal of businesses that seek to gain competitive advantage throughout their supply chain.

CASE STUDY 5.3

asserta home

OVERVIEW

asserta home represents a revolutionary new way for consumers to take the stress out of moving home, and for estate agents to promote homes for sale and capture new listings. Using the power of the internet, the property portal connects thousands of prospective homebuyers and sellers with an extensive, searchable database of available properties and property agents in the UK.

As the company name implies, asserta home is about giving customers control of the house hunting and purchasing process. Accessible from home by computer or interactive digital TV (iDTV), or on the hoof through mobile telephony, the web site provides a simple, speedy, hassle-free resource for consumers, and an additional 'shop window' for estate agents. A customer-friendly contact centre staffed by knowledgeable service operatives supports the wealth of online information. The company makes revenue from selling the range of home-related products and services featured on the site, including a new range developed specifically for estate agents, and from on-site advertising.

A subsidiary of insurance giant, CGNU, the company has to serve, in parallel, the respective interests of its parent, estate agents as intermediaries, and buyers and sellers. By combining superlative technology with skills in building strategic relationships and a long-term outlook, asserta home is creating a prominent place for itself in the highly competitive world of property e-services.

Key learning points

This case demonstrates the commercial and customer benefits of building the business model around existing market behaviour and an appropriate media framework. asserta home intended from the outset to become the definitive online information provider for everyone contemplating moving home, and sought competitive edge by combining traditional values with emergent technology. Acknowledging the essential role performed by estate agents, the company exploited it, rather than endangering it, by making estate agents the 'founder' customers en route to the end consumer target audience.

Aligned to this intelligent channel strategy is an integrated multi-media strategy that capitalizes on the different platforms available to maximize convenience to the customer and the performance of the company. The internet is the prime medium, but iDTV allows the family to see what's on offer, mobile phone text messaging alerts house hunters to new offers or deals, and the customer contact centre helps resolve problems. Using these selected media in an interlinked fashion, asserta home can provide the customer with a better experience than they would get using any one medium independently.

CRM issues

- Maintaining excellent customer service while managing rapid growth can test any organization. However, maintaining a customer perspective can help keep the organization's vision, mission and action on track.

asserta home is dedicated to satisfying and anticipating the needs of customers, as it demonstrates by building its business on the belief that it generates revenue on the back of well-established consumer trust and market penetration.

- 'Do what you do best' is simple advice but well worth remembering. Expanding into areas outside your competence and capability can destroy rather than create value.

asserta home carefully designed its interactive home moving service to generate qualified leads, and left fulfilment to the experts (the estate agents and ancillary home-related service providers, and the outsourced contact centre).

Channel and media integration process issues

- To provide a consistently positive customer experience an organization needs to focus on the benefits customers get from the way the product or service is delivered, as well as from the substance of the product or service itself.

The synergy between asserta home's channel and media strategies provides estate agents with the best possible platform to promote their business and attract customers, and provides consumers with the best possible platform to research the widest selection of properties.

To achieve cost-effective, forward-looking CRM, companies need to consider which media are most appropriate for different types of customers and different types of interaction (communication, transaction, research, browsing and so on).

Because asserta home's target customers are web-proficient, time-pressed business people, the web site forms the core of an integrated multimedia strategy that works both to remove 'non-value-added' activity and to offer greater flexibility through a choice of appropriate platforms. The company will not introduce new technology unless it actually helps users – it has to offer them a significant benefit, and they have to be equipped, able and willing to use it.

- Businesses that operate predominantly through the consumer-controlled electronic environment of the internet must ensure that their web sites offer sufficient personalization and customization. If they don't, prospective and potential repeat customers may turn away, feeling undervalued or dissatisfied by what looks like mass-oriented treatment.

A key priority for asserta home is to develop its web site. Measures to improve navigation of the site and benefits to individual users include a 'personal folder', and a refined search and selection facility and a new layout template. asserta home also operates to high standards, ensuring it handles online interactions professionally and securely.

- Many organizations aim to improve their operational and financial performance by creating more direct routes to market – disintermediation – but others may benefit from forming alliances with existing market players.

By partnering with, rather than competing against, estate agents, asserta home has profited from their longstanding role and provided consistent and sustainable superior customer value. This has produced a 'win–win–win' situation for estate agents, consumers and shareholders.

- Using channels and media that are complementary, compatible and minimize potential conflict, can reduce the demands on management as well as enhancing the customer experience.

asserta home gives estate agents the appropriate software and uploads data nightly, so that they can quickly transfer information from their databases to asserta home's online, searchable database, putting extensive up-to-date information at home-hunters' fingertips. The electronic system means that estate agents don't have to 'upload' the data themselves and guarantees that asserta home is always providing the best choice of properties available.

Introduction: A win–win–win with asserta home

asserta home,[5] a comprehensive home-buying portal that works to 'address the stress' of moving house, is the UK's leading interactive property service. Moving home is notoriously fraught, and asserta home seeks to turn what can be a complex and nerve-wracking ordeal into a positive, seamless experience.

Building a brave new brand

asserta home Limited is a subsidiary of CGNU plc,[6] the world's sixth largest insurance group and the largest insurer in the UK. Launched in May 2000, asserta home became the first of CGNU's new e-businesses to adopt a customer-oriented view of transactions linked to major life events. asserta home offers a 'one stop shop' service to the home-buying, lettings and new-build markets, uniting homebuyers with a comprehensive array of high-quality service providers in an interactive, dynamic environment. asserta home's core asset is a huge searchable database of domestic properties fed daily by electronic uploads from estate agents' databases. The database can also pass back to estate agents enquiries about specific properties from site visitors, and even engage their services on behalf of customers.

asserta home describes its target audience as time-pressured businessmen and women aged 25–54, along with users of internet, interactive TV and mobile technologies, who are contemplating buying, renting or improving a home. To reach these customers, and to encourage them to use the service fully and repeatedly, the company created a compelling customer service experience across multiple media. By leveraging partnerships with estate agents to provide an outstanding register of properties, and by offering a choice of communication media to customers, asserta home has taken the hassle out of home buying. Key to its clever channel strategy and skilful use of new media is an in-depth understanding of market needs and trends.

---

[5]This case study was developed and agreed with asserta home management in July 2001.

[6] CGNU plc has more than 15 million customers worldwide and over £200 billion of assets under management. CGNU is the result of the merger of Commercial Union and General Accident in 1998 (CGU), and its subsequent merger with Norwich Union on 30 May 2000 (CGNU).

A triple challenge

Extensive groundwork research had revealed that it is far harder for estate agents to get people into their branches and properties onto their books than it is to close sales. So to recruit estate agents, the property portal had to deliver not only innovative marketing support and sales channels, but a reputable brand that would prompt home sellers to choose agents linked to its web site. This presented a triple challenge.

To be of benefit to estate agents, asserta home had to become a property market lead-generator, but crucially, a non-threatening one. It had to be seen by estate agents as a 'co-petitor' which would add value to them, rather than a competitor which would take revenue from them. To be of benefit to home-buyers, asserta home had to become a consumer champion serving a critical mass of property content, but without being perceived as pro-estate agent. Estate agents rank among lawyers, doctors, car mechanics, bankers, insurers and other requisite service providers who do not enjoy the trust of the general public principally because they engender a feeling of disempowerment. What's more, to be commercially viable, asserta home had to provide a good return on investment for its chief backer – a financial services company – without prompting the property industry to question its motives.

An intuitive solution

Meeting these challenges head on, asserta home set out to build profitable relationships with homebuyers by establishing and retaining profitable relationships with estate agents. 'Estate agents represent the lion's share of trade in the property market, a trend we expect to continue', notes Simon Phipps, Head of Customer Proposition and co-founder of asserta home. This business solution of forming pivotal partnerships with property retailers in order to provide superlative breadth of choice, depth of information and height of convenience to home hunters and browsing property enthusiasts serves the interests of estate agents, consumers and investors. However, asserta home needed skills and technology to create a compelling customer value proposition capable of winning both content and custom (see Figure CS 5.3.1).

To gain competitive advantage quickly, the company needed to acquire insider knowledge and know-how about the way the property market behaved and estate agents operated. In December 1999 it bought UK Property Gold, then a top-ten property portal, capturing key people and IT resources. It enhanced its

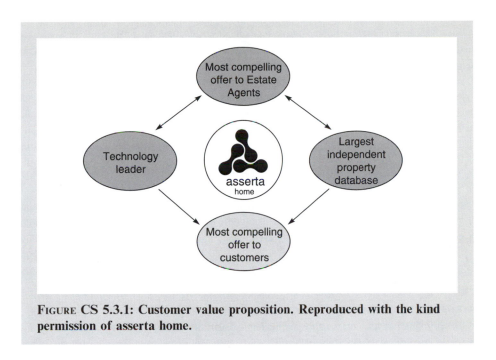

FIGURE CS 5.3.1: Customer value proposition. Reproduced with the kind permission of asserta home.

skill set further by buying smove.com,[7] a fledgling property firm, in November 2000. Smove, as it was known, had a strong editorial team, which, admits Phipps, 'would otherwise have taken us 12 months or more to build up'. Smove's founders, Nancy and Jim Cruickshank, are now, respectively, head of business development and head of marketing at asserta home. asserta home's strong editorial contingent, currently led by the former editor of the *Daily Telegraph*'s property section, draws on a wealth of experience of what customers want.

The company also established an enviable network of top technology partners to construct an infrastructure capable of attracting the widest audience to the widest choice of properties. The web site, developed and designed by Sapient, is now fully in-house and is managed and hosted by IBM. Sun Microsystems provided the hardware, Oracle and WebLogic the software, and Telewest provided interactive digital television (iDTV) distribution. asserta home has signed tenancy agreements, giving it promotional precedence on other web sites, with a range of major search engines and internet service providers (ISPs), including Freeserve, Excite, Altavista, Lycos, AOL, and Yell.com.

---

[7] Smove, pronounced 'smooth' in a Cockney accent, was launched in July 2000 and based in the dot.com-capital, Clerkenwell in Central London.

asserta home applied this considerable competence and market and media understanding to arrive at the right channel strategy and media mix – essential components of a viable business.

Channel strategy

Channel partner recruitment

asserta home recognized early on that it had to list more properties and provide better quality information on those properties than its competitors if it was to become market leader among property portals. Getting a wide range of properties on its books was the only real way to save consumers time and hassle. The company bought itself a head start. Phipps recalls: 'The first big question was, "there are 12 000 estate agents out there, how do we get to them?" There was no comprehensive list of estate agents' details, so we bought the best list available.'

Using this list as a springboard, asserta home then engaged in a dialogue with estate agents, gathering their details over the telephone and determining what professional accreditations they held. Approved agents, including members of The National Association of Estate Agents (NAEA), The Royal Institution of Chartered Surveyors (RICS), and The Guild of Professional Estate Agents (GPEA), along with those which could handle daily uploads of information, became the prime focus for recruitment. asserta homes also directed its initial efforts at the biggest players (franchises owning hundreds of branches) in a bid for quantity as well as quality.

The company invited estate agents to join and benefit from high-profile, multi-million pound advertising and marketing initiatives, along with state-of-the-art systems and implementation technology – all expertly designed to complement estate agents' existing (mainly traditional and terrestrial) promotional activities. It costs estate agents around £200 to generate every lead (a typical estate agency spends on average £20 000 per annum per branch on marketing alone to achieve 100 home sales per annum per branch). Registering with asserta home's 'one stop shop' service represented a more cost-effective and less labour-intensive way of reaching prospective home vendors and buyers.

asserta offered agents an incentive to register early in the form of what was then a unique package deal of ongoing support. This included: promotional materials and multi-media platforms; free listing of property data on the web site; and, for qualified members, the right to opt for shares in the new enterprise. It was an attractive offer. While other portals charged estate agents a fee for listing their properties, asserta home chose not to, offering the chance to share in the business' success instead.

Estate agents saw the logic in linking up with a no-cost, high-quality lead generator: within six weeks asserta home signed up approximately 50 per cent of the trade market – and its web site got five million hits in the first week it went live.

asserta home charges no commission on the core product (quality property listings for consumers and qualified property leads for estate agents), and generates revenue from advertising sales, commercial partnerships, sales of software from vendor GMW, and services offered on the 'asserta business' web site. The company makes most of its income from banner advertising (there were over 18 million page impressions in the first quarter of 2001); commissions on transactions involving move-related products and services (mortgages and insurance, utilities, removals, professional service referrals, and so forth); and software sales/support for estate agents through wholly-owned subsidiary GMW. From June 2001, contributing estate agents and non-members have also been able to purchase industry-specific products and services through asserta business Limited. These include: web site design by asserta home specialists, and, by arrangement with a company called Datagraphy, digital photographs of properties which can be incorporated online to give customers a '360-degree experience', or virtual tour, of any property.

Channel partner management

asserta home has increased the number of property listings and the richness of data held since forming a sales and relationship management team to nurture relationships with estate agents. asserta home's main concern is to 'keep the property cycle fresh', says Philip Caterer, head of estate agency relations, and previously managing director of UK Property Gold. asserta home attributes its ability to grow relationships with property retailers and maintain the most extensive and up-to-date property database to its focus on quality control.

asserta home screens prospective estate agent partners through an application and selection process, and then asks them to sign a contractual agreement to abide by certain performance rules. To qualify, estate agents must: be a current member of a nationally recognized scheme, and adhere to an approved code of conduct for professional estate agents; have Professional Indemnity Insurance cover to a minimum of £250 000 for any single event; be able to update their data electronically every 24 hours; and be willing and able to reply satisfactorily to customer enquiries (including complaints) within one working day.

Caterer's dedicated team manages member estate agents according to size, ranging from the top five corporates with some 500 branches each to 8000 'one-man bands'. All editorial content is produced in-house and the relationship management team manages estate agents' technical updates, so asserta home can constantly monitor and regulate the content of its site. Specific measures and mechanisms for quality control comprise IT and support infrastructures and the nightly upload process referred to above (see Figure CS 5.3.2).

asserta home is also vigilant about providing an impartial, independent service. There is no favouritism or preferential treatment. Providing a fair and inclusive service is particularly important in an industry where small independent agents feel threatened by large multi-branch agents and where size – in terms of the number of property listings – really counts.

asserta home extends this code of neutrality to the way it deals with sister brands such as Your Move.[8] Your Move (www.your-move.co.uk) is a separate company within the CGNU group and one of the major chains of estate agents in the UK, with its own web site and profit centre. 'Your Move received the same commercial pitch as all the other major chains', says Caterer. 'In fact, Your Move was probably one of the hardest agents we've had to recruit.' asserta home is conscious of the need to dispel any suggestion that it is 'Your Move in disguise'.

asserta home's strategy of being non-threatening to the estate agency community is further evidence of its neutrality. 'The last thing we did was say that we won't accept private listings', recalls Phipps. The significance of this claim was to reassure estate agents that asserta home had no intention of replacing their 'intermediary' role, but sought rather to augment it. But the strategy works in the company's favour too: the estate agents' professional qualifications represent a cost-effective quality filter.

By closely managing and monitoring its relationships with estate agents, and working with them rather than against them, asserta home has created a cooperative channel strategy which is free from potential conflict and adds value. This value is added through a consistently positive customer experience and achieved through an integrated multimedia strategy.

Media mix

The media mix – the assortment of platforms through which asserta home and its customers interact in order to create and impart value – makes the home-moving service readily available, accessible and useable. asserta home uses multiple media – internet, iDTV, mobile telephony and a contact centre – rather than

---

[8] Your Move is a trading name of your-move.co.uk ltd, the Estate Agency Division of Norwich Union. It has over 340 branches in the UK.

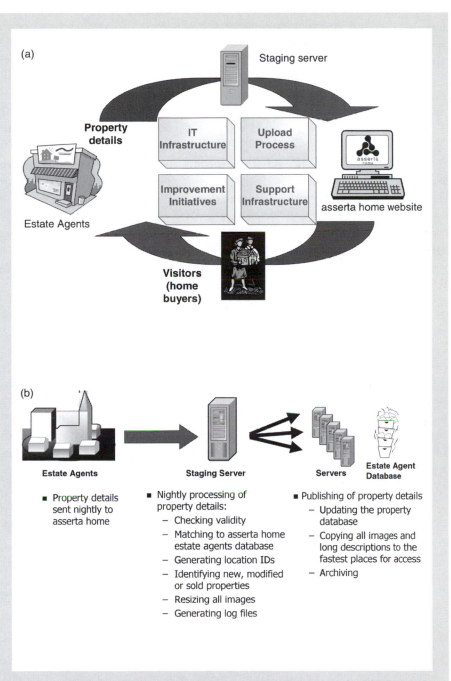

FIGURE CS 5.3.2: (a) IT and (b) upload process. Reproduced with the kind permission of asserta home.

just one medium, in order to enhance the relevance and attractiveness of the service for its target customers, and ultimately boost the company's performance and profitability.

asserta home's understanding that buying a new home tends to be a family rather than an individual's decision, is at the heart of its unique and growing appeal. The company assembled an integrated delivery and communications programme using a sophisticated multi-media approach to address people's varying interests and information-gathering habits. Deploying different media for different purposes demonstrates asserta home's understanding of the strengths and weaknesses of individual media as well as customers' propensity to use media selectively and in combination.

Internet

The internet is asserta home's core medium, serving as a one-to-one promotional tool, information resource and communication device. The internet is adept at presenting masses of textual and graphical data in immediate and customizable form through user search and selection facilities, as well as being accessible every hour of every day. As such the internet enables asserta home to provide web-savvy home hunters with an efficient and convenient alternative to pounding the streets or trawling through weekly and monthly newspaper ads. Property details can be easily updated or expanded on the web at a fraction of the cost (and time) involved in reprinting property brochures. Enquiries from all over the world can be handled speedily and inexpensively through e-mail, and customer comments stored and reported to asserta home's marketers and developers.

Located at www.assertahome.com, the company's web site provides access to an extensive computerized register of available UK properties, and direct connection to the respective estate agents via e-mail and hyperlinks to their own web sites. It also enables people to research local information and a wide range of home-related services. The sum total is a topical site packed with well-informed and well-organized 'intelligence'. Special offers from mortgage lenders and DIY stores are publicized alongside consumer advice reports and recent media commentary on asserta home.[9] Bulletins featuring the property of the week, celebrity homes, and popular-interest stories such as 'How to feng shui your home' or 'How to speak builder', add a timely touch. Helpful guides outline things to consider when planning the move, negotiating the sale (from the perspectives of

---

[9] Independent research by UK-based Media Measurement (July 2000) found asserta home's PR ratings to be overwhelmingly positive: press comment to date was 92% positive, 8% factual (neutral), and 0% negative.

both buyer and seller), and changing utility providers. There are even practical checklists and competitive price lists.

asserta home has actively sought to reinforce the consumer's confidence and sense of control by maintaining the security and privacy of personal information and transactions. The company adheres to the Data Protection Act as well as internally imposed standards to respect the rights and preferences of customers. Site visitors remain anonymous to asserta home and its strategic partners, except where they elect to disclose their identity in order to receive text messages, or electronic property updates and weekly newsletters. Even at this point, however, asserta home limits the details required to process correspondence to name, e-mail address and property specifications. If site users want information about the value added products and services, or to contact the service providers directly, they do so of their own accord: asserta home simply makes it easier for them by supplying the e-mail and site links online.

Fostering a direct interface with the public, the site invites customer feedback, and solicits and exhibits home-buying success stories. Offline consumer focus groups and an online forum for member agents provide further means for exchanging views, and pooling ideas to improve content and drive more traffic to the site and more leads to estate agents.

At the moment asserta home can only measure the number of referrals generated by the site by tracking e-mail and web-link usage. For example, it can see that x e-mails were sent from the site to member estate agents during y period, but cannot identify the senders. And, of course, it has no way of knowing when leads are followed up by telephone. However, the company does track share of product and, according to Phipps, 'only a small percentage of all home-buying traffic needs to transact here for the company to meet its targets'. This inability to 'close the loop' in measuring value further underlines asserta home's stance of offering a non-intimidating, non-exclusive service to estate agents.

iDTV

The convergence of television and conventional internet access has created a new medium for services suitable to interactive television, namely, those that thrive on home-based, group participation. iDTV is a natural component of asserta home's media mix because it supports both the evaluation of property options as a family and the more personal search for information against individually defined criteria. The ability to move results of a net search to television means home hunters can search during the day and view together at night. The popular 'personal folder' feature on the web site enables users to store information on their favourite properties for later review or comparison via the web and iDTV.

However, people can only be encouraged to embrace iDTV if the web site content is excellent and is transferred skilfully to interactive television. asserta home got involved early on with appropriate experts so that it could integrate the necessary material and technical expertise with programme scheduling, advertising and viewing behaviour. Immediately post-launch, asserta home developed an iDTV platform with Telewest to enhance the customer experience. The service lets homebuyers search asserta home's property database, examine photographs, explore neighbourhood facilities and contact estate agents. A partnership with Upmystreet, which provides local information to viewers using the interactive TV platform Open, has allowed asserta home to list more than 100 000 houses for sale in the programme's classified ads section.

Despite iDTV's slow start in the UK due to complexities surrounding connection and coverage, asserta home is confident that the growth in digital TV subscriptions and interactive commerce will see iDTV usage soar in the next few years.

Mobile telephony

Mobile telephony also plays into the media mix. Users of the asserta home service can sign up to receive automatic updates via e-mail or mobile phone text messaging. Text messaging by SMS (short message service) gives the mobile phone user a message confirming that x number of newly available properties matching their requirements have been added to their personal folder for review at www.assertahome.com. Through this tactical use of mobile phones, those on the property prowl who are technologically equipped can opt in to receive immediate text message notification of homes matching their expressed criteria – a 'must have' where properties sell sooner than you can say 'house for s–'.

At the moment, mobile phones are only really suited to providing quick alerts. While asserta homes can sensibly exploit the current popularity of text messaging to benefit its customers, it will wait for Wireless Application Protocol (WAP) technology to become more sophisticated and reliable before going on to adopt third-generation (3G) mobile technology into its media mix. In the meantime it will confine its choice of viewing property details and photographs to the more reliable web and iDTV.

Contact centre

asserta home's communication with estate agents and members of the public has, since its launch, been concentrated at its outsourced customer contact centre in London, which handles telephone calls and e-mail during normal business hours seven days a week. Past research has shown that while asserta home's customers are internet-savvy, they value telephone contact due to the nature of the business and the fact that property represents such a big investment. The centre's contact details feature prominently on the web site.

The contact centre allows the company to build customer affinity and consumer confidence by affording real-time human dialogue, a feature absent from the automated and self-assisted forms of communication of the web and iDTV. Customers who prefer to interact person-to-person or who have more difficult questions that cannot be adequately addressed by the information given online can speak to or e-mail a skilled customer service representative. However, the amount of information that can be exchanged is limited to the extent to which it can be conveyed verbally or through e-mail and retained by the listener or recipient. Customers are therefore encouraged to browse or read about a complex proposition on the internet.

Jo Huntington, customer relationship manager at asserta home (she previously held the same job at Smove), regards the contact centre as 'a key differentiator in the market place'. She explains: 'We answer all e-mails within two hours during opening hours and offer a telephone contact number. The Frequently Asked Questions section of the web site is reviewed regularly to enable customers to self-serve. Working alongside our marketing department we are building upon a customer communications strategy to keep in regular contact and personalize information to customers' individual needs relative to where they are in the home moving stage.' The contact centre team meets weekly with Huntington and visits asserta home's head office frequently to ensure internal communication flow. The team is actively involved in testing and launching new web site products, and receives ongoing training, which both empowers them with product knowledge and encourages 'ownership' and 'accountability'.

The level of help and/or complaint-related queries to the contact centre has fallen, probably because, as the website improves, more questions are being answered online (see Figure CS 5.3.3). Consequently the company has focused more closely on expanding revenue streams through developing its database, and is aspiring to one-to-one marketing activities. It has initiated a programme to integrate its database to link the separately held customer and property databases and produce a data warehouse capable of supporting behavioural modelling and other analyses. With a unified and immediately accessible view of each customer, asserta home can better ensure that customers' problems are resolved and their preferred methods of interaction are respected at every customer touchpoint.

asserta home's customer contact centre

An average week of inbound contact equates to a breakdown of 55 per cent of queries/communications delivered by e-mail and 45 per cent delivered by telephone.

Below is a category analysis of inbound communications:

– Suggestions make up 13 per cent of contact total. 60 per cent of these arrive by e-mail.

– Problems make up 23 per cent of customers' contacts. 79 per cent arrive by e-mail.

– General queries make up 25 per cent of contact. These are evenly split across both channels

– Complaints make up only 8 per cent of contacts. 88 per cent of these arrive via e-mail.

– Other/miscellaneous contact makes up the remaining 31 per cent. Contact is made 70 per cent of the time through e-mail.

FIGURE CS 5.3.3: **Category analysis of inbound communications. Reproduced with the kind permission of asserta home.**

Achieving results

By teaming up with the nation's leading estate agents, in little over a year asserta home was listing more than half the total number of properties for sale in the UK – over 200 000 properties from over 4000 'approved' agents. Further, at the time of writing, not one of these 4000-plus estate agents has left the asserta fold voluntarily, although a handful have gone because they failed to meet asserta home's quality standards and/or have closed.

asserta home's growing portfolio of services is helping estate agents to compete more effectively, as members testify. Philip Jordan of Burford Jordan Estate Agents claims: 'I believe assertahome.com is the most effective property portal and has already generated a significant amount of business for us.' Charles Raymond of Charles Raymond Estate Agents is convinced that membership is getting his firm noticed. 'We have been very impressed with the new enquiries we have received and our vendors are delighted how quickly their properties appear on asserta home', he says. Sue Brown of Castle Estates is seeing the benefits of a good match. She says: 'Since being associated with www.assertahome.com we have found their dynamic professionalism, innovative ideas and efficiency complement our own high standards and this has resulted in increased business, both from prospective purchasers and buyers.'

Industry accolades highlight the company's accomplishment in terms of customer value proposition. Website watchdogs, thenet.co.uk, metro.co.uk, house-about.co.uk, and Financial Times Connectis have all awarded asserta home a top five-star rating for performance and usability. The figures themselves speak volumes. The number of monthly unique visitors and properties on the web site doubled six months after launch. Of the 1.24 million unique visitors to the site in the first year of operation, 27 per cent went through to an estate agent web site. Visitors spent an average 15–25 minutes on the site, looking at some 25 pages. The following year, visitors spent an average nine minutes on the site, looking at over 17 pages. These figures are still higher than average for web browsers, but the fact that they fell from the previous year may be explained by users being more familiar and comfortable with the site, and improved site navigation. Today the site attracts more than 20 million hits a week, which equates to 1.25 million page impressions, and the figure continues to rise.

Consumer feedback further substantiates the excellence of asserta home's service and its wide appeal.

'With all the useful hints and tips on items such as moving, security, gardening, packing, legal fees, etc., I believe the site is outstanding and the updating of data is excellent.' I. Curtis, UK.

'If you're like me and too busy to get onto the internet every day, asserta home e-mails you when a property matches your search criteria, and can also send you a text message to your phone! What more could you want?' J. Patel, UK.

'Without your information we would have spent many a wasted hour and loads of cash on phone bills gathering estate agents' names, telephone numbers, etc., not to mention [the site] giving us an advantage to preview homes available in our price range and our desired location [before] we visited [the UK] for two weeks in June., C. Watters, USA.

'My husband and I registered with all the estate agents in our local town [but] we never found the right place. Then my mum suggested asserta. Wow – how easy to use, and what choice! One night I stumbled across a property which sounded just right. We e-mailed the estate agent, and had a phone call the next day to set up a visit. From that, we made an offer, and moved in this March. It was great that my extended family could also look on the site to see where we were moving to.' G. and P. Woodruffe, UK.

asserta home's strategy of partnering with estate agents and optimizing new media to build consumer trust and market penetration first, rather than simply revenue, seems to be working. Its parentage helps, as Phipps readily acknowledges. 'One of the benefits of having a very strong financial services company for a backer is the long-term perspective. Life companies are used to making money eight or nine years down the road, not on day one. This said, we [the asserta management team] are acutely aware of the need to deliver real shareholder value within the time scales agreed, and for us this begins with breakeven by the end of Year 3 and meeting traffic referral targets along the way.'

Making the next move

asserta home is building on its foundation stones of customer focus, technology, quality, marketing and partnerships in order to consolidate its leading market position. Channel and media integration continues to form an integral part of company development, enabling asserta home to fulfil both its operational goals of managing technology and the quality of information provision, and its strategic goals of business competitiveness and customer relevance.

To date the company's recruitment strategy has focused on the home-buying market, which offers most scope for leveraging value. However, it recently launched a separate home-lettings section on the web site, together with a new search facility that allows people to choose either 'to buy' or 'to rent'. New-home developers account for 5–10 per cent of all property sales in the UK each year, and 10–15 per cent of the site's property content is currently directed at this section of the market.

asserta home continues to develop its web site to ensure that quality is not sacrificed to quantity. A new site template allows standard items such as property search options and service directories to be anchored in familiar, reliable positions, while special promotions and editorials can be interchanged easily without considerable expense or disruption to the layout of the site (see Figure CS 5.3.4). Site navigation will be improved by adding further category tabs and colour coding, and by separating the money section from the mortgage and insurance section. The IT architecture is being reviewed to accommodate a wider range of subject matter and to facilitate greater personalization through serving adverts and content relevant to individual users. asserta home is pursuing these developments in anticipation of the arrival of advanced new PDAs (Personal Digital Assistants) and mobiles – although it understands that adoption of these new technologies will depend on a variety of factors, including IT capability and compatibility with existing platforms and technologies.

asserta home is seeking to manage and grow its relationships with estate agents more effectively through a superior benefits package that will both attract more members and enable it to gather the data and insights necessary to tailor services to estate agents on an individual or segment basis. The launch of asserta business Limited was a direct response to member estate agents' call for affordable, new ways to streamline their operations and obtain competitive advantage. By offering web site design and virtual tours, asserta home hopes to surpass its current record of 20 000 e-mail requests to estate agency branches for property details and delivering at least 50 000 click-throughs to estate agents' own web sites.

Conscious that it needs to serve estate agency and consumer interests simultaneously, asserta home will continue to leverage its considerable size and standing to identify, negotiate and provide products and services that improve estate agents' commercial performance and enrich the home mover's experience. By aggregating ever more relevant content through a 'one stop shop' asserta home will, says Phipps, continue to 'push customers where they choose to go, by taking progressively richer and more tailored information to them through platforms of their choice and at times which suit them'.

The result will be a win–win–win situation: more property listings and consumer choice, more qualified leads and instructions to estate agents, and more company profit. In the process, the company may even help to enhance the reputation of estate agents among the general public. After all, modifying the behaviour of customers is predominantly about stimulating affinity and trust, and this means making the most of every opportunity to add even greater customer value.

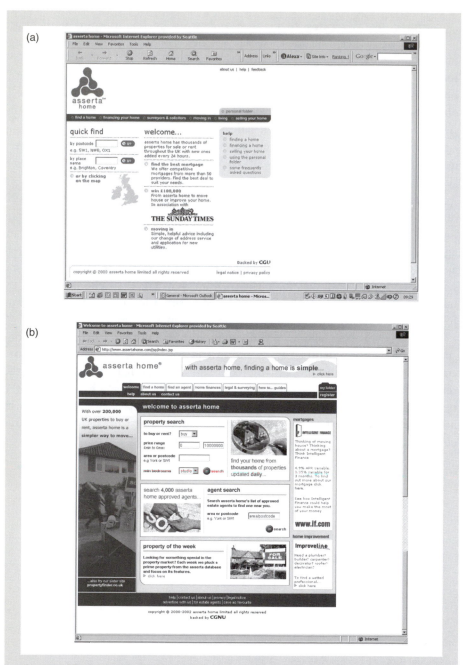

FIGURE CS 5.3.4: Web site development: (a) original home page; (b) current (June 2002) home page. Reproduced with the kind permission of asserta home.

FIGURE CS 5.3.4: Web site development.

Chapter 6

Information management process

The effective management of information has a crucial role to play in a CRM strategy – not only for supporting each of the CRM processes but also as the glue which integrates these processes, giving coherence to this strategy. If we examine the strategic framework for CRM introduced in Chapter 2, we can explore the role that information plays within each process.

Strategy development process. Developing an effective customer strategy depends on having information that provides a clear understanding of both the marketplace and its characteristics. Industry structure, market and customer attributes and profiles, buying behaviour, and the value of the customer base can all be assessed if appropriate information has been collected. Information for strategy development comes from both internal and external sources. Customer databases across the organization can provide a wealth of information about the behaviour, buying patterns and value of existing customers. Information from sources external to the organization, such as consultancy reports and market research analysis, provides market intelligence. All this information enables strategic decisions to be made – product/service positioning, segmentation granularity, approach to communication, channel and media development, etc. Of course, the actual strategy ultimately developed depends on analysis and interpretation of all the information coupled with insight, judgement and inspiration.

Value creation process. Information is crucial for addressing the three key elements of this process: determining what value the company can provide to its customers – the value proposition; determining customer value – the worth of the customer to the organization; and determining how to successfully maximize the lifetime value of desired customer segments. Information is also necessary for product and service innovation and tailoring, particularly in information intense industries such as financial services, media and music.

Channel and media integration process. We have seen that decisions regarding the choice and development of the most effective combination of channels and media requires information. In addition, it is the integration of information across all channels and media that enables a consolidated view of the customer to occur in real time – a key cornerstone of CRM. Customers should be known everywhere – for example, in retail banking – if they phone, if they go to their local branch, if they use the Internet, if they visit a different branch. The customer should also be able to begin a transaction using one media (e.g. Internet), completing it using another (e.g. branch) in a seamless fashion.

Performance assessment process. Information is required to assess performance both in executing the CRM strategy and assessing its effectiveness. Metrics are required to determine the value both the organization and customer is receiving, to calculate retention and churn rates, to indicate customer satisfaction levels, to assess the result of marketing campaigns, etc. An effective performance assessment process can also identify areas for improvement across all four processes.

The central role of information has seen organizations look towards the deployment of information technology (IT) for the collection, processing, transmission and storing of information. Technologies such as data warehouses, the Internet, imaging, workflow, mobile phones, personal digital assistants (PDAs) and data mining and analysis tools provide many opportunities in designing and implementing a CRM strategy. While the key tenets of CRM have been around for many years, it is only through the use of technology that many can become a reality. Software such as business rules engines, process middleware, personalized content, browser sharing and real-time profiling, make a 'one-to-one' customer experience a possibility; and today's technology is powerful. Data analysis tools can enable patterns to be discerned in massive customer and transaction databases – patterns that can be impossible for humans to observe. Internet technology enables 'self-service' direct from the customers sitting room. Consumers can browse the websites of competing organizations, compare prices and conditions, order and pay for products from books and CDs to furniture and electrical goods to groceries. While some products still require physical fulfilment, many others can be digitized and delivered immediately directly to the consumer.

CRM technologies fall into two categories: operational CRM and analytical CRM. Operational CRM brings relationship management, customer service and fulfilment into the front-office. Example applications include: delivering customer information to front-line staff; managing customer information across different channels and media; managing customer contacts; managing campaigns; and managing tasks and workflows resulting from customer interactions. It also includes automated tools for a mobile sales forces – also known as 'sales force automation' (SFA). Analytical CRM includes tools to analyse customer information to support marketing decisions. These include data mining technologies, analytical processing, statistical applications and modelling tools. More recently, vendors have been developing tools based around artificial intelligence (AI) concepts, such as neural networks, to enhance the analysis capability.

We have seen companies set out to buy CRM software, assuming that this is all that is required to have CRM. CRM is a business strategy not a technology. Technology, however, can support the proposition. To determine what technologies support the CRM strategy requires an understanding of the information and system requirements of the four key processes (the information systems strategy) – as outlined above – and how they relate to each other. Once this has been ascertained, the technologies that will collect, process, analyse, manage and store this information can then be determined (see Figure 6.1). Some of these

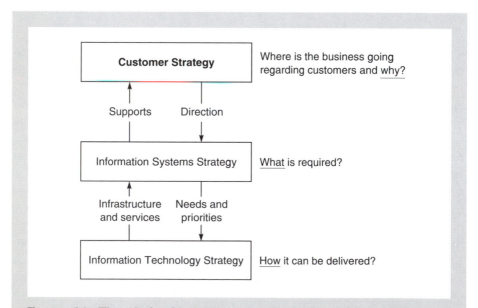

FIGURE 6.1: The relationship between the CRM, IS and IT strategies.

technologies will be located in the front-office, others will reside in the back-office. This will ensure that there is alignment between the CRM strategy and investments made in technology.

CRM software is powerful. Figure 6.2 illustrates a screen from a CRM package that provides information about a customer of a retail bank. It shows basic information about the customer, such as name, address, portfolio summary, preferred method of contact, and details of the nature and content of the last contact. By clicking on any of the tabs – contact history, relationships, portfolio, extra information, and mortgage details – a branch teller or call centre operator can access additional details about the relationship which the customer has with the bank. As a result of an interaction with a customer, tasks, such as to send out a brochure or to organize an appointment with a financial adviser, can be logged and routed to the relevant department for action.

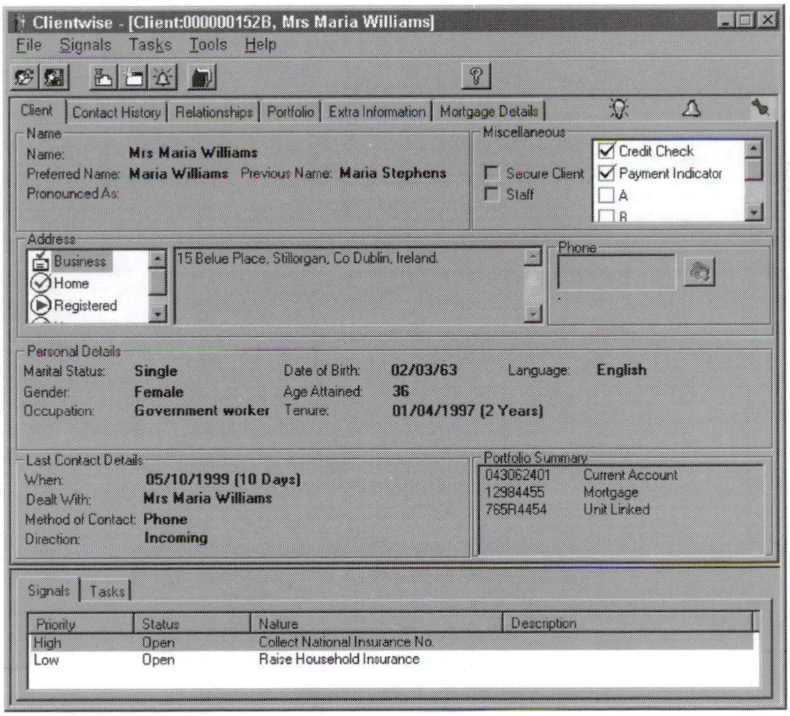

FIGURE 6.2: **Screen showing basic customer information.**

Figure 6.3 illustrates an example contact history screen which logs the date and time of contact, method and direction (i.e. inbound or outbound call in a call centre) of contact, as well as a description of the nature of the contact with the customer. The bottom of the screen highlights the tasks that have been raised as a result of the interaction with the customer, their current status and target for completion.

Behind these front-office screens lies a variety of back-office systems and technology. Customer requests and enquiries may need to be routed to relevant staff; processing may be required for products, for example calculating interest on an interest-bearing account; statements and invoices may need to be sent to customers; tools may be used to analyse customer behaviour and buying patterns; imaging software can capture paper-based customer correspondence, enabling them to be immediately retrieved during interactions with customers.

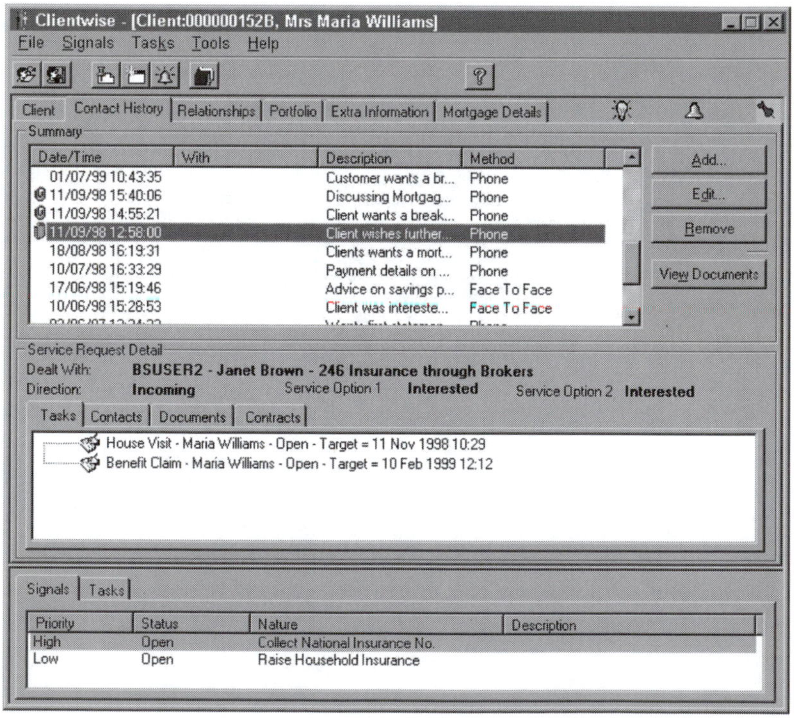

FIGURE 6.3: Contact history screen.

While the CRM strategy will be supported by IT, investments made over the years in IT can severely inhibit the execution of the CRM strategy – particularly in the back-office. What we find in many organizations is that customer information is stored in multiple locations; it may be different in each of these locations; it is often stored in different formats. Systems and technology have traditionally been designed to support individual channels/media or products, not customers. For example, many retail banks know products or even account profitability but not customer profitability. Different systems may have been built on different technologies that are not easily connected to each other – of course, such investments in IT were not made for this reason.

The four cases included in this chapter illustrate different aspects of the information management process. The Derbyshire Building Society case study outlines the information requirements prior to implementing IT to support a customer strategy. Canada Life (UK) highlights the problems encountered when acquisitions result in a myriad of different technologies existing in the organization and the implication for the CRM strategy, particularly in integrating the legacy systems. The CRM implementation at Dutch insurer Reaal Particulier illustrates the case of using technology to support its field sales force, to improve customer service. The NatWest case highlights the role of IT in CRM to support business and customer strategy, not to define it. NatWest Cards' creation of a data warehouse, analytical and reporting tools (performance models), and new statementing and communications systems was predicated on the identified need to realize potential as well as current customer value.

CASE STUDY 6.1

The Derbyshire Building Society: Putting the customer at the heart of business

OVERVIEW

As it approached the new millennium, The Derbyshire Building Society had a number of challenges to face as a consequence of the processes and systems that it had in place. First and most compelling, there was a lack of integrated, centralized customer information, which meant that achieving a seamless, one-stop service for their customers was not possible. Like many financial services organizations, its processes and systems were account-driven not customer-based. As a result, interactions with customers over the telephone and in branches were handled inconsistently, and leads and cross-sell opportunities were not communicated rapidly across the organization. This resulted in diminishing customer loyalty and loss of potential revenue. New channel development was suffering from problems that stemmed from legacy systems. Additionally, all work was paper based, which was time-consuming and had significant margin for errors. This and the high operational and personnel costs meant that it was time for a change: to orient around customers, making significant investment in technology.

Key learning points

This case illustrates an organization that recognized that to deliver on its promise and meet the demands from customers it needed to radically re-focus its operation structures. It had to leave behind the account driven structures of a traditional retail financial services provider and become a customer-centric organization. This also required a cultural change within the Society.

CRM issues

- To serve your customers you have to know your customers.

One of the key issues the Society had to address in becoming a customer-centric organization was the lack of customer information – they did not know their customers. In addition, there was no way of identifying, recording, monitoring or following-up business opportunities.

- Not just customer service – efficient customer service.

Having information was just one aspect. The Derbyshire also needed to deal with inefficiency in its business processes. Essentially, this meant finding better ways to handle routine day-to-day tasks and by extension, helping to reduce operating costs.

- CRM is not just a front-office issue.

The Derbyshire recognized that to be successful with its CRM strategy, it was not just about purchasing customer and contact management software. It demanded not just a new organization but a new set of corporate values.

Information management process issues

- Becoming customer-centric requires customer information.

This simple fact is lost on many organizations and CRM software alone does not address this challenge.

- Exiting IT infrastructure severely limits a company as it moves from an account-focus to one with a strong focus on the customer.

Not unlike many financial services institutions, the existing IT infrastructure was built around product and had a strong account-focus. This meant that it was impossible to get a consolidated view of customers' holdings with the society.

- Decisions about technology should be driven by the customer strategy and its underlying information requirements.

Technology is just an enabler, supporting the customer strategy. It is therefore important to first define what it is that is to be supported before making decisions regarding the purchase of technology.

Introduction

The Derbyshire is one of the UK's largest independent building societies. It provides a variety of products, including mortgages, savings and investments, insurance, loans, as well as providing a financial planning service. Founded in 1859, it has total assets in excess of Stg£2.75 billion and a network of over 50 branches. The Society is strongly committed to remaining a mutual organization and has maintained that stance throughout the '90s, a decade that also saw radical change and intensifying competition in the financial services industry.

Today, as financial services providers everywhere jockey for position in a technology-enabled, increasingly global and deregulated marketplace, customer service has emerged as a key differentiator. It is an issue that reflects a core value of The Derbyshire – to place its customers at the heart of its business.

However, technology, in particular, has left a significant imprint on customers, whose service expectations are growing in line with technological capability. The Derbyshire recognized that to deliver on its promise – and meet new demands from customers – it needed to radically re-focus its operational structures. It had to leave behind the account-driven structure of a traditional retail financial services provider and, instead, become a truly customer-centric organization. This would require a significant mindset and behavioural change amongst staff at all levels.

A new approach

The Society's Corporate Plan 1997–2001 noted that it had 'to reshape our business to deliver a higher standard of service at each point of customer contact. To achieve the latter will require changes to organization structure, attitudes and skills as well as further systems developments.' Yet the society recognized that redefining business processes, changing work practices and introducing new technology would have little effect unless accompanied by cultural change.

A corporate vision was established to capture the change in focus: 'You are welcome at The Derbyshire – our customers really are special to us. We always work hard to do more for them.' To underpin this vision, a set of core values were articulated. These gave guidance to expected attitudes and behaviours and were expressed as follows: 'The Derbyshire's way is to'

- *put the customer at the heart of our business.* We truly want to put the customer at the heart of our business across the whole of the organization – without our customers, we are nothing.
- *have respect for each other.* It is too easy to ignore someone else's point of view. We must have respect for each other all the time. We need to listen to each other and recognize that everyone has a point of view. It is as important to understand as it is to be understood.
- *help our people grow and achieve our success through teamwork.* We are all individuals and we all want to perform well. But together as a team, we can achieve so much more.

- *celebrate being a winning organization.* Too often in the past we've been shy of saying 'we've really done well'. In future, when we do well we want to celebrate the success and give appropriate recognition to those who achieve good things. We are winning as a business – we should all celebrate that.
- *be an enjoyable place to work.* The Derbyshire must be an enjoyable place to work. Everyone should enjoy their jobs and if they do, they are more likely to delight our customers so that they can enjoy doing business with us.
- *be driven by the opportunity to make a difference.* Everyone who works at The Derbyshire should make a difference. There is something we can all do to add value to the customer experience.
- *have integrity in everything we do.* There is no long term future for this organization if we don't believe in what we do. We should never betray our values. People must be respected for what they say and we must have integrity in the way we do things.
- *use mutuality and financial strength to enhance member benefits.* We are proud to be a building society – not having to pay dividends to external shareholders gives us a real chance to give real value to customers. If we don't enhance member benefits, we should not be surprised if they say in a few years time 'so what's different about The Derbyshire'. We've got to deliver real value, both in the products we offer and in the way we serve our communities.

Meeting the challenges

Putting the customer at the heart of its business would mean re-focusing every business process to ensure it revolved around the customer, rather than around the requirements for the management of the organization. To get to that point, The Derbyshire pinpointed two major challenges that had to be addressed.

- To service your customer, you have to know your customer.

Chief among these was the issue of customer information, or more accurately, the lack of it. The absence of a shared, single point of reference on customers across the enterprise meant that a seamless, one-stop service was just not possible. As there was no consolidated view of the customer, across all channels and products, this made building a complete relationship with them very difficult. In addition, there was no way of identifying, recording, monitoring or following-up business opportunities. The resulting losses in potential revenue, and the knock-on effects of diminishing customer loyalty, were not easily measurable. It was clear, however, that opportunities were being missed.

The gulf between information needed and information available was also having a significant impact on business development and growth. Increasing the revenue yield from existing customers was not a simple process. Sales and marketing opportunities were being hampered, while new channel development was suffering from problems to do with both capturing and integrating with information from legacy systems.

Another shortcoming was in the area of rewarding customer and member loyalty. Lack of customer knowledge meant The Derbyshire had a limited view of how many customers held multiple accounts and what history they each had with the Society.

- Not just customer service – efficient customer service.

Information, nonetheless, was not the only concern. The Derbyshire also needed to deal with inefficiencies in its processes. Essentially, that entailed finding better ways to handle routine day-to-day tasks – and by extension helping to cut down on operating costs. Logging contacts with customers, or dealing with their enquiries and requests, apart from being costly, were largely paper-based processes that simply took too long. And because inter-departmental tasks were passed along manually, mistakes and delays were inevitable.

In addition, calls were not being handled in a consistent manner, which meant the customer had a variety of experiences with the organization. The fact that the Society's customer service advisers had to navigate multiple systems without integrated support wasn't helping the situation.

Such inefficiencies were also leading to higher operating costs and higher personnel costs, while the overhead involved in capturing and maintaining a clear customer history was unacceptable.

The Customer Services Division

It was decided that a new Customer Services Division, incorporating a customer call centre, would spearhead the drive to put the customer at the heart of its business. If the Society was to achieve its corporate objectives ('To become the home loans, savings and investment retailer that our customers recommend to others, without reservations'), then there was the need for a step change in the quality of service they provide, particularly to those customers who prefer to deal with The Derbyshire directly by telephone. The society concluded that better service would come from:

- competent and informed management continually researching 'customer satisfaction';

- staff training programmes;
- empowerment of staff at their desktop;
- support of the above with suitable technology.

The strategy stressed that establishing a call centre was not about herding together good administrative staff into a room stocked with modern telephony handsets. To the caller the Call Centre would be The Derbyshire Building Society, and the call centre agents would be ideally placed to affect, influence and measure customers' perceptions of the organization. In the call centre equation, people are more important than technology, and the project team saw that establishing a team whose skills are predominantly in handling customers over the telephone was one of the key challenges that the project would face.

The Call Centre Feasibility Study noted that the Call Centre, which they named 'The Careline', supported the Society's Corporate Plan in a number of ways.

- *Customer retention.* Many of the Society's customers rarely visit a branch once they have made the initial purchase. With such people the best opportunity to strengthen their relationship with The Derbyshire is by telephone.
- *Customer orientation.* The establishment of a Call Centre would begin to introduce into Head Office the process, attitudes and skills needed to meet customers' changing expectations about service delivery.
- *Operating costs.* The re-engineering of processes necessary to establish a Call Centre would not only lead to service improvement but also identify opportunities to reduce operating costs through, for example, streamlining workflows.
- *Low balance/high transaction customers.* This entails a shift of emphasis towards 'proper' savers and investors who have less need to visit a branch and are therefore more likely to find the telephone an attractive alternative when they wish to make contact.
- *The retail funding challenge.* Postal/telephone products were beginning to be a permanent feature of the marketplace and if the Society was to compete effectively for a share of that business it required a high quality telephone service, operating outside normal hours.

Within this new Customer Services Division, it was obvious to the management team at The Derbyshire that they needed to implement an operational CRM and workflow solution, one that would enable the Call Centre and customer service staff to perform their jobs rapidly, professionally and efficiently. They saw this system becoming the single point of access, input and update for all customer information.

The Society researched the outcome of not having an IT based CRM solution. In effect there would be no desktop system for the agents, who would be forced to rely on their skill at navigating diverse legacy systems, all accessed by different methods. Tracking of calls (i.e. up to and including wrap-up) would certainly be manual, and processing of service 'follow-ups' would also be paper based. Any tasks resulting from a customer interaction would be improvised on the spot, with little regard for efficiency, repeatability or consistency. In summary, the absence of a CRM system would impact the Service Centre in the following ways:

Higher agent costs and lack of efficiency savings:

- manual identification of service issues;
- manual resolution of service issues, resulting in large numbers of agent call backs and large numbers of transferred calls;
- need to consult paper procedure manuals;
- delay in searching and finding customers across systems.

Little support for building customer relationships:

- agents forced to be reactive;
- no access to customer contact history;
- no ability to consistently record valuable customer data;
- difficult to measure and therefore manage call wrap-up;
- no information exchanged with marketing database.

Little support for generating revenue:

- difficult to identify the point where a service call can be turned into an opportunity;
- remains a cost centre.

Inconsistent call handling:

- affects caller's experience;
- cannot help in building loyalty;
- difficult to manage agent performance;
- complexity of legacy systems.

New channels are held back:

- extended hours access to core administration systems could be restricted;
- Internet/Kiosk access requires flexible approach.

The CRM solution

To solve both their customer information problems and their operational challenges, The Derbyshire's operational CRM system would need to offer both complete contact history functionality and flexible task management capability. In addition, a number of other requirements were identified. The system would have to:

- provide unified, updated customer information across all customer access channels and contact points;
- shift the service focus from 'the account' to 'the customer';
- raise levels of service quality while reducing the cost base;
- enable easier and more comprehensive customer information capture;
- improve the effectiveness of customer acquisition and retention programmes;
- offer end-to-end customer management;
- be flexible enough to accommodate future changes in business strategy;
- permit easy integration with other acquired systems;
- support existing and future channels for sales and service by building a future-proofed customer service infrastructure.

The Derbyshire wanted a package solution that could be configured to match their requirements and be delivered quickly. Speed was an important factor as the Society wanted to see returns from the new system well in advance of implementing the rest of its change programme. Equally importantly, the system had to be one that was easy to understand and use. This would be key to its overall success – staff had to be comfortable with what was chosen. The Society could minimize the length of the required training programme to attain quick implementation to a live situation.

Once The Derbyshire began to search for a suitable CRM vendor, Fineos Corporation, with its CRM and workflow components, was identified as having the best fit with their requirements. A specialist financial services focus, the ability to integrate with its legacy ICL mainframe environment, the potential for incorporating future channels and a rapid deployment capability were some of the criteria used in the selection.

In March 2000, The Derbyshire went live with both CRM and workflow throughout their customer service centre – Phase I of its implementation. The project was successfully completed within budget over a six-month period. The second phase of the project saw the roll-out of the CRM solution into the branch network. This was completed during 2001.

Providing the answers

Having successfully completed the rollout, The Derbyshire now has the potential to deliver increased customer satisfaction and to do so more efficiently. In addition, better management information can be made available to better understand customer relationships.

The CRM software has proved a powerful tool for The Derbyshire's call centre, customer service staff and branch staff. They now have access to a single integrated view of the customer, from a full cross-product portfolio to the history of each contact made with The Derbyshire. Now, staff can use each contact with the customer to reinforce their message of customer care, improve customer satisfaction – and identify new sales opportunities.

- By viewing the customer's full product portfolio, staff can make decisions about service and sales opportunities. At the same time, the customer's satisfaction is increased by being confident that The Derbyshire 'knows' them.
- Staff can now answer a high percentage of customer queries on demand.
- With a fully integrated contact history, the user can see full details of the customer's previous contacts with The Derbyshire. This minimizes the need to check back with other departments on previous contacts, avoids duplication of calls or tasks and boosts customer satisfaction.
- Complete customer information also means a single point of access, input and update of customer data. The result is easier information capture and a significant reduction in data duplication.
- Sales or customer contact personnel can easily log all contacts with the customer both during and after the sales process.
- Presented in a user-friendly manner, the contact history is easily maintained with minimal input by the user.
- Because it's now easier to capture powerful 'soft' customer information, such as preferred times phone, sales effectiveness can be improved.
- With better information and more knowledge about the customer, sales opportunities can be identified more easily and customer retention programmes can be effectively implemented.
- Marketing is also enhanced. The CRM solution can link leads, contacts and tasks to a specific marketing campaign, and analyse its effectiveness in considerable detail.
- Delays or waiting times are no longer a problem because the customer search dialogue makes it quick and easy to call up customer information.

The workflow processes are vital to the success of relationship management at The Derbyshire. Without efficient servicing follow-through and back-office support, increased customer satisfaction and sales effectiveness cannot be delivered.

- Tasks are carried out faster now that they are created and routed electronically between departments (e.g. mistakes and delays are cut down). Requests originating from the call centre and branches can also be tracked to ensure that they are responded to.

- There have been significant time savings by cutting out the paper-based processes that impede efficiency
- Scripting facilities, complete systems support to telemarketing activities and a facility that automates production of integrated customer correspondence provide essential work tools for all servicing and support processes.

Through the CRM and workflow solutions, staff satisfaction levels have improved. The Derbyshire is seeing more ownership and responsibility being taken for calls and more attention being paid to identifying sales and customer care opportunities. Simon Theobald, Project Manager for the Phase I implementation, sums up the advantages of CRM and workflow. 'This integrated solution is an enabler. It enables us to better understand our customers' needs and truly put them at the heart of our business. By using this solution, we are able to get closer to our customers and give added value to the service we provide them.' Peter Richardson, CEO at The Derbyshire, is quite clear on the consequences for his organization. 'This integrated system really has become the main focus for our new approach to customer care. As it is developed, it will have a direct impact on almost every part of the Society's business. We now have the information to connect with customers on a one-to-one basis, so we can deliver service that is truly special to them.'

Leveraging the CRM infrastructure

Over the last few years The Derbyshire has invested a very significant amount of money in its CRM solution and associated programmes. What it now seeks to do, before spending any more money, is to leverage business value from this investment. At the beginning of 2002 it implemented an initiative to ensure that this investment was being leveraged and to prepare for further investment in 2003. This initiative has 4 key objectives.

1. Despite the list of benefits outlined above, the society is keen to see a *tangible* return from is investment in CRM. There is a general perception that the implementation has been successful but there is no hard evidence or metrics in place to prove this is the case. In particular, its impact in terms of new business has not been seen. The society is keen to explore the opportunities that it has from these new relationships that it has established with customers. It is now beginning to explore customer churn, prospect acquisition for new products, conversion rates, response rates to campaigns, etc.

2. Borrower retention has been a perennial problem and presents the society with a number of challenges. The society has traditionally been geared more towards customer acquisition rather than customer retention. One project that has been kicked off is exploring the relationship between customer retention, loyalty, and profitability. The society also does not have any predictive modelling in place, yet there is a generally feeling that customers give the society an early indication that they are considering leaving the society, but that the society doesn't recognize these warning signs and therefore does not react in a proactive way to retain the customer. The 'lost customer' project has been established to research this issue and will seek to identify ways forward. For example, their preliminary research suggests that when customers start asking for certain documents they are considering leaving the society; there is a high correlation between requesting these documents and defection.

3. The third objective is centred around the issues of customer profitability. The society is trying to establish the economic worth of each customer or household – information they just don't have at present. This information will then be used to refine its customer segments. During 2001 the society defined 11 customer segments; however, the information used to develop these segments was product based and needs to be refined. Indeed, there is a feeling within the society that eleven is possibly too many segments. Segmentation development will be an ongoing activity for the society that will improve as more appropriate information becomes available.

4. The final objective is to make CRM 'feel real' for all staff. When the roll of the CRM solution to branches was complete a user survey was administered, and in addition to questions relating to ease of use and system response times, there was a question regarding what CRM actually meant for that individual. While 50 per cent responded with an answer suggesting that they understood what the society was attempting to do, 50 per cent also viewed it as jargon and/or technology and didn't understand why The Derbyshire was going down that route.

   Work that is being undertaken is developing a series of 'customer experience statements', linked directly to the mission and values of the society. The society wants to define some sort of cultural or behavioural objective that articulates what it is that The Derbyshire is attempting to do with its CRM programme. The Human Resources Department is involved as they hope to align the CRM objectives with performance measurement and link into the appraisal process, so that CRM is not just something that is considered on the periphery.

   The society is attempting to move to a situation where customer contact staff can have meaningful conversations with customers. The technology to facilitate this is there. However, without the necessary behavioural changes little is likely to be achieved. 'Destination Excellence' was a programme that was implemented in the Customer Services Division during the roll out of the CRM solution and has proved very successful. This now needs to be affected enterprise-wide.

Rosie Grant, who is leading this initiative, is well aware that it could be argued that these four objectives should have been addressed prior to implementing the CRM solution in the first place. However, she is philosophical: 'you are where you are', noting that it has been a tremendous journey and learning experience for all involved. She points to the difficulty in getting the branches involved when defining requirements: 'They just wanted a system to process transactions quicker and get the customer out of the branches as quickly as possible. It would have been difficult to get engagement and buy-in at that time. Staff can now see what is possible.' She is adamant that cultural change is the key, not just for the success of the CRM solution but ultimately for the success of the society. 'By getting buy-in to the vision and values and the philosophy of the customer, The Derbyshire wants to have relationships with the customer that cannot be emulated by any of our bigger competitors.'

CASE STUDY 6.2

Canada Life (UK): Leveraging value from legacy systems

OVERVIEW

Although technology is advancing at breakneck speed, the reality for many organizations is that their core systems are often running on 'older' legacy technologies, some of which have been in place since the 1960s. These systems were probably leading edge when first implemented, but today's technology is faster, more flexible, and cheaper to maintain. Merger and acquisition activities have also led to situations where there can be a myriad of different technologies and systems present in an organization.

This situation is particularly true for many financial services organizations, where the wave consolidation that has taken place in the industry has seen companies acquire different legacy systems running on different technology platforms. This presents a challenge when these once separate companies now seek to present a single face to the customer. This issue is compounded when newer channels, such as the Internet and Digital TV, enter into the equation. In particular, information has tended to be stored in systems not on a customer basis, but on a product or account basis. While the replacement of old systems might seem an obvious solution, this is not always the clear-cut option that it might seem at first as there are many issues to be considered.

Key learning points

This case considers the strategy followed by Canada Life (UK) whilst it considered how to deal with a number of legacy systems as it sought to be more customer oriented in its business. Many of these systems were the direct result of its acquisition strategy. In particular, the case explores the advantages and disadvantages of total replacement versus the use of 'middleware' to enable a CRM solution 'front-end' legacy system, providing the perception of totally integrated front- and back-offices.

CRM issues

- It is important to understand the role of information in CRM.

The case demonstrates that without appropriate information even a well inten-
tioned CRM strategy will achieve little on implementation. A customer service
focus also requires access to appropriate information.

- Legacy IT systems can have a negative impact on a CRM strategy.

As the back-office provides processing, contract administration and storage
functionality, it must be considered in the development of a CRM strategy.

Information management process issues

- Software 'middleware' can provide the glue to integrate back-office legacy
  systems.

Using middleware can be an effective way of dealing with legacy systems, providing the mechanism to integrate data from disparate back-office systems.
However, it should be seen as a step in the journey towards full front-to-back
integration.

- Develop a migration strategy that focuses on the front-office for quick wins.

It is possible to begin the migration strategy by first implementing a CRM system
in the front-office (for example, call centre or branch) for quick wins, but recognize that this is not the final solution, only a step on a longer journey.

- Automating the front-office does not solve problems of the lack of information integration in the back-office.

Organizations must consider developing a Front-to-Back (F2B) strategy for
integrating the front-office and back-office. Just because the use of middleware
can give the impression of seamless integration, the old IT systems still have to be
maintained. This is generally costly, and can severely limit product offerings to
the marketplace.

Introduction

Despite the fact that information and communications technologies continue to
advance at a breakneck pace, financial institutions still find that many of their

core systems are running on 'older' technologies. This is not a criticism but the reality that looks set to remain with us as we move further into the twenty-first century.

There are a number of possible reasons for this situation. Previous uncoordinated investment decisions often mean that there is a variety of technical platforms and architectures scattered throughout the organization. Locally developed applications often don't integrate very well or easily with other corporate applications – particularly as most were designed to serve local requirements. But as their value and usage increased and there was a push for corporate integration, the result was a portfolio of applications often held together by little more than 'sticky tape'. In addition, the wave of mergers and acquisitions that has characterized much of industry and commerce over the past decade has exacerbated the problem, with many companies now in possession of diverse and incompatible applications running on diverse and incompatible technologies.

The implications of this situation are profound. Ironically, while these disparate systems all seek to support the organization in serving the customer, they can seriously affect the organization's competitiveness.

Replacement: an obvious but impractical solution

The obvious solution might appear to be replacing older systems with newer technologies. This is no easy or clear-cut task; indeed, many legacy systems process back-office transactions adequately. Cost is a major consideration: replacing legacy systems is not cheap. Further, companies need to set aside considerable time, estimated in years per system, for any migration. And then there's the disruption to day-to-day operations that all this can cause. What's more, the organization might have limited application and data knowledge of mainframe applications: some could have been developed 30 years ago and have evolved subsequently with poor, if any documentation. The applications work but nobody is quite sure how!

Insurance company Canada Life (UK) sought to address the problem of its legacy heritage in 1998. The company had multiple systems running on multiple platforms, many of which were the result of its acquisition of Manulife and Albany Life. Canada Life had five key policy processing systems (the oldest dating back to 1964) and three different computer platforms. On their own these presented a considerable maintenance overhead for the Information Systems department. Couple this with the need to address Year 2000 compliance issues and the ongoing Euro conversion work, and you can begin to appreciate the predicament they faced.

The business implications

This legacy systems situation presented many problems for Canada Life. It held poor information about its customers. Although the company had 1.4 million policyholders, it estimated that in reality it only had about 400 000 customers. Customer related information was crudely maintained across each of the policy systems, with all the inherent difficulties of duplication of data and inconsistencies. One particular customer's address was held in 30 different locations! The company also estimated that 30 per cent of customers were 'orphans' – that is, did not have agents assigned – but it couldn't easily identify who these were.

To gain access to details held by the policy processing systems, the end-users needed expertise in navigating through multiple systems, each with information maintained in a myriad of formats. This drastically increased the learning curve for new employees who were expected to liaise with customers, and it meant that the company had to maintain a pool of experts who were experienced in the difficult detail of the way each system operated.

This legacy problem meant that Canada Life (UK) couldn't provide a 'one stop service' for customers. Customers often found that they were 'passed around' the organization and there was no record of previous correspondence or conversations. Promises made by Customer Service staff were often not acted upon as they fell through the cracks of an increasingly brittle situation. Indeed, sales and branch staff often had to phone the call centre to acquire customer information.

All this prevented the company from 'knowing' its customers and building one-to-one relationships with them, which it saw as critical to future growth.

This lack of information about customers and their dealings with the company presented the marketing and business development areas of the business with considerable problems in terms of 'farming' the existing customer base. Relatively simple tasks such as identifying lapsed policies was almost impossible in this arcane environment. Targeting marketing campaigns proved difficult, while calculating the effectiveness of marketing spend was impossible.

Canada Life (UK)

Canada Life (UK) is part of the Canada Life Group, which was founded in Toronto in 1847. The group provides services to more than eight million policyholders throughout Canada, the United States, Ireland and the UK and has assets in excess of £20 billion. Its core business is offering products and services to meet clients' needs for:

- the accumulation of assets in the form of annuities, pensions and investment products;
- financial and investment management;
- financial protection in the event of certain risks, including life, medical, dental, disability and general insurance.

The company has been operating in the UK since 1903, where it provides a range of products including life assurance, income protection, pensions and investments. These products are distributed through direct sales channels and independent financial advisers (IFAs). The company is headquartered in Potters Bar and has a total staff of 800 head office people and 800 sales agents. Operating locations include 24 business centres, three regional sales offices and three group offices. Following the take-over of Manulife in 1995 and Albany Life in September 1997, Canada Life UK has become one of the UK's largest life and pensions companies.

The customer service programme

The company recognized that in the financial services sector no single insurer can offer a product that is significantly different from or better than those of its competitors. The key differentiator between providers is the quality of customer service, and Canada Life recognized this as being central to engendering customer loyalty and winning new business.

In late 1996 the company instigated a programme to improve customer service. It set itself the challenge to:

- use the power of information to understand customers;
- increase the effectiveness of acquisition and retention programmes;
- reduce its cost base while increasing the quality of service;
- provide customer information to distribution channels.

The company sought a way forward that allowed it to make the best of the systems and resources it already had, while at the same time allowing it to deliver new system functionality rapidly as demanded by the business. To accomplish this it recognized that it needed the best use of:

- modern mainstream 'open' technology;
- rapid systems development tools;
- intuitive user interfaces providing 'familiar' systems that are easily learnt;
- component-based development providing re-use of systems building blocks.

At the same time it needed to leverage off its existing policy processing systems.

Blueprint for the Customer Information System

The company's IS department considered two options in order to address the problem of inadequate customer information. The first strategy was to build or buy a new policy processing system, which would include a customer database to replace all its existing systems. The second was to maintain the existing systems but to provide a 'wrapper' in order to present a common front-end to the business with a separate customer database.

Given its problems, the logical approach might appear to be to procure a single policy processing system to maintain all its customer policies and then migrate everything from its old system to this new single system. However, the Strategy Review Group identified a number of difficulties with this approach.

- The time and effort required. Conservative estimates suggested that implementing full functionality on a new system would take at least two years. Past experience indicates it would take much longer. Migrating existing systems to the new system would take at least a year per system – and the company had five systems.
- It was likely that Canada Life would acquire further systems (through company acquisitions) that would also need to be migrated, probably adding systems more quickly than it could remove them.
- The implementation would take so long that by the time it was complete the business' requirements might have changed.
- The company's market intelligence suggested that insurers were no longer focusing their main systems activities on new policy processing systems. The logic is that each insurer typically has significant investments in a handful of systems, and is looking for cheaper and quicker ways of leveraging extra value out of these old and inflexible systems with modern web-based tools.
- The final consideration was effective customer relationship management. A policy processing system is, by its very nature, specifically designed to manage policies. But the business wanted to focus more closely on 'knowing' the customer and managing its relationship with them. This meant it needed a system that could capture and manage customer information and provide functionality beyond the scope of a traditional policy processing system.

The development of 'wrappers' provides a common, easy to use front-end to the policy processing systems that allows users to access information without needing in-depth knowledge of each legacy system. This approach:

- takes advantage of new technology to provide a common front-end for all policy processing systems, enabling the business to make enquiries across a number of different platforms without needing to be an expert in any of them;

- enables the business to rapidly integrate other policy processing systems in the future by simply 'wrapping' the system with the common front-end;
- significantly reduces the training period for customer support staff from six months and lets them concentrate on servicing the customer rather than navigating through multiple legacy systems;
- supports, via the single point of entry to all legacy systems, the concept of having a single customer database that maintains much of the information the business needs to 'know' about the customer. This information includes home address, business address, details of previous telephone conversations, correspondence history, manner, preferred contact times and so on;
- provides the flexibility to embrace other business technologies quickly and easily, including imaging and workflow systems, quotations, new business, telephony and the internet.

While this approach has its merits, it doesn't resolve the need to maintain and support multiple systems over multiple platforms, which requires the IS department to retain a wide skill base that can embrace the numerous legacy systems as well as new technologies.

The company concluded that it could adopt and adapt both strategies because they were not mutually exclusive or contradictory. Its decision reflected its need to support multiple policy processing systems. The benefits are as follows.

- The 'front-office' can use all policy processing systems effectively, regardless of platform, through a single, easy to use common front-end.
- Any policy processing system that may be acquired or developed in the future can be 'wrapped' through the common front-end, allowing the business user community to continue to provide good customer service, regardless of where that system is maintained.
- The company could develop a rationalization strategy to reduce the number of policy processing systems in the future without affecting the daily operation of the business and the critical interaction with the customer.

The Customer Information System project

The solution Canada Life (UK) chose was to 'wrap-around' existing legacy systems. This would provide one view of the customer, providing basic information, a database to store all contacts the company had with that customer, the ability to track all interactions with that customer, including copies of all correspondence, and the ability to capture 'soft' information such as the contents of telephone conversations. It needed the additional implementation of an imaging system (from FileNet) to capture letters and other paper-based documents.

The primary focus of the CIS project was to design and build a customer service infrastructure for the future. A central feature was to support existing and future sales and service channels, which meant it needed the flexibility to respond to opportunities that might arise as a result of the internet or digital TV.

The key challenge was to provide a single integrated desktop view of the customer across all policy processing systems. This infrastructure was also to be flexible enough to accommodate any changes in business strategy. Further, given the ambitious growth strategy of the company, it should also permit easy integration with legacy systems of any acquired company.

Figure CS 6.2.1 illustrates the range of functionality required of the CIS in supporting front-office activities. These include contact management, a single integrated client profile including portfolio summary, task management, campaign management and user prompting.

Canada Life (UK) also needed to support back-office administration. Policy data should be selectable from a customer perspective rather than a policy number. Updating policy information (such as a change in an address) should only require one task no matter the number of policies held by the customer. In the medium term the company believed that this would enable back-office paper processing clerical staff to move to a front-office customer support role (see Figure CS 6.2.2).

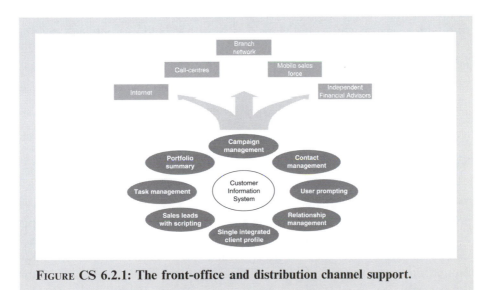

FIGURE CS 6.2.1: The front-office and distribution channel support.

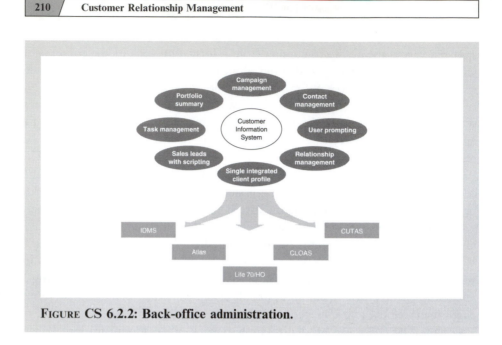

FIGURE CS 6.2.2: Back-office administration.

Partnership not package

While Canada Life (UK) decided not to develop a bespoke CIS, nor did it want to purchase just an off-the-shelf software package. Rather, it wanted a partnership with a vendor who would work closely with it both as it implemented the CIS and in the future. It selected Fineos Corporation because its CRM solution met all Canada Life (UK)'s requirements and because the insurer felt Fineos had breadth of vision. Figure CS 6.2.3 illustrates the technical architecture of the chosen solution.

Where Canada Life is now

The CIS has been rolled out to call centre and customers service staff. The application provides full inbound and outbound support for telephone, paper and electronic communication. The company is now beginning to collect information about customers that is helping to understand how to keep them and to grow. Critically, customer information is now available across the business from the desk-top.

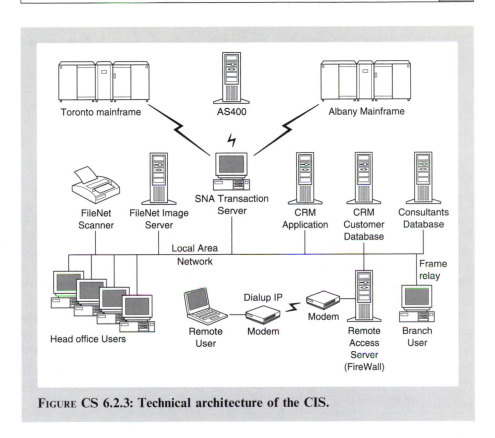

FIGURE CS 6.2.3: Technical architecture of the CIS.

Task management is being used to manage business processes. Tasks, such as sending out brochures or phoning customers next week, are recorded and routed to relevant personnel.

Benefits

The company is already seeing the benefits of its investment. In the call centre the quality of the interaction with the customer has improved significantly. Customers no longer need to repeat the gist of their last interaction: the call centre agent already has a record. This has completely eliminated the 'who spoke to Mr Jones earlier?' syndrome. The seamless integration with the FileNet imaging system has ensured that customer information includes a record of all paper correspondence (by permitting access to all scanned documents) relating to the customer. By enabling a wide variety of customer contact information to be captured, the new system allows the company to engage in an informed and intelligent dialogue with customers regardless of who they are or how the last contact was made.

The standard user interface has meant that both call centre and customer service staff can now concentrate on customer requirements rather than navigating multiple legacy systems. Customer service representatives now have full customer information when they take calls. They can see policy details from a customer perspective rather than having to search for each individual policy the customer holds with the company. The time it takes to train call centre operators has fallen significantly, and staff morale and satisfaction has increased as a consequence.

The new business department now finds it much simpler to identify previous policies the customer may have had or has with the company. All previous documents, including medical records, relating to the client can be easily accessed as they are stored against the client and not just the policy. The new CIS is also helping the company identify 'orphan' customers, thus enhancing its relationship building capability.

Additionally, the CIS is benefiting the marketing department by laying the foundations for more focused marketing campaigns. Coupled with detailed tracking it is expected that campaign management will increase significantly. Detailed trend analysis will permit a better understanding of marketing spend. Canada Life is also beginning to use the CIS to record and use data on prospects, including IFAs.

Management reports

Canada Life's CRM solution runs on an Oracle database. This has meant that data are easily accessible for management reporting purposes. So far, the company has defined 14 report types. For example, the Task Management Report includes information on tasks outstanding, tasks complete, number of quotes issued and payments issued.

Contact method (phone, fax, mail, for example) can be logged, and the reason for the contact recorded. Complaints can be tracked so that weaknesses in both service quality and business processes can be identified quickly and improved.

The journey continues

While the CIS project was the response to a legacy technology problem that was damaging the business, a business-driven CRM strategy is evolving in order to exploit this new customer information. The company is also in the process of constructing a customer value model. The customer base is being segmented to enable Canada Life to provide focused service to the different requirements of each segment. The company is also evaluating the product offerings in each of the segments. The next phase of the project is to roll out the CIS to branches and sales agents.

CASE STUDY 6.3

Reaal Particulier: Improving customer focus through field sales integration

OVERVIEW

One of the big problems that organizations with a mobile sales force face is ensuring that information flows freely between agents who spend most of their time on the road away from the office and all other areas of the companies operations. Agents require a full and comprehensive picture of the customer before a visit. A promise to deliver more information on a particular product, or fresh leads generated while out with a client, can easily be forgotten if there is not a mechanism in place to capture and route this information efficiently. This case describes how Reaal Particulier addressed this issue.

Key learning points

This case presents an example of the particular issues that an organization with a mobile sales force faces. These include sharing information with others in the company, following up on lead generation, cross-selling, and campaign management. Field sales integration is just one element of a CRM strategy that brings together information from diverse systems to give the entire company a single consolidated view of the customer.

CRM issues

- CRM is about information integration!

Mobile sales agents require as complete a picture as possible of the customer before meeting with customers. In addition, tasks generated by the mobile sales agent during a customer interaction must be communicated efficiently back to 'the office' for action.

Information management process issues

■ Information integration can improve process performance.

As all documentation at Reaal was paper-based, there was a long lead-time between a customer contact and follow up with an appointment. In addition, service levels to customers were hindered by the fact that the hand-off of tasks was a slow process. Using IT, there was a significant reduction in this time, greatly improving both responsiveness and quality of customer interaction.

Introduction

Mobile sales agents, although an important distribution channel for the insurance industry, can sometimes act as an information sieve between the insurer and the insured. The sales agent, who has direct access to a rich source of account details, such as current income, occupation, address and, possibly, the customer's current financial plans, may neglect to communicate some of this information to head office, call centre or back-office functions. A promise to deliver more information on a particular product, or fresh leads generated while out with a client, can easily be forgotten if there is no mechanism in place to capture and route this information correctly. Reaal Particulier is one insurance company that has overcome these problems by implementing Field Sales Integration (FSI) through its front- and back-office.

FSI is just one strand of a customer relationship management strategy that brings together information from diverse legacy systems to give the entire company, from the mobile sales force through to the call centre and administrative back-office, a single consolidated view of the customer.[1] FSI makes it possible for sales agents to share data with others in the company who are selling to or servicing the customer, across the entire customer life-cycle. With FSI, tasks generated while out on site can be queued in a task manager function and progressed automatically to the right person in the organization when the mobile adviser 'docks' into the network, whether from home or over a mobile phone.

Reaal Particulier, a specialist in both life and non-life insurance, merged with SNS Bank in 1997 to create SNS Reaal. Combined, the company now occupies the sixth position in financial services in the Netherlands. Through its direct distribution channel, Reaal is a strong player with a wide range of insurance

---

[1] Field Sales Integration is often referred to as Sales Force Automation (SFA).

products, and a total of over 900 000 customers. The group sells mortgage loans, pension plans and investment-linked insurance.

The Reaal challenge

The Dutch market is highly competitive as pension deregulation and the privatization of welfare benefits have contributed to growing numbers of new entrants to the market. According to a recent report on the European Life Insurance Industry by Moody's Investor Services, the Dutch life market is comparatively mature and has experienced lower growth than in other European countries over the past five years. Its pension funds and protection products are well developed and unit-linked policies are developing fast.

Reaal, which is highly focused on direct sales through its mobile advisory team and call centres, recognizes the importance of customer service in its strategy to improve customer retention and thereby increase direct-selling and cross-selling opportunities. Managing director Frans van Dorp outlined the group's objectives when reviewing its requirements for customer focused processes as being:

- to gain a consolidated view of all customer information;
- to improve customer service levels;
- to improve operational efficiency in lead generation and sales appointment creation;
- to improve marketing campaign management.

Reaal had to overcome a number of obstacles to achieve these objectives. The systems used to generate and deliver appointments to the sales force were not integrated. Data were scattered across four legacy systems, which led to complexity, inefficiency, data duplication and data obsolescence. Consequently, all documentation was paper-based and there was usually a long lead-time between a customer contact and a follow-up appointment. Service levels to customers were hindered by the fact that the hand-off of tasks was a slow manual process.

Reaal's marketing operation, which accounted for a large proportion of new customers, lacked a campaign tracking system. Although the company had many systems to effectively support the marketing and sales effort, the lack of integration made it very difficult to analyse the resulting sales or lack of sales.

The mobile solution

In Reaal, the mobile advisory team, which consists of 130 people, acts on leads generated by the marketing team and in the call centre. However, the advisory team's view of the customer was often sketchy and was largely limited to their own knowledge of the customer and basic facts such as time, date and location of visit.

The mobile sales team now have access to a CRM solution on their laptops. The advantage of this, according to sales manager Hans Schoondermark, is that a sales agent can get a complete profile of the customer 'in one system', while out with a customer or before visiting a customer. In Reaal, no one sales agent owns a customer; the direct sales team, through the call centres and the mobile advisory team, all work at selling to and servicing the customer. By dialling into the network from their homes, the mobile sales team can synchronize their profile of the customer with the company's and therefore be assured of knowing all the company's previous contact with the client.

A challenge for the sales agent is to cross-sell to existing customers. The CRM solution aids this process by using prompts and scripting to highlight areas the sales agent needs to address when out with a customer. This might be, for example, a gap in the customer's portfolio of products or a complaint that the customer has previously registered. Any data that the agent captures while on a visit is fed back to the legacy system when the agent dials in remotely. Agents can also generate tasks, such as request that a brochure be sent to the customer, and these are queued and allocated to the correct person, progressing automatically through the organization.

The next phase of the implementation will include integration with a full quotation system and underwriting, using third party software products. This will improve the group's ability to speed up transaction processes, improve customer services and spot fraudulent claimants by linking into a central database.

Call centre integration

The open architecture of the CRM solution means that it can be integrated with a number of off-the-shelf end-user tools, such as word-processors, spreadsheets, e-mail and a scheduler package, as well as being linked with fax and telephony services. In the past, the call centre set up appointments for sales agents and notified them by phone or fax. But the call centre relied on the sales agent informing them of any change of plans, for example if they had organized a meeting independently of the call centre. Now the team can quickly identify which sales agent is available by accessing Microsoft's Outlook Express, and set up an appointment with a client immediately. This process eliminates much of the paper trail that existed previously. Reaal estimates that the old process took up to 15 minutes, as the information had to be updated in various systems. With its CRM solution this process has now been reduced to less than one minute.

At present Reaal relies for over 50 per cent of its sales on its mobile sales team. As part of the company's distribution strategy, its CRM solution ensures that alternative distribution channels can be used to respond appropriately and rapidly to customer needs. Reaal's more in-depth understanding of customers and prospects enhances its cross-sell/on-sell opportunities and improves retention of its most valuable customers. Reaal's call centre in Utrecht employs 50 people, but it also houses 13 service teams totalling 150 staff, made up of service and telesales advisers.

Marthijn Slotboom, an adviser from the inbound call-centre, sums up the use of CRM in Reaal. He says: 'I have all the customer contact details in one place. I can answer the majority of queries myself and also create tasks that are routed to the relevant department. When requests are more complicated, I'll pass the query on to either a member of the advisory team or set up an appointment with a sales agent.'

Campaign management activity

Reaal prides itself on offering an innovative product range. It places a heavy emphasis on market research and communication with the market. Branko RB Driessen, who manages the group's marketing campaign activity, says that 80 per cent of targeted customers in campaigns are new customers. So keeping track of responses to campaigns is hugely important.

Whereas all responses to campaigns used to be captured on separate databases, Reaal's CRM solution means that all contacts can be stored in a single location (see Figure CS 6.3.1). 'Through Fineos Front Office we can gather a lot of information in one place on age, family, income', says Driessen. 'We are still building on the information.'

The CRM solution has improved campaign management within the group by ensuring that Reaal now tracks campaign activity from the launch of the campaign, through to gathering responses from various channels, to the eventual outcome – whether the campaign produced the desired results. Driessen notes: 'So if we have three letters being issued for one campaign, we can now track which letter produced the best response and we can also link a contact to a campaign. This offers us the scope to do more niche marketing.'

FIGURE CS 6.3.1: Screen shot depicting how Microsoft's Word integrates with Fineos Front Office, to allow a customer's details to merge with template documents.

Campaign tracking has also improved as campaign responses can be entered by the marketing team, call centre staff or the sales team. All entries have to be assigned to a campaign, and the CRM system helps by defaulting to the last campaign run. Customer service levels will benefit from heeding customer requests not to be targeted, either for a particular product or through a particular medium, for example phone, e-mail and so on. The CRM solution can also facilitate the filtering of name according to customers' demands.

From remote users to back-office, and everything in between

The financial services industry is finally waking up to the importance of customer retention and customer relationship management. Frans van Dorp notes that 'Through the use of Fineos Front Office, we have been able to support all

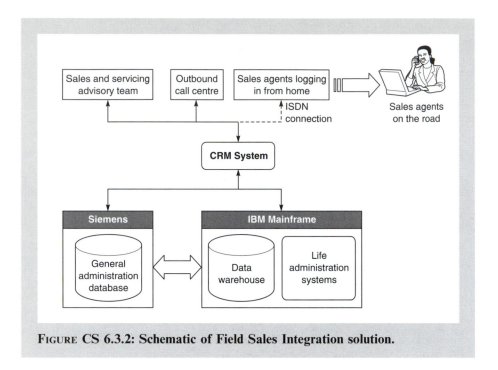

FIGURE CS 6.3.2: Schematic of Field Sales Integration solution.

our business processes with the same customer information.' This facility, which spans the entire operation from remote users to front- and back-office operations, gives Reaal the opportunity to respond innovatively and intuitively to an increasingly intelligent customer base.

Acknowledgement: Lorna Daly made a significant contribution to the development of this case.

CASE STUDY 6.4

NatWest: Bold new statements

OVERVIEW

The management of information is a crucial activity in CRM as it is that which provides an indication of performance and the bases for decision-making – underpinning all the other CRM processes.

The widely accepted strategy of placing customer interests at the core of business activity requires that responsibility for customer relationship management be shared collectively across the company and not confined to a single department, typically marketing. Shared responsibility, however, demands shared access and input to sources of customer information: a radical departure from the traditional practice of operating disparate 'pockets' of knowledge. For many organizations, achieving customer-centricity also means shifting company focus from growing 'share of market' to growing 'share of customer', necessitating a complete rethink of the value and utilization of customer data.

In an effort to extend product penetration across the brand, NatWest tackled both these challenges by introducing, initially within its Cards business, a new strategy based on obtaining and reflecting a unified, integrated understanding of customers. Problems posed by legacy systems and inappropriate management practices were overcome through IT investment and internal restructuring. The creation of an accessible and scalable data warehouse and a targeted communications programme enabled NatWest Cards to design and deliver segment-specific customer strategies. Pivotal to the relatively swift shift from a product orientation to a customer orientation within Cards was the well-defined use of customer data and the well-managed partnership between Marketing and IT.

Key learning points

This case is an outstanding example of how customer data can be exploited to produce customized communications that enhance profitability. Building on the inherent personal interface and flow of customer data, and variable profitability of credit cards, NatWest Cards was able to acquire and act upon a greater understanding of the drivers of profit (the business's perspective) and the drivers of cardholder engagement and satisfaction (the customer's perspective).

The case illustrates how NatWest's goal to gain a greater share of customer spend, or 'share of wallet', demanded an understanding of segment transience, and acceptance of the reality that some segments may decline and some will be actively protected or grow. The company's customer behaviour modelling capability needed to be developed to not only predict customers' propensity to default but also their predictive profitability; what products/services they were likely to purchase and what level of profit this would yield for the bank. Crucially, a means for establishing effective dialogue with customers was necessary to both accumulate and demonstrate a detailed, dynamic knowledge of customers.

CRM issues

- 'Start small, prove quickly.'

NatWest's adoption of CRM principles through a pilot programme in NatWest Cards made optimal use of the business's wealth of customer data and its direct marketing channel. As a result, Cards' CRM projects could be implemented and successes quantified in the immediate term. Earlier attempts to introduce data-driven CRM across the brand failed to deliver or impress due to the enormity and complexity of approaching the challenge at a macro level. The extent to which change is needed to shift from an entrenched product- to customer-centricity, ironically requires a product by product, and often business by business, approach.

Capitalizing on marketing expenditure is essentially about matching the right customers with the right promotions. Appropriate and expertly targeted messages are more likely to be a 'turn on' and less likely to be a 'turn off' for customers, maximizing customer responsiveness and minimizing any resource wastage or inadvertent relationship damage.

The targeted communications programme of NatWest Cards helped the company to align the marketing mix more closely to the diversity of need and value potential of its vast customer base.

- Measure what you value rather than value what you measure.

The revised segmentation of NatWest Cards, and then development of segment performance and segment satisfaction models demonstrated the company's recognition that profitability had more to do with customer experience than product features. By identifying the drivers and levers of customer satisfaction and performance through examining cardholder behaviour, Cards gained the ability to more accurately measure and monitor the impact of customer strategies on profitability margins.

Information Management Process issues

- The ability to leverage customer relationships stems from being informed and making informed decisions (i.e. the value of information lies not in its existence but in its use).

For a long time NatWest Cards had gathered valuable customer data but never used it, except to assess credit risk and process transactions. By collecting all the data relating to cardholder activity into a single scalable and accessible resource, and analysing and applying the information proactively, Cards was able to tailor customer strategies and manipulate customer performance.

- The transformation of raw data into the strategic delivery of an enhanced customer experience often means challenging the status quo and taking risks.

The radical changes made by NatWest Cards to internal technological and organizational infrastructures in order to manage and exploit customer information produced more positive results and segment management models that were transferable.

- The role of IT in CRM is to support business and customer strategy, not to define it.

NatWest Cards' creation of a data warehouse, analytical and reporting tools (performance models), and new statementing and communications systems was predicated on the identified need to realize potential as well as current customer value. The investment in technology considered the future integration of e-CRM and CRM strategies.

Introduction

Since late 1999 more than four million NatWest cardholders have been receiving bold new statements. The new-style statements not only provide a clearer presentation of their transaction details and account summary, but also highlight special savings and promotional offers. While the redesign looked like a simple cosmetic exercise, it actually marked a milestone in the company's strategic development. NatWest was traditionally a very 'black and white' bank, right down to its monochrome logo, and the 'new look' reflected profound changes in the way NatWest Cards looked at its customers and at its relationship with them.

Background

National Westminster Bank plc (branded 'NatWest') was created from the merger in 1968 of the National Provincial and Westminster Banks. In March 2000 the company was acquired by The Royal Bank of Scotland Group, one of Europe's leading financial services groups and one of the largest banks in the UK, with global operations. This case study focuses on key issues and events at NatWest before the RBS takeover.

Customers often perceived NatWest as a single brand, but it was, in fact, managed largely as a set of five independent businesses: Card Services, Retail Banking Services, Insurance Services, Mortgage Services and Corporate Banking Services. Each had its own marketing function and ran on a separate operating platform. Systemic and cultural differences between each operating unit meant that the bank would only notice by accident if any customer held more than one NatWest product.

The most autonomous member of the group was the Cards business, which was considered the 'jewel in the crown' in terms of profitability. NatWest Cards was the third largest card issuer in the UK, handling over 3.2 million customer accounts. It issued cards for both personal and corporate customers on the platforms of all of the plastic giants: MasterCard, Visa, American Express and Switch. NatWest Cards also incorporated STREAMLINE Merchant Services, which served commercial customers who wanted to accept plastic card payments. Personal Cards made most profit for NatWest Cards. This was primarily due to the inherent variation in the profitability of credit cards, which provided a key lever for improving customer service and increasing revenue. Within the cards industry, NatWest Cards boasted the highest value of business per card – 50 per cent ahead of Barclaycard.

Challenges facing the brand

NatWest Group

By the late 1990s the retail financial services sector as a whole was under increasing pressure to find new ways of generating competitive advantage. Traditional determinants and descriptors of winning performance were becoming obsolete as markets matured, fragmented and globablized. The internet, in particular, had given customers greater choice and power to choose, and made it easier for them to switch providers. What's more, customers' heightened service expectations had forced companies to raise their minimum service levels. Loyalty was at a premium.

The pace of change had forced NatWest to confront a number of outmoded attitudes and operations. Its banking structure was rigid, legacy systems impeded progress, and marketing management in the decentralized business units was determinedly product-centric. Managing directors were driven by how many products they could push into their individual markets rather than by how much more demand they could create from the NatWest brand franchise and the numerous customer relationships they already had. The focus on building market share rather than share of customer wallet helped neither internal collaboration nor the forging of a brand-wide relationship with customers.

Prevailing legacy systems perpetuated the disparate strategies and the diffusion of customer knowledge, preventing NatWest from creating and exploiting a single customer view. It undertook a couple of group-level initiatives in 1999/2000 to redress this situation, but these proved inadequate in the face of such an enormous challenge. For example, it built a central information database (CID) by wiring together the different legacy systems, and initiated projects to identify the value of customers visiting branches. However, these programmes didn't take account of customers' motivations or their potential value, consequently running the risk of treating low value customers with high potential very poorly.

NatWest's historical orientation towards pricing and risk management, rather than customer value management, presented another barrier to achieving effective CRM across the brand. The bank defined customer risk in terms of a customer's propensity to default or to close. Using credit rating information from the credit reference bureau, Experian, NatWest scored a customer's account-holding behaviour to determine their level of credit risk, and adjusted their credit limit accordingly. However, there was a ceiling to how far people's personal allowances in products such as credit, loans, and overdrafts could be raised before their risk level became unacceptable. The bank then asked itself what else it could do to enhance service and boost profit. It identified one potential avenue to create value and generate revenue: in addition to maximizing the value of individual products and groups of products, it could maximize the value that exists in the linkages between products. This reasoning underpinned a key driver of change at NatWest: the Group's ambition to increase the number of products its customers held across the group.

NatWest had fewer customers holding a number of products than any of its high street rivals. While 84 per cent of credit card holders also held current accounts, just 30 per cent of current account holders had NatWest credit cards, compared to the key competitor average of above 40 per cent. There was clearly a case for pursuing a recruitment drive to extend current account relationships through core current accounts.

NatWest Cards

NatWest Cards' main challenge, however, was to continue to sustain a price premium offset by the Air Miles reward scheme, in an intensely price-driven market. Price (largely interest rate) remained a key weapon of differentiation in cards services, and companies battled to win market and customer share by offering lower rates. NatWest's chief competitors on price included the American brands Capital One and Morgan Stanley Dean Witter, and Barclaycard in the UK, which enjoyed by far the largest market share. Other new market entrants, such as supermarkets, compounded the challenge of winning and keeping customers.

Adoption of CRM principles

Because the Group's overall objective to extend product penetration was clearly too difficult to achieve across all its products and customers in a single pan-company effort, NatWest looked to its Cards business for ways of securing deeper customer relationships which it could later build on. Cards was considered the best test bed for CRM development because it was data rich, had most contact with customers, and, less encumbered by legacy systems and Group 'compliance' than its counterparts, was 'fleeter of foot'. Cards offered the most scope to realize significant short-term benefits; it could influence customers' behaviour on a weekly and monthly basis, compared to other products in the NatWest portfolio, which were typically annual subscriptions or longer-term products.

In mid-1999, with the Group's blessing, NatWest Cards embarked on several initiatives in support of a new CRM strategy, which it called Customer Value Management (CVM). Cards wanted to prove that the business could be managed better by refocusing strategy towards managing customers rather than products. Cards had a high-performing customer base, but no scientific understanding of why customers behaved the way they did, and an abundance of data that could help it understand customers' motivations. It realized that reconciling these two factors could help it deliver a more customized approach to incentivizing customers to use their cards more profitably. Forging more targeted, personalized relationships with customers would lead to improvements in customer satisfaction, business efficiency and profitability.

Tony Davis, Head of Customer Marketing at NatWest, says: 'NatWest is grasping the CRM concept with both hands, and looking to capitalize on its experience and customer performance history to customize its proposition in order to offer benefits beyond the generic features of credit cards. In doing that, it can achieve not only the maintenance of market share in a fast-growing market, but the growth of profits through increased customer satisfaction and usage.'

Davis sees 'the heart of the challenge' as 'the management of information'. Davis, the champion and architect of the Group's approach to CRM, had previously spent time reviewing how the businesses could work together in dealing with customers with a single voice, and subsequently constructed the Cards pilot.

The IT department fully supported Marketing's strategy to build a data-driven business that acknowledges customers and their card usage preferences. IT created the technical capability to allow the business to achieve its aim of delivering a customized proposition. CVM was composed of several discrete but interlinked projects to improve the way customer information was managed so that Cards could develop more personalized customer strategies and deliver them through more personalized communications, thus enhancing the customer experience and ultimately customer profitability. These projects: created an unprecedented central repository of customer data; consolidated the marketing themes of segmentation, segment performance (profit), satisfaction and management; and culminated in revolutionized statementing and communications platforms. Together they challenged the underlying culture of a previously product-driven business.

Data warehouse

A new customer database within Card Services was central to the events leading up to the new statements being issued. The Cards Customer Database (CCD), created in early 1999, was an enormous historical archive, or data warehouse, of all customer activity relating to the use of NatWest credit cards. As CCD Programme Manager Bob Newton explains: 'When a customer uses his card in a travel agents, for instance, all that information is captured because we have to know it in order to raise the bill and get the settlement. It's a standard activity, but no one was holding it before we built the database.'

To construct the data warehouse NatWest's IT constituency looked to the leaders in database technology – the United States – for guidance. Bank of America and Chase Manhattan helped reveal the way forward. The state-of-the-art data warehouse gave Marketing access to a depth of customer data which allowed it to segment its customer base and, later, track behaviour and profitability through campaign management software.

Customer segmentation

CVM's objective was to group customers in like-minded behavioural segments. However, understanding current customer value was only half the story: the company needed to understand the current motivations and potential value of customers if it was to move from a short-term transaction focus to a long-term perspective of relationship building. It could only segment customers according to their behaviour and underlying preferences, rather than basic demographics, if it managed their recruitment, activity rates, borrowing levels and defection. Most defections were measured by product type, and the goal was instead to cut and report customer data segment by segment.

Utilizing the powerful data warehouse, and identifying and researching key behavioural differences, the CCD was used to identify ten core segments, eight large, two small, containing New Accounts and Co-Branded Cards. Segments were based around: (a) spend and borrowing; (b) promotional engagement (particularly collection of Air Miles); and (c) card type/the payment of a fee. While simple, this initial approach was to be a significant first step in dealing with customers as people rather than account holders.

Segment Performance Model (profit)

Once it had developed the segmentation, Card Services then identified key 'drivers' of customer value, such as retention, additional products, turnover and borrowing. By determining the relationship between these drivers and customer income, such as the link between borrowing and net interest income, Cards also identified appropriate 'levers' (Air Miles, cash advance, fee waiver or card upgrade, for example) for increasing income through each driver, for each segment. The net result was a methodology to help segment managers measure and manage customer value (see Figure CS 6.4.1). This Segment Performance Model, based on customer data, provided a much more sophisticated view of customer behaviour than the previous practice of managing

A map of drivers and levers of Customer Value:

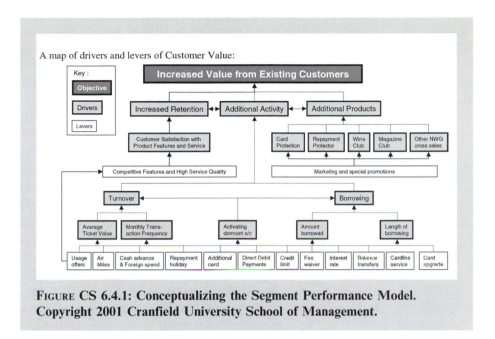

FIGURE CS 6.4.1: Conceptualizing the Segment Performance Model. Copyright 2001 Cranfield University School of Management.

account performance by product alone. It also represented a tool for increasing customer profitability.

Segment Satisfaction Model

NatWest's strong market position had long been attributed to its Air Miles 'loyalty' scheme, which was a major component of the way it managed its segment performance. Cards Marketing carried out extensive research in October 1999 (via telephone surveys, customer focus groups, and internal data analyses), which found that linking customer satisfaction with loyalty was not straightforward, and equating the two could be dangerously misleading.

The research, which measured satisfaction about price, service, product features and flexibility, showed that price performance was a major source of customer dissatisfaction and had a high impact on satisfaction levels overall. The research also revealed a very low correlation between satisfaction and loyalty in the unsegmented customer base.

The company had always assumed that Air Miles were a popular customer benefit, but the customer satisfaction study showed clearly that the scheme wasn't motivating all customers, particularly those who didn't spend very much and who might never accumulate enough points to redeem them. For example, it would take a customer who spent more than £2000 a year (a typical 'convenience' transactor) over eight years to get two return flights to Amsterdam. The proliferation of cheap flights available through low-costs airlines such as EasyJet diminished the perceived value of Air Miles yet further. Cards needed a more personalized approach to stimulate emotional engagement and loyalty, and motivate long-term profitable behaviour.

Segment management

In late 1999 Cards created a new team of 'segment managers' within CVM to direct and deliver the new strategy by managing the volume (account numbers) and value (income and profitability) of defined segments. These individuals assumed responsibility for data analysis and campaign management, which required both customer-centric and commercial expertise. They used the CCD for data mining and other analyses to identify patterns of customer behaviour, which lent themselves to specific strategies for growing particular segments.

Cards gave the segment managers the status and authority to act and plan, empowering them to respond to evident and predicted customer needs. This migrated responsibility from the outdated Product Management function, and Davis describes the team dynamic as 'creative tension' whilst the separate Product and Customer Marketing areas initially concentrated on different aspects of product and broader customer performance measures.

Targeted communications

The capacity of NatWest Cards to interact across media and channels focused mainly on statements, direct mail, and telemarketing. Statements, in particular, were seen as an increasingly important medium through which to build customer relationships. Statements supported a two-way dialogue with customers, allowing the bank to demonstrate high responsiveness to customer needs and preferences expressed via other channels (telephone, fax, e-mail, 'snail mail', etc.). Inserts, vouchers and messages could be included in target customers' monthly statements for little or no extra cost by 'piggybacking' the existing statementing process. 'What we were doing was maximizing the opportunity of contact with the customer', says Davis.

To exploit this medium fully depended on the company's ability to build a store of data about customers, to analyse and interpret the data unambiguously, and to use the resulting 'intelligence' to leverage value proactively. In this respect, NatWest Cards possessed distinct advantages. For one, financial services, especially credit card providers, could collect a meaningful level of data because of their very frequent contact with customers. Their data were also very accurate, because cardholders check the data themselves. Further, by their very nature, personal cards permit a personal interface between companies and customers, representing a direct communication and delivery channel.

In late 1999, NatWest Cards launched a targeted communications programme to establish a mechanism to deliver, via customer statements, the customized propositions devised by the CVM team. The platform solution was put out to tender, and the system was developed by a combination of external and NatWest capability. It comprised two major components:

- *New statement platform.* The first part was a radical change in the way statements were printed. Historically, a pre-printed statement went through a machine where it received the transaction and balance entries. With the new system, each statement was a dynamically printed white sheet-fed piece of 'word document' that was wholly customized. It presented customer account information alongside selected promotions for other value added services, such as eligibility to receive extra Air Miles or to make cheaper calls through taking advantage of one of NatWest's growing number of partnership agreements. The message was that being a NatWest cardholder carried a host of benefits that went beyond core transaction services (see Figure CS 6.4.2).
- *Campaign management.* The second part was using a sophisticated piece of campaign management software (based on Prime Response's 'Vantage') to enable the segment managers to link to the CCD. Customer profiles (pre-identified segments and subsegments) were matched with lists of products, offers or messages of specific relevance and value to them. These were then included in the designated piece of communication or correspondence.

The system, known as TCP, originally stood for Targeted Communications Platform, but was renamed Targeted Customer Propositions because it moved beyond the remit of communications. At a cost of £5 million, the system allowed products and marketing initiatives to be tailored to individual customers through statement messages, inserts, outbound telephony and other media. TCP also allowed feedback on marketing promotions to be captured on the CCD, informing Cards Services about the effectiveness of targeting particular types of initiatives at particular groups of customers.

Results fast!

Before it adopted the CVM strategy, NatWest Cards could only target communications at customers based on limited and one-dimensional segmentation, such as 'age' or 'sex'. With TCP, the CVM team could make informed

⋩ NatWest   Credit Card

000049/000097/22   002

MasterCard number	
Visa card number	
Cardholder	
Total Credit Limit	£ 600

Did you overlook your payment last month? If so, please make a payment of £5.00. A late payment fee may be applied to your account. If you have already paid please accept our thanks.

Summary   22 June 2002

Balance brought forward from previous statement	£ 106.32
Payments to your account	£ 0.00 -
Spending on your account, plus any adjustments	+£ 1.79

New Balance   = £108.11

Minimum Payment   £ 10.00

Pay overdue sum £5.00 now, remainder as below

Your minimum payment should reach your account by 17 JUL 2002.

1 of 2

bank giro credit ⋩

Paid in by	....
Date	....

⋩ NatWest

NatWest
London
E77 1SE

Total Cash*	
Cheques etc+	

Fee	Items		9	62-19-70		73	£
Please do not write or mark below this line				Sorting code number		Transaction Code	

<   621970+< 73   X

Figure CS 6.4.2: NatWest Credit Card statement. Reproduced by kind permission of The Royal Bank of Scotland

decisions about which offers should be sent to which customers in their monthly statements. It deployed customized segment strategies through the sophisticated campaign management system that offered direct, cost-effective delivery and the means for measuring successes in terms of both customer satisfaction and performance.

Figure CS 6.4.2 (continued) NatWest Credit Card Statement. Reproduced by kind permission of The Royal Bank of Scotland

Within just four months of launching TCP, Cards could point to an improved use of cards and increased customer retention. Spending and borrowing increased as a result of the company's new-found understanding of and response to the reasons for which customers held and used a NatWest card. Based on these results, the programme's total technical investment was on track to repay investment in a third of the time the business case had been justified on.

By adopting CRM principles in a micro-programme, Cards quickly proved that focusing customer-facing operations around customer behaviours rather than company products realized even short-term benefits. Greater understanding of and engagement with customers naturally led to improved satisfaction, card usage, retention and profitability.

'Ultimately, more informed and deeper relationships will also lead to a more active loyalty and advocacy of key customers, through which the strategy realizes further unseen benefits', concludes Davis.

Lessons learnt

The introduction of a data-driven and technically proficient CRM approach brought about a sea of change in the way NatWest Cards managed its customer relationships. 'I think we were mass marketers before', reflects CCD Programme Manager Newton. 'We didn't seriously manage our customers. Segmentation was virtually non-existent, seeing customers as basically upper class, middle class and lower class.' Now, with refined segmentation and a robust profitability model based on indicative behaviour, Marketing can ensure that customers are viewed – and treated – as individuals. Customers are *people* rather than accounts.

Mind change

NatWest's adoption of CRM appeared to be a marriage of the right psychology with the right technology, coupled with a close understanding between Marketing and IT. 'We found that engaging the business visionaries in IT helped both to sell the investment to the board and ensure the delivery of a project with cross-business implications', says Davis. This collaboration between two disparate functions was unprecedented, but even more impressive was the way the collective mindset was transformed. NatWest Cards now focuses on achieving a balance between customer satisfaction and profitability, delivered across both front- and back-office functions.

New management information helped effect the cultural change, particularly among senior management. For Customer Marketing to oust Product Management from its plum position at the marketing table, it had to demonstrate performance. Management had traditionally assessed campaign, business and specific product success through regular well-established product-based reports. Revising the format of these reports to incorporate customer-based information was a dramatic and high profile demonstration of changes in the way the business was run and performance measured. Initially, NatWest ran the new set of MI in tandem with the old, to make absolutely sure the new reporting system was watertight.

IT investment

From an IT perspective, Newton sees the move to modern technology as 'a CRM capability in its own right'. For Cards, he says 'one of the main limitations in establishing full CRM and linkage to the full operational systems is its operational environment in technology terms'. Through introducing a fresh IT approach, the TCP project cleared the common hurdle of trying to deliver CRM using a 'mixture of old and badly integrated, poorly designed technology'.

On the issue of justifying big technology projects, Head of IT Strategy, Sean McGarr, is succinct. 'If it doesn't add shareholder value, doesn't add customer value, don't do it', says McGarr. He is clear about what it takes to manage customer relationships effectively. 'CRM is about looking after customers. It's not a technology problem. It's an internal culture of the organization problem', he says. 'From a CRM point of view, unless you are putting a specific message across to a specific group of customers, it's a pointless exercise, so you've got to move away from throwing mud at the wall to be very specific and put the message to the right customer group.' To own the customer relationship, he adds, 'you have to plan at segment level'. Moreover, agrees Head of Customer Marketing Tony Davis, the goal of consistently meeting customers needs profitably is one of 'sophistication, not necessarily complexity'. He points out: 'CRM is simply using customer information to deliver the basic marketing principles.'

The future

As other groups within NatWest realize how fundamental CRM is to business sustainability and growth, buy-in grows. Being able to differentiate customers according to their value to the organization is seen increasingly as being about analysing and interpreting data rather than simply acquiring raw data. As Davis says: 'If we don't exploit data, we're only as good as the new competitor who possesses no historical data.'

Articulating customer value in cardholder statements meant changing the view of the customer from 'What the bank might lose in terms of possible default or fraudulent behaviour' to 'What the bank might gain in terms of opportunity to grow value, extend product holding, or cross-sell'. In short, 'risk' was now about profit as well as loss. But Davis identifies further potential from CRM: 'CRM can become the core business strategy because it doesn't use the word "marketing"', he says. 'People can rebel against the word marketing.'

At NatWest, the case for CRM that prompted redesigning the statements was constructed around future capability rather than quantification of precise cost–benefit. Eventually, customer statements will also be sent electronically, and the self-customization feature of the company's web site will be integrated with the statementing process to further personalize account and service information.

NatWest Cards has actively pursued its belief that effective CRM is about recognizing and rewarding customers, sending them relevant communications, and motivating them to be profitable transactors through carefully managed relationship interactions. The extent to which customer behavioural data will be used to guide the development of future propositions and promotions is subject to growing concerns about the protection of customer privacy and security of information. For long-established banks such as NatWest, which have traditionally enjoyed a relatively high level of consumer trust, future codes of conduct, be they voluntary or compulsory, will pose new challenges for managing customer relationships. New players, who are not so data rich, are not open to such scrutiny.

Davis is confident that the investment in CRM will continue to deliver substantial, positive change. 'With a marketing team now focused around segments based on attitudes and behaviours (not just product types), and technology enabling the attaching of offers, benefits and communications at an "intimate" level, NatWest Cards looks set to continue to build on its strength as one of the biggest, most successful card issuers in Europe', he says. The key to achieving brand-wide CRM, he emphasizes, is to start small and prove quickly: 'It is important to remember that differentiation is only achieved through the *delivery* of the strategy, and evidence of success requires bold action in the first instance.'

7

Performance assessment process

In Chapter 2, we suggested that the CRM services market was still growing fast, despite the downturn in other IT sectors. Gartner (Nairn 2001) predicts that the market will triple in size in the next four years. It also predicts that fail rates for CRM projects will rise from 65 per cent today to more than 80 per cent in two years. The reason is that more and more companies are embarking on CRM initiatives without understanding the full extent of the business changes required, without an appropriate methodology for developing CRM and without relevant performance metrics to measure – and manage – the impact of CRM investments. Ultimately, these measures, or KPIs (Key Performance Indicators), need to reflect the two drivers of shareholder value: productivity and growth. Productivity – cutting costs, investments or price rises – may prove the easier to measure and arguably the first to deliver results, but it is growth that delivers shareholder value based on improved customer retention and acquisition.

Companies need both types of measure to assess the performance of CRM, and to identify how to link and manage them to gain short-term efficiency and create longer-term value. In Chapter 2 we identified how firms can link and measure these performance metrics across four main categories:

- strategic integration;
- output effectiveness;
- customer value; and
- operational efficiencies.

When it developed its enterprise performance model, the US retailer Sears, Roebuck and Company (the first case study in this chapter), used metrics spanning all four categories. Using over 60 measures of employee behaviours, customer impressions and financial performance, Sears, led by Arthur C Martinez, was transformed from a loss maker to a $1billion+ net income generator during the 1990s. To implement the employee–customer profit chain model successfully, senior management needed to take greater responsibility for the company's culture and the effect it had on customer satisfaction, retention and revenue growth, which drive improvements in profit and shareholder value. Sears uses these performance criteria to manage its vision to provide 'a compelling place to shop, work and invest in'. The retailer has established causal links between the performance measures; for example, a 5 unit increase in employee attitude leads to a 1.3 unit increase in customer impressions and a 0.5 per cent increase in revenue growth. Towards the end of the 1990s, earnings per share and return on employees (ROE) were increasing year on year and 30–70 per cent of its executive incentives were linked to these measures.

In similar fashion, Nortel Networks transformed its business performance and the metrics it used to measure the effectiveness of its CRM activities, to emerge as a major competitor in the global telecommunications market. During the 1990s, the Canadian company moved from being a manufacturer of telecommunications equipment to being mainly a service organization offering network solutions. Nortel established a causal link between customer relationship management, employee motivation and shareholder value creation. It built a value cycle model to establish a measurement system spanning customers, employees, internal processes and shareholder returns on investment, drawing these measures from each of the four performance metrics identified above. Like Sears, Nortel places a great emphasis on the key value of its employees: it attributes 52 per cent of customer satisfaction to employee satisfaction. Nortel delivers CRM on the back of motivated employees and an appropriate leadership style, and has redesigned its recognition and reward system to reflect customer loyalty, employee satisfaction and business results.

The final case study, Siemens, is perhaps less holistic in approach than Sears or Nortel. Nonetheless, it provides insights into operational and customer metrics that have been significantly improved in recent years through the use of internet technology, and which accompany big improvements in business performance. Operationally, Siemens CT division has transformed its supply chain – from customer relationships to supplier management – and improved the productivity of its employees by over 100 per cent. The use of web cameras and computer networks, to transfer data about orders and parts availability, has provided a fail-safe way of relaying information in the order fulfilment process.

Customer service performance indicators have also improved as closer relationships with new and existing customers have been established through the use of the internet. As a consequence of these productivity gains and improvements in customer value, the division's profitability has greatly increased.

CASE STUDY 7.1

Sears, Roebuck and Company

OVERVIEW

Sears, Roebuck and Company has been an eminent US retailer for over 100 years. A household name, Americans associate it with quality and value. However, during the past twenty years Sears has had to fight hard to overcome the difficulties inherent in operating in a mature market and to combat adverse trading conditions.

This case study describes the events of the past ten years. It focuses on how the senior management tackled the company's problems in the early 1990s, when Sears faced gigantic financial losses. Part of management's remedy was adopting a new approach to managing business performance. This model links the performance of management, employees and customers directly to company profits and so provides some important insights into the value of adopting CRM.

The case study also looks at recent innovation at Sears, including two very successful advances into electronic trading. Sears.com has been named the number one 'clicks and bricks' retailer in the world, and GlobalNetXchange has been hailed as one of the most successful business-to-business web sites in the world.

Key learning points

This business-to-consumer case study at Sears, Roebuck and Company demonstrates how effective CRM depends on managing relationships with other important stakeholders as well as customers. The case describes the roles played by three stakeholder groups: employees (including senior managers), customers and suppliers.

Initially, Sears focused its CRM activities on managing face-to-face relationships between employees and customers and on building a large data warehouse. More recently, CRM activity has been extended to embrace innovative technology to provide customers with a widely acclaimed e-retailing channel. In addition, through GlobalNetXchange,

Sears has taken the lead in business-to-business exchanges, making the supply chain more efficient by linking suppliers with retailers.

CRM issues

- Successful CRM involves managing important stakeholder relationships.

Sears acknowledged that successful relationships with customers depended upon successfully managing employees. Senior management identified key profit indicators that allowed them to manage their business more efficiently. They monitored three key areas involving many metrics, including 25 employee measures, 20 customer measures and 19 financial performance indicators.

- The employee–customer–profit chain can be used to manage a business-to-consumer company.

Sears has integrated the service profit chain, developed by researchers at Harvard, into a cohesive performance assessment process that identifies causal linkages between its constituent elements.

- Implementing CRM often involves changing the attitudes and behaviour of senior management as well as other employees.

The CEO and his top team recognized that to implement successful CRM, they would have to change the behaviour of senior managers. Managers' leadership skills created the culture of Sears and this had an important impact on revenues.

Introduction

The turnaround of Sears, Roebuck and Company between 1992 and 1995 has been described in some detail (Rucci et al. 1998; Sherman, 1997). Sears is almost certainly the best and most powerful illustration of an organization that has implemented a service profit chain enterprise performance model.

In 1992, Sears, Roebuck and Company reported massive losses of $3.9 billion on sales of $52.3 billion. A new CEO, Arthur Martinez, was appointed in 1992 to head the merchandise group and he began to streamline the business. He closed 113 stores and terminated the 101 year old Sears Catalogue, which was a household institution in the US. He also set about changing the service strategy, focusing on women, who were the most important buying decision-makers. As a result, in 1993, the company reported a net income of $752 million – a dramatic reversal of fortunes for such a mature company.

Martinez set up four task forces – customers, employees, financial performance and innovation – to define world class status in each specific area, identify obstacles and define metrics for measuring progress. The task forces spent months listening to customers and employees, observing best practice in other organizations and establishing measures against objectives. Gradually it became apparent that a model was needed to show 'direct causation' from employee attitudes, through customer satisfaction to profits. The company needed to know how management action, such as investment in sales force training, would directly translate into improved customer satisfaction, retention and higher revenues. It needed to operationalize what it termed 'the employee–customer–profit chain'. The revised model of this is shown in Figure CS 7.1.1.

Sears defined a set of measures based on its objective of making Sears 'a compelling place to work at, to shop at and to invest in'. This objective reflected the company's focus on three value domains: employees, customers and shareholders. Sears identified relationships between changes in key metrics using causal pathway modelling. CFI Group undertook the econometric modelling of the relationships.

Sears built its enterprise performance model using data from over 800 stores. It used 20 customer measures, 25 employee measures and 19 financial perform-

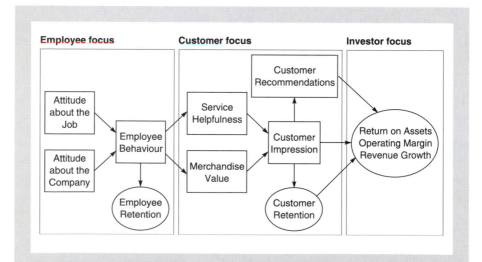

FIGURE CS 7.1.1: The revised employee–customer–profit chain at Sears.
Source: based on Sears, Roebuck and Company.

ance indicators, including productivity, revenues, margins, payroll costs, number of transactions and so forth.

The results of this work were impressive. Sears identified direct causal links between employee measures, customer measures and revenues, allowing it to establish total profit indicators for the company. It found that employee attitudes towards their job and company were critical to employee loyalty and behaviour towards customers, while the impression the customer received of the company directly affected customer retention and the likelihood that they would recommend it to others. After further refinement, the model was used to predicting revenue growth: a 5 unit increase in employee attitude drives a 1.3 unit increase in customer impression, a 0.5 per cent increase in revenue growth and a quantifiable increase in the profitability of the store.

To implement the service profit chain model successfully Sears had to change the behaviour of its senior managers and encourage them to take responsibility for the company's culture and understand what effect this had on revenues. In addition, the company aligned employee rewards to the model for financial and non-financial measures.

Later, the analytical CRM system was streamlined. Previously there were 18 separate legacy databases; today there is a single, integrated data warehouse of over seven terabytes, as shown in Figure CS 7.1.2.

In the period following the implementation of the enterprise performance model, employee satisfaction at Sears rose by 4 per cent and customer satisfaction by almost 4 per cent, netting the company more than $200 million additional revenue. Figure CS 7.1.3 shows the relative performance improvement in profitability, customer satisfaction and associate (Sears' term for employees) attitudes between 1992 and 1998.

Sears was so confident about its data that it computed 30 per cent to 70 per cent of its executive compensation from these measures. Sears delivered earnings of US $1.3 billion in 1997. In terms of shareholder value, the total return to investors between September 1992 and April 1997 was 298 per cent – a remarkable improvement for a firm in such a mature business. Sears now uses its measurement system to improve future revenues and profits.

By 1998 Sears faced a new challenge in the form of lack of sales momentum. Sears was in a very difficult and highly competitive sector and to address the challenge it needed a fresh approach to managing its relationships with customers. In 1999 Martinez said: 'Now, what we need is renewed energy. We need what I'm calling a Second Revolution – a second revolution and our marketing communications to our customer to send a stronger message about who we are and what our value proposition is.'

A new reorganization followed, along with a major new marketing campaign and other initiatives. US financial analysts were impressed.

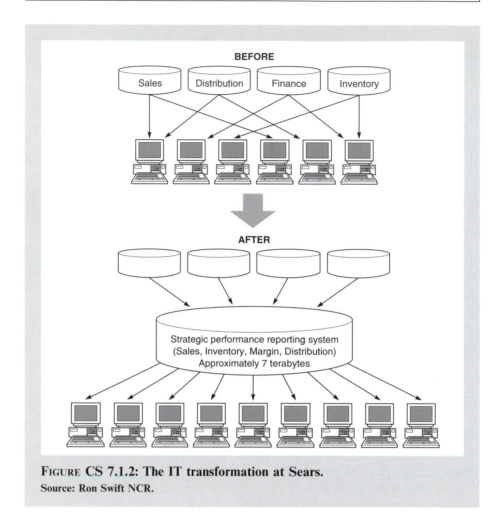

FIGURE CS 7.1.2: **The IT transformation at Sears.**
Source: Ron Swift NCR.

Martinez has also been a driving force behind e-commerce activities at Sears. These began in 1996 with the launch of Sears.com which, by December 1999, was rated by Nielsen as the fourth fastest growing shopping site. However, the site was not user friendly, and was relaunched with enhanced capabilities – improved searches, smoother navigation and simplified shopping, for example – in July 2000. The results have been very encouraging, with Sears.com named the number one e-retailer in the world.

Another important development was GlobalNetXchange, the first business-to-business marketplace for retail, launched in February 2000. The site unites technology partners with retailers, making the supply chain more efficient. Initially, the company has focused on the relationships Sears and other retail giants have with their suppliers, partners and distributors. The exchange pro-

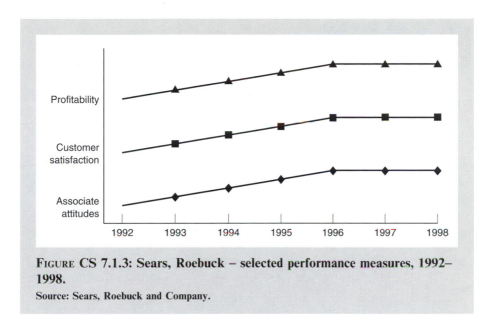

FIGURE CS 7.1.3: Sears, Roebuck – selected performance measures, 1992–
1998.
Source: Sears, Roebuck and Company.

vides these companies with a common place to buy, sell, trade or auction goods
and services online, allowing them to buy more effectively and to manage their
supply chain better. The companies pass these advantages on to the customer in
the form of a better value proposition – something Sears knows is critical to
driving sales and profits in the company.

The results have been significant. Even Wall Street has acknowledged that
Sears' financial performance has exceeded expectations. However, financial analysts agree that the retail giant must continue focusing on a growth strategy to
overcome the difficulties inherent in the troubled retail sector. Measuring and
managing critical relationships with employees, customers and suppliers is likely
to continue to be central to this strategy.

CASE STUDY 7.2

Nortel Networks

OVERVIEW

The Nortel Networks case illustrates the issues faced by a business-to-business company competing in the aggressive global telecoms market. In such an environment it has been particularly important to closely monitor and assess CRM and its contribution to the company.

This Canadian corporation operates in the global telecommunications market, and made revenues of US$30 billion in 2000. While Nortel is currently suffering from the malaise that has beset the telecoms sector, the company's performance over the past ten years has been impressive.

This case describes how Nortel has developed a sophisticated process to assess the performance of CRM, a critical tool especially during its period of rapid growth during the 1990s. Understanding how value is created and delivered has played a vital role in the company's success.

Nortel was transformed during the 1990s from being primarily a manufacturer of equipment to being mainly a service organization offering network solutions. This change in focus required very different skills and resources, and put pressure on the organization to be extremely flexible while continuing to deliver high quality customer service.

Key learning points

This business-to-business case study illustrates how CRM can be successfully managed across a global business. It explains how Nortel Networks tested CRM initiatives in one country and then adapted them in other countries, helping to share knowledge about how value was created across different parts of the business.

Initially Nortel focused on the key role of employees in creating value. More recently, it has turned its attention to understanding the links between customer satisfaction and shareholder value.

CRM issues

- Critical to the success of CRM is understanding where value is created in a business.

Nortel understood that its relationships with customers would be threatened unless it understood its value creation process. To do this, senior management identified the need for a sophisticated measurement system. This allowed the value created by people and processes to be closely monitored so that managers could allocate appropriate investment.

- Employees play a key role in creating value.

Nortel has found that employee satisfaction accounts for 52 per cent of customer satisfaction. Realizing that this measure is critical to successful CRM, the company has developed an employee recognition and reward system that is closely linked to business results and customer loyalty.

- Service profit chain approaches can be utilized within the business-to-business sector.

Nearly all the examples relating to the service profit chain are drawn from the business-to-consumer sector. Nortel Networks illustrates how such CRM approaches can be extended to the business-to-business sector.

Introduction

Nortel Networks is a Canadian corporation operating in the global telecommunications market. Despite the recent problems in this sector the company had a record year in 2000, when revenues grew by 42 per cent to over US$30 billion. However, the company grew most rapidly in the 1990s when, prompted by intense competition and enormous change in the market, Nortel recognized that it needed to move from being primarily a manufacturer of equipment to being mainly a service organization.

Nortel knew it needed to understand how value was created and delivered within the business so that it could focus on the most critical areas, and it developed its own model of value creation. The approach senior managers adopted was influenced by work they had done on benchmarking leading organizations such as Xerox and Disney, and from their work on quality. They have won a number of quality awards and are strong supporters of the US Baldridge and the European EFQM awards. They have worked with leading external experts (including Brad Gale of the US Strategic Planning Institute, the leading econometric modelling firm CFI Group and Ray Kordupleski, a US expert in customer value), to develop aspects of their sophisticated model.

Gale, well known for his recent research on value, was an early influence on Nortel. His work on value creation caught the attention of senior management, and led to their realization that value was created through a linked system of mutual benefit to shareholders, customers and employees.

Nortel realized it needed a sophisticated measurement system to identify where value was created in the company. It developed the Nortel Business Value Cycle, shown in Figure CS 7.2.1, to link resources, internal and external processes and shareholders. Although this model looks rather different on paper from the service–profit chain, there are many similarities. The service–profit chain is a model developed by researchers from Harvard Business School, which links factors including internal service quality, employee satisfaction, customer value, customer satisfaction, customer loyalty, and profitability. The Nortel Business Value Cycle extends the service–profit chain model to incorporate the processes that create value. It also emphasizes the important role of leadership.

Establishing such a measurement system and then extending it across the global organization presented a major logistical challenge. The effort has been repaid in the way in which knowledge has been shared across different parts of the business. For example, comparing the satisfaction ratings of a customer in one country with scores in another country has helped integrate management

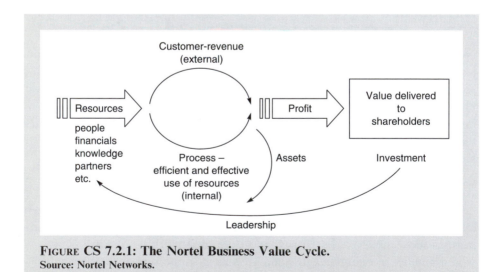

FIGURE CS 7.2.1: The Nortel Business Value Cycle.
Source: Nortel Networks.

processes across the global operation. Also, initiatives to improve value creation that are tested in one country can, if successful, be adopted elsewhere.

Nortel's use of a linkage model has helped it identify many statistically valid relationships across its version of the service–profit chain. For example, it has identified three key drivers of employee satisfaction: leadership, perceived customer focus of the business, and the extent to which an employee sees obstacles hindering job performance. Leadership accounts for 31 per cent of employee satisfaction and 18 per cent of customer satisfaction; management recognized that developing the appropriate leadership style and supporting processes was vital. Nortel clearly identifies leadership behaviours that every manager has to demonstrate and evaluates their performance in regular appraisals. The organization places strong emphasis on individual empowerment aligned to a carefully formulated and well-communicated business plan.

The value cycle model strongly emphasizes the key value of employees to the corporation. Understanding that appropriate rewards linked to market factors are critical to motivate employees, Nortel redesigned its recognition and rewards system, linking it closely to business results, customer loyalty and employee satisfaction. Seniority was dropped as a reward criterion. Employees were grouped into two teams: the first was a strategic development team that is rewarded on product 'time to market' and market success; the second was a customer-facing team that is rewarded by market share and 'share of customer wallet'. Rewards were therefore closely aligned to the value cycle model, so individual employees could understand their specific contribution to creating value for the business.

Nortel found that employee satisfaction accounts for 52 per cent of customer satisfaction. Understanding that effective internal processes are critical for succeeding in its customer markets, Nortel has begun to refine its employee satisfaction measures. For example, it identifies 'high flying' employees and monitors their impact on customer satisfaction compared with other employee segments.

Nortel also draws comparisons between the impact of very satisfied and merely satisfied employees on customer value creation. It compares different employee jobs, such as customer interface workers and account managers, to identify those that have the strongest impact on customer satisfaction.

The company refined its data further to predict future events – aside from business performance – such as changes in customer behaviour.

Nortel has also been concerned with understanding the relationship between customer satisfaction and shareholder value. Its analysis suggests that there is a positive correlation between customer satisfaction and revenues and the share price. Figure CS 7.2.2 shows the relationship between share price and customer satisfaction between 1993 and 1996. The share price continued to rise in 1997; it

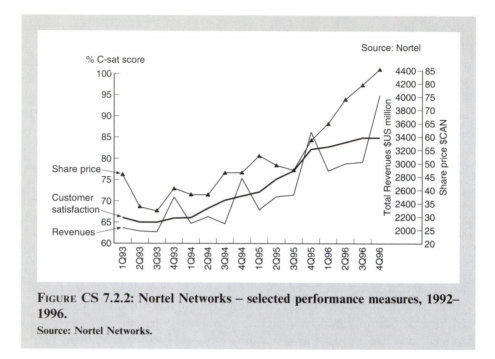

FIGURE CS 7.2.2: Nortel Networks – selected performance measures, 1992–1996.

Source: Nortel Networks.

dipped at the beginning of 1998 because of a board decision to split the shares and re-issue them on a 2 to 1 basis.

Nortel Networks has reaped many benefits from understanding and managing the linkages between employees, customers and shareholders, using a formal linkage model. The work does not measure causality, but the correlations appear to be highly significant. Nortel can anticipate events more effectively, allowing it to chart a smoother course – a vital capability in the fast changing telecommunications environment.

In 2000 Nortel achieved record results, with adjusted net earnings increasing by 61 per cent and earnings per share by 42 per cent. But the following year, struck by the dramatic downturn in the telecoms sector, it made a loss. Many of its major customers, the telephone companies, cut back on their spending, while some of the weaker phone companies went out of business altogether. Nortel has been forced to lay off one third of its worldwide staff and lower its cost structure so that it can return to profitability. In this climate, managing CRM effectively has become even more critical for the company.

The market continues to change rapidly and players must be agile to compete. For example, new products are frequently introduced into the market, often by smaller, innovative companies. These pose a considerable threat to the larger operators which struggle to change their technology. Nortel has responded by listening to its customers and developing new technology, but massive investment required to do this has not been matched by customer spending.

Nortel recently announced it was looking for a new leader. John Roth, the CEO who has led the company through massive change, has announced his retirement and a successor is now being sought. Analysts suggest that Roth has done an excellent job but it is now time for a change. The new CEO faces considerable business and CRM challenges, including winning new customers and encouraging loyalty from old ones in a turbulent market environment.

CASE STUDY 7.3

Siemens CT Division

OVERVIEW

To develop a business case for CRM investments, companies need to clearly articulate and monitor the appropriate performance metrics as they implement the programme. In Chapter 2, we argued that the performance assessment process should measure improvements in the business' added value activities – its effectiveness – and its cost base – its efficiency. The degree to which either is achieved will vary according to the nature of the investment and the business' underlying objectives. When Siemens moved its computer tomography (CT) division into the internet age, it became both more effective and more efficient in a dramatic business turnaround.

Siemens is a world leader in electrical engineering and electronics, employing over 450 000 people in 190 countries. It prides itself on being the principal provider of IT solutions for the healthcare market, where two-thirds of its products and services are less than three years old. However, in the mid-1990s Siemens CT division was under-performing and lacked creativity and innovative flair. More importantly, its relationships with its customers – hospitals and clinics throughout the world – were uncoordinated. Consequently, customers' experiences of dealing with the business through the product lifecycle of installation, maintenance and upgrade, was inconsistent. Siemens CT's customer service levels and responsiveness were not enhancing its reputation as the world's second-biggest maker of CT scanners.

This case study provides insights on how the business used internet technology to forge much closer relationships with is customers, and how it measured its improved performance through its supply chain.

Key learning points

In this business-to-business case study, Siemens CT division shows how using the internet creatively, through webcam technology, can lead to improved customer relationships and competitiveness, while increasing the productivity of the workforce and supply chain partners.

From a CRM perspective, the company's new performance assessment centres around customer lifetime value and cost reduction throughout its supply chain, from the cost of serving customers to the productivity metrics of agile supply. Since the mid-1990s, the division has become much more profitable, a key performance indicator of shareholder value, and has built much closer relationships with its customers and suppliers. How has it achieved this, and what CRM performance measures did it use?

CRM issues

- Measure customer satisfactions throughout the product life-cycle.

The business establishes relationships with new customers, before shipping products to them, via internet-linked web cameras it installs in the hospital's designated scanner room. By discussing installation specifications and viewing work-in-progress with customers as the room is prepared, the company can monitor customer satisfaction throughout the installation process.

- Internet linkages can extend customer lifetime value.

Siemens CT has increased customer lifetime value by maintaining the internet links with customers in case the equipment should fail, or upgrading it with new operating software.

- Facilitates lean supply and transparency in components supply.

Siemens CT has doubled the efficiency of the production lines in its own factory and those of its major suppliers, by using web cameras to check the availability of components. Over the past few years, it has reduced the time it takes to assemble a new CT system from 13 to six days.

Introduction

Keeping your customers happy is a well-rehearsed way to achieve business success. If you can do this using much the same process that you use to manage suppliers, you probably have a good chance of turning your company into a winner.

That has been central to the philosophy of a division of Siemens – the large German electrical goods company – and has allowed it to dramatically improve its business performance over the past few years. The story illustrates how manufacturers are increasingly looking at all aspects of their activities – from product design to improving distribution of their goods to the customer – as they strive to increase their efficiency and competitiveness.

The computer tomography division of Siemens (Siemens CT) recently won a global award for excellence in manufacturing operations in a competition organized by management consultants AT Kearney, for its achievements in introducing new practices into many parts of its business.

Siemens' CT division is the world's second-biggest maker of computer tomography equipment, after General Electric of the US. CT systems are highly complicated medical scanners costing up to €900 000, which use X-rays to look at sections of the body to diagnose or monitor diseases such as cancer. The German operation – based in Forchheim, near Nuremberg – achieved sales of around €700 million in 2000, 85 per cent of which were derived outside Germany.

Improved profitability and productivity through the internet

In the past three years, the division has become much more profitable – it hasn't disclosed the exact figures – as part of an effort led by Siemens group chief executive, Heinrich von Pierer, to turn around the company's previously lacklustre financial performance.

Richard Hausmann, president of the CT division, claims that the productivity of workers in his unit has doubled since 1996, largely due to rethinking the supply chain and getting closer to customers.

A novel use of the internet has facilitated these improvements. Siemens has installed web cameras – small TV cameras linked to the internet – on the premises of selected suppliers of parts for its CT machines, to monitor production lines and check availability of components.

This provides a fail-safe way of relaying information about the flow of components to the division's Forchheim plant, the world's biggest CT factory and home to 500 of the division's 1200 employees. Hausmann is now using a similar concept to help the division move closer to customers.

Camera links with customers: Building customer value

About a month before the company installs a CT machine in a room at a clinic or hospital, anywhere in the world, technicians will install internet-linked web cameras to provide instant feedback to Forchheim on the customer's preparations for the rooms.

Installing the CT equipment is a lengthy process which often involves technical and manufacturing staff from Forchheim. According to Hausmann it can frequently be delayed because the rooms do not have the required electrical wiring or are not properly painted.

He says that the web camera system will keep such delays to a minimum, maintaining customer satisfaction as well as improving the efficiency of the division's internal operations.

After the CT machines are successfully installed, the internet links (although not the cameras) remain. These are used to connect the customers' systems to the Forchheim headquarters so that technicians can help solve equipment problems or download new operating software.

The efforts the company has made to improve links with its customers follow from the strides Siemens has made to improve its supply chain.

Camera links with suppliers: Shortening the lead times

Since the mid-1990s, the CT division has made two big changes in the way it manages its supply chain. For one, it has outsourced much more of its parts production – nowadays 80 per cent of the cost of the parts in each CT machine is accounted for by outside suppliers, compared with around 50 per cent four years ago. Additionally, in an effort to reduce the complexity of its supply arrangements, Siemens has reduced the number of suppliers from 100 to about 30, of which roughly half are in Germany.

Techniques such as the web cameras on the suppliers' production lines, plus the use of computer networks to transfer data about orders and parts availability between Forchheim and outside contractors, has significantly reduced the time it takes to make a complete CT unit. According to Hausmann, assembly time for a new CT system has been cut over the past few years from 13 to six days.

Because Siemens CT division has switched more of the overall manufacturing responsibilities onto suppliers, only 150 directly-employed Siemens employees work in production jobs at Forchheim. They spend much of their time on assembly or in logistics, working on links with either suppliers or customers.

This case study is © Financial Times, 25 October 2000. Reproduced with kind permission and adapted from Peter Marshall's original article.

References

Laabs, J. (1999) The HR Side of Sears' Comeback. *Workforce*, March, pp. 4–29.

Nairn, G. (2001) A fast-moving bandwagon attracts new passengers. *Financial Times IT review* 13, July 4.

Rucci, A. J., Kirn, S. P. and Quinn, R. T. (1998) The employee–customer–profit chain at Sears. *Harvard Business Review*, January–February, pp. 83–97.

Sherman, S. (1997) Bringing Sears into the new world. *Fortune*, October, pp. 183–184.

Siemens Annual Report (2000) Medical Solutions (Med).
   http://w4.siemens.com/annualreport_2000/business_segments/medical/med.shtml

Siemens AG Medical Engineering – Products and Solutions.
   http://www.med.siemens.com/medroot/en/prod/index.html
   http://www.med.siemens.com/medroot/en/prod/diag/ct/index.html

Chapter **8**

CRM investments and shareholder value

Summary of cases

The cases highlighted in this book illustrate the five processes we have identified as being key to successful CRM: strategy development; value creation; channel and media integration; information management; and performance assessment.

The companies in the case studies are at different stages with their CRM, and are enjoying variable benefits. Some have been highly successful, while others have learnt from the mistakes they have made and are now in the position of being able to use this learning for their next surge forward. Every company is different, faces different challenges, and has different objectives, and therefore every company sets about CRM differently. Nonetheless, while CRM is clearly not a one-size-fits-all, off-the-peg solution, other firms considering embarking on CRM can learn considerable lessons from the successes and failures of this first tranche of pioneers.

A number of factors prompt companies to embrace CRM. These include competition, more demanding customers, the need to manage corporate growth and an expanding customer base, and the need to retain as well as attract customers. However, those companies that have enjoyed the most success started small, and are now poised to roll out CRM to other parts of the organization. Don Peppers, the US one-to-one marketing guru, and one of the CRM 'opinion leaders' we go on to interview in Chapter 9, says: 'In our client work, almost all the successful implementations are the result of rolling out from a series of pilot projects.' The experiences of our case study companies certainly bear out Peppers' hypothesis. Orange, Friends First and The Derbyshire Building Society realized that creating a customer relations department which would build an integrated view of the customer and enable them to establish and meet customers' needs more effectively, was an obvious first step to becoming customer-focused.

Other companies focused on those parts of their business they believed would bring them quick wins. This, in turn, would give them the understanding and the confidence to roll CRM out into other areas. NatWest, for example, chose its cards division as a testbed for CRM, exploiting both its position as a direct marketing channel and the wealth of customer data it held. CRM could be implemented quickly, and the results quantified quickly. Earlier attempts by NatWest to introduce data-driven CRM across the brand failed because of the complexity and enormity of the task. Insurance company Wesleyan, which deals directly with customers primarily through its sales force, dramatically improved the productivity of its sales force, with disproportionate effects on revenue and profits, by giving them laptops linked to a central customer management system. Each salesperson's sales tripled within three years, and the success of the sales force automation project encouraged Wesleyan to embark on a more broad-reaching CRM programme the following year.

However, the Wesleyan case also exemplifies another factor, which is key to the success of CRM: people are just as important to value creation as systems and processes. The best sales people were redesignated 'financial advisers' and trained accordingly, and the pay structure was revised so that they were rewarded for keeping customers rather than acquiring them. Sun Microsystems also recognized the value of its people, giving account managers more strategic roles that created value for the company. Staff buy-in was an important component of the successful CRM programme at Canada Life (Ireland). Staff rate the new CRM system, which provides a much deeper under-standing of customers, highly, both because of the image it conveys of the company's commitment to service, and its user-friendliness.

Rolling out into the rest of the business, however, may not be plain sailing, as Orange's experience suggests. Despite Orange's enormous success, growing competition and the pace of technological development forced it to reassess its strategy and switch its focus from gaining new customers to keeping existing ones. The new Customer Relations department fostered a new two-way com-munication with customers that reaped substantial benefits for both sides. Advocates in Customer Relations are struggling to drive CRM throughout the organization – not least because the pace of change within the industry and the frantic race to acquire customers allow scant time to consider or analyse the benefits of a different approach. But Orange is pressing ahead, knowing full well that subscriber numbers don't tell the full story and that success is more meaningfully measured in terms of the value of the customer to the business and the business to the customer.

The three cases highlighted in Chapter 4 on value creation – Friends First, Canada Life (Ireland) and Sun Microsystems – demonstrate just how important value is in building, managing and sustaining profitable, long-term customer relationships.

Financial services group Friends First created a new strategic vision to be customer-centred, trustworthy and easy to do business with. Its customer service centre was central to its value creation process, with the guiding principle that 'if we look after our customers better than the competition then everything else that is important will follow'. In a market where trust and reputation are critical to success, Friends First built a brand virtually from scratch, with a customer-focused strategy backed up by a CRM technology solution. Resolutely customer-focused, committed to continual improvement, and enjoying a strategic partnership with its software supplier, Friends First is set to build on its successful implementation of CRM with a customer value model.

Prompted by more demanding customers, and driven by its long-held commitment to delivering on customers' expectations, life and pensions company Canada Life (Ireland) adopted CRM to help it boost its retention and acquisition strategies. It has increased customer and company value by integrating the information spread across three legacy systems into a new CRM system, which has given it a much deeper understanding of its customers.

Sun Microsystems, one of the world's leading enablers of customer relationship management, decided to practise what it preached, and adopted a CRM strategy in its own business to help it switch focus from acquiring to retaining customers. In the process, it discovered that CRM can lead to far-reaching changes in the way companies manage their supply chains: it developed more effective value-adding communication with its employees, suppliers and partners, as well as its customers.

The value lesson is one that Homebase learnt only with hindsight. Homebase's decision to fight off competition in the DIY market by launching a 'virtual store' to complement its bricks and mortar presence created value neither for itself nor its customers. Indeed, the venture demonstrates all too clearly the penalties of moving into a new area very quickly.

Homebase's experience taught it some valuable lessons – lessons that could be invaluable to others considering a similar approach. First, you can't just throw money at CRM. Homebase invested heavily to build a retail website, which almost from the start showed scant sign of being able to generate the expected Return on Investment (ROI). Secondly, e-strategy must be incorporated with corporate strategy. The virtual store was set up independently of the rest of the company, so, without the support and input from other areas of the business, it struggled to meet customer and commercial demands. Subsequent moves to integrate e-commerce with the rest of the business have delivered benefits to Homebase, Hombase.co.uk and customers. Thirdly, internal talent and expertise must be fostered and developed. Homebase.co.uk initially outsourced many of its e-commerce operations, losing an opportunity to develop in-house expertise.

In March 2001 Schroder Ventures bought Homebase from Sainsbury's and set about changing it from a stand-alone operation intent on capturing market share into an integral part of a business-wide initiative to improve the company's bottom line and commercial viability. This about face is a radical revision of Homebase's initial e-commerce priorities and the assumptions on which they were based. Above all, the Homebase case is a lesson in not allowing customer focus to cloud commercial judgement.

All the cases demonstrate the value of information to a customer-focused organization. You simply can't give customers the products and service they want if you don't know what they want – or indeed, who they are. Information management both underpins CRM processes and integrates them into a coherent strategy. The Derbyshire Building Society and Britannia Building Society cases perhaps highlight the need for customer information most clearly, while the Canada Life (UK) and Sun Microsystems cases are a stark reminder of the barriers to successful CRM posed by legacy systems.

The Derbyshire Building Society case outlines the information a company needs before implementing IT to support a customer strategy. In a climate of increasing competition, Derbyshire was struggling to deliver on its core value of putting its customers at the heart of its business, because it lacked a single point of reference on customers across the organization. Creating a new Customer Services division and equipping it with a central CRM system gave it a new integrated view, which resulted in better customer service, higher retention and faster growth.

The Britannia Building Society decided to remain a mutual despite the rush by its competitors to convert to plc status. It then decided that to remain competitive it would build on its strengths as a provider of competitive products in a friendly and approachable way, while refocusing on the loyalty of its core customers and building a new differentiated strategy around that.

It enhanced its members' bonus scheme, incentivizing members to provide updated information about themselves to qualify for eligibility. This information helped the company build a comprehensive customer database, which has allowed it to segment its customers and target its products and services to them accordingly. Customer service staff have an at-a-glance knowledge of a customer whenever they talk to them, which helps the customer's sense that the company understands them. The average number of products held per customer has increased from 1.3 to 1.8.

Despite this early success, Britannia then faced the challenge of improving its products and services further, and found its IT systems not up to the task. The next phase of Britannia's CRM strategy was to upgrade its IT structure. After its initial CRM win, it found itself in the same situation as Canada Life (UK) – its ability to know and build one-to-one relationships with its customers was severely constrained by its legacy systems. The Canada Life (UK) case illustrates the problems of integrating legacy systems. At first sight, the obvious solution would be to replace older systems with newer technologies, but this is expensive, time-consuming and disruptive, particularly when many legacy systems process back-office transactions adequately. Canada Life (UK) found that using middleware can help integrate back-office systems, but should be seen as a step in the journey towards full front-to-back integration, rather than as an end in itself. Likewise, installing a CRM system in the front-office – a call centre or branch, for example – can achieve quick wins, but should be recognized as a step on the journey rather than a final solution.

Sun Microsystems found there was no alternative to changing its legacy systems to create a single view of the customer.

Simon Kelly, head of marketing at BT Major Business, and another of the 'opinion leaders' we speak to in Chapter 9, believes that 'integrated channel management is a bigger part of CRM than most people realize'. The most important thing CRM technology should do, he says, is '[give] customers the touchpoint to interact with the company when and how they want to'.

The Wesleyan, RS Components and asserta home cases in Chapter 5, demonstrate the experiences of companies at different stages on the road to integration. Wesleyan improved media quality within its existing channel structure by automating its sales force. RS Components extended its media to improve the customer's experience, reduce costs and attract new customers. The company traditionally supplied office components to a wide range of businesses through a catalogue and call centre, but recently added a website to make it easier for customers to buy, and to attract new customers. It is also cheaper for the company to serve its website customers, allowing it to grow faster than it could through its traditional media.

asserta home is essentially an online marketplace for customers buying homes and estate agents selling them. It demonstrates a real channel partnership and offers an integrated multi-media experience to customers. Rather than seeking to disintermediate estate agents by selling online, it capitalizes on their inventory and reputation, understanding that excellent media mean nothing without a good stock of property. Estate agents benefit through asserta's ability to qualify leads and reduce their sales and marketing costs, while customers benefit from an imaginative media mix which supports all the different aspects of buying a house.

Phill Robinson, vice-president international marketing for Siebel Systems, and another opinion leader featured in Chapter 9, points out that CRM is 'a very good example of an initiative designed to grow revenue rather than cut costs', and urges companies to build their business case based upon that fact. The problem is that too many companies have just not got their heads round the measurement issue at all – neither how much CRM is going to cost them, nor how they are going to measure its impact. Little wonder then that, despite the rise in the CRM services market, Gartner predicts that within the next two years, more than 80 per cent of companies' CRM investments will fail.

Yet, as the cases in Chapter 7 demonstrate, those companies that do measure their CRM investments are demonstrably more successful than those that don't. For example, US retail giant Sears, Roebuck and Company saw its fortunes transformed from losses to $1 billion-plus income during the 1990s, through using over 60 measures of employee behaviours, customer impressions and financial performance. The company established causal links between measures – for example, a 5 unit increase in employee attitudes leads to a 1.3 unit increase in customer impressions and a 0.5 per cent increase in revenue growth.

Canadian telecoms company Nortel Networks transformed its business performance in a similar fashion. It identified that 52 per cent of customer satisfaction derived from employee satisfaction, and places great emphasis on motivating employees and fostering an appropriate leadership style as a consequence. Likewise, Siemens has improved the profitability of its CT division by using internet technology to improve its customer and operational metrics.

In the next two sections of this chapter, we go on to examine in more detail how companies should value their CRM investments, and ask whether CRM does indeed create shareholder value.

Valuing CRM investments

The cases in this book illustrate the wide range of companies engaging in aspects of CRM and the impact that introducing CRM can have on an organization. However, CRM projects are often both extensive and expensive. Faced with a decision about whether or not to implement CRM, business managers are increasingly asking themselves how to make the business case for investing in CRM.

Although we have managed to identify and present some cases where companies have been able to value the return on their CRM investments, all too often companies can't assess its impact. The data are hard to come by and, as we shall see, some traditional means of estimating the benefits of CRM are flawed. Yet measurement is critical to understanding why and how these companies which are good at CRM achieve their startling results. We argue that the impact and the real value of CRM lie in the contribution it can make to shareholder value.

The impact of CRM

As the case studies demonstrate, CRM is concerned with the way companies manage their relationships with their customers in an integrated fashion. It is about the way companies identify, satisfy, retain, and maximize the value of their best customers, using customer information to increase both customer and shareholder value. CRM helps companies improve customer service by tailoring their offer to the customer and providing greater convenience, including speed and ease of access, and by avoiding needless repetition of the same basic data. The resulting growth in customer retention and/or increased purchases creates shareholder value.

However, CRM pioneers have tended to put more emphasis on the role technology plays in forging better customer relationships, than on the increased shareholder value that ensues from those healthier relationships. Only relatively recently – since companies have begun to address how they will justify their CRM investments – has the importance of shareholder value creation been acknowledged.

The cases in this book illustrate four important principles underlying CRM (Kutner and Cripps 1997):

- Customers should be managed as important assets.
- Customer profitability varies; not all customers are equally desirable.
- Customers vary in their needs, preferences, buying behaviour and price sensitivity.
- By understanding customer drivers and customer profitability, companies can tailor their offerings to maximize the overall value of their customer portfolio.

If companies are going to apply these four CRM principles, they need close contact with, understanding of, and responsiveness to their customers. As we saw in Chapter 1, CRM investments are often very substantial, with projects routinely costing tens of millions of dollars. This makes the payback on CRM investments an issue, and companies need to consider whether it is worth investing in such a huge project, and how they will value the payback.

Approaches to valuing CRM investment

Many of the case studies deal explicitly with the problems and issues surrounding performance measurement in CRM. One clear advantage of IT-based CRM is the opportunity it gives organizations, sometimes for the first time, to monitor and appraise their performance against the measures that are important to customers and to the company.

A recent survey of published accounts of how companies measure the payback on their investment in CRM projects (Ryals et al. 2000) has revealed four different approaches. When evaluating the success (or otherwise) of their CRM investment, companies are measuring:

- improvements in customer service, satisfaction and retention;
- the return on investment on CRM systems themselves;
- changes in overall company profitability and performance; and
- increases in customer profitability.

Improvements in customer service and satisfaction is one of the most popular measures of CRM success, probably because these are relatively easy to measure. We know that customer satisfaction leads to customer retention and, in turn, that increased customer retention is linked to an increase in the lifetime value of that customer. That said, however, companies need careful and sophisticated measurement systems to link customer satisfaction – a non-financial measure – directly to profitability. Moreover, just because you can measure things doesn't necessarily mean they will improve. For example, companies may find that customer complaints are higher than they thought, once they develop systems to record and analyse them.

As we discussed in Chapter 1, companies sometimes try to measure Return on Investment (RoI) in CRM systems. RoI is deceptively simple; the problem lies in correctly identifying the relevant investment. The appeal of using RoI to measure the effectiveness of campaign management software systems, for example, is that the increased effectiveness of targeted marketing campaigns which such systems deliver, comes hard on the heels of the CRM investment. The downside of this method is that some of the apparent successes of such packages actually stem from earlier investments in other aspects of CRM, such as a data warehouse, data feeds, de-duplication exercises and so forth. Attributing all the success to a single software investment may understate the true costs of the investment and hence overstate the RoI.

It is difficult to attribute changes in overall company profitability and performance to investment in CRM, because it is hard to tell what would have happened without CRM. Some companies adopt CRM as a defensive investment to protect their existing business, in which case profitability would scarcely increase, if at all. The benefit of CRM under these circumstances is that, without CRM, profits would have fallen (in some instances, it is claimed, catastrophically). In other companies, industry sector-specific factors have driven profits down or up substantially over the period of the CRM investment and masked the effects of the CRM investment itself. Companies would need to do careful 'what-if' forecasting to isolate the effects of CRM, if that were possible.

Because of the shortcomings of these approaches to valuing CRM investments, the fourth method – measuring increases in the profitability of customers or segments – is currently attracting most interest as a way of understanding what impact CRM is having on an organization. Customer profitability is directly linked to the actions that companies take to tailor their offerings to customers. In principle, the more profitable a customer is, the more valuable they are to a company and the higher the level of service they might receive. Marketing managers intuitively believe that there are significant differences in profitability between customers, and that these could be important in implementing CRM. Customer lifetime value is now widely regarded as one of the most important measures of business performance; it has emerged several times as a major consideration for the companies studied in this book. Consequently, we will now go on to explore it in some depth.

Some customers are more valuable than others

As Garth Hallberg (1995) has pointed out, a small proportion of customers account for a large proportion of turnover and hence profit. In packaged and soft goods, for example, 33 per cent of buying category accounts for at least 67 per cent of volume: this is the high profit segment. Similarly, just 21 per cent of film-goers account for 80 per cent of cinema attendance; and a Coca-Cola-sponsored survey found that the top third of grocery shoppers were responsible for 80 per cent of grocery spending in a supermarket. Kraft foods found a similar pattern: across all its brands, the top third of households accounted for almost 70 per cent of the company's sales volume. In some categories the split was even more extreme: in yogurt, the top 16 per cent of households delivered 83 per cent of the volume, for example; and for Diet Coke, 84 per cent of volume comes from just 8 per cent of households. This volume picture is also reflected in profits, with higher-spending segments being more profitable.

These spending patterns have encouraged suppliers to segment their markets, prioritizing the most attractive customers, and identifying low-margin, low-profit customers from the outset. Segmentation permits companies to target their marketing efforts more closely and develop tailored products and service propositions, to improve customer retention.

However, to segment their customer base, companies need to be able to measure its profitability. Unfortunately, existing management accounting systems are often constructed along product lines, rather than customer lines, making it enormously complicated to calculate the value of a customer.

Customer profitability versus product profitability

Management accounts are often based on an analysis of product profitability. Direct costs are attributed to the products to which they relate, with central costs such as sales and general administration (SGA) allocated in some other way, often in proportion to the sales volume of different products. However, the problem of allocating costs in proportion to volume is that some customers use more service time than others, so the result tends to overstate the profitability of heavy users of the service, and understate the profitability of lighter users. The inherent unfairness in this method is compounded if overhead costs, such as costs of service, are substantial. Costs of service are very complex to allocate, but they are critical. Profitability is largely determined by how effectively these costs of service, incurred after the product is produced, are managed.

The focus on product profitability implies that products, rather than customers, generate profits. But this provides an unreliable guide for management action. For example, a company may decide to continue to produce an unprofitable product if, by doing so, it retains a profitable customer. This is logical if profits are generated by customers not by products, but irrational if products, not customers, are the key drivers of profitability.

To calculate the profitability of a customer or segment, organizations with product-based reporting systems will have to identify profits on the product mix held by that customer or segment, then determine an effective way to allocate other significant costs that affect the relative profitability of that customer. These will normally include SGA and logistics costs.

Logistics costs can be a key determinant of profitability, and simple cost allocation by volume can be seriously misleading. Crookes Healthcare, which makes over-the-counter healthcare products such as Nurofen and Strepsils and supplies chemists chains, wholesalers and grocery retailers, found a 600 per cent variation in distribution costs between its customers, depending on their delivery requirements. The 'pocket price' – the amount the seller actually realizes from the sale – is key. Invoice prices do not reflect payment terms, claims records or delivery charges, items that are specific to the customer and which can have a major impact on profitability. Constructing a customer database is usually the first step towards identifying the pocket price.

To allocate SGA and logistics costs accurately companies may need to use Activity Based Costing (ABC), a measurement system which allows a business to measure accurately how much time and effort it spends on serving certain customers or segments. ABC projects themselves can be expensive and time-consuming to implement. Fortunately, CRM systems can help companies calculate customer profitability. The automatic monitoring of staff interactions with customers can help companies understand the actual costs involved.

Calculating the profitability of a customer today is not straightforward, but CRM is about managing the lifetime relationship with a customer. If companies really want to understand the value of their investment in CRM, they need to not only calculate the profits from a customer or customer segment in a single year, but in future years too. The value of CRM needs to be expressed in terms of a stream of value over the lifetime relationship with any given customer. The concept of customer lifetime value is critical for understanding the benefits of CRM to a company.

Customer lifetime value

Customer lifetime value can be calculated as the stream of profits (i.e. revenues minus costs) for the forecast period. In valuing customer relationships, the forecast period is usually taken to mean the likely lifetime of the relationship with that customer or segment.

Customer lifetime value is problematic because it involves forecasting what amounts of what products customers will buy in future years, and what the sales, administration and logistics costs will be. Then, because profits in future years are progressively less valuable (because of inflation) and less certain, a discount rate has to be applied. The higher the discount rate, the less valuable future profits will be. A customer lifetime value calculation is shown in Table 8.1 for a customer who is expected to remain loyal for four years and whose revenues less costs will result in profits of $100 per year for each of the four years for which the relationship lasts. Assuming a discount rate of 10 per cent, this customer has a lifetime value of $317 today.

Table 8.1   Calculating customer lifetime value.

	Yr 1	Yr 2	Yr 3	Yr 4
Customer profit	100	100	100	100
Discount Rate	10%	10%	10%	10%
Discount Factor	0.91	0.83	0.75	0.68
NPV	91	83	75	68
				= $317

As we have seen, information systems for CRM can help to collect cost data to calculate customer profitability. In addition, data mining tools and techniques can be used on the customer information held in a data warehouse to help determine customer lifetime value. Among these tools are: cluster analysis, which can identify which segment a customer belongs to and how long the relationship might last; predictive modelling, which can help ascertain what products a customer might buy, and when; and predictive algorithms, which can detect customers who might be on the verge of defecting to another supplier. These 'potential defectors' can then be channelled to a special team charged with saving the relationship. Such tools have been particularly important in the financial services industry. Insurance companies, banks and brokerage houses are keen to realize the benefits of CRM through call centres or the internet by trying to provide the most accommodating environments possible to please their customers and to eliminate expensive customer turnover, which can cost as much as $400 per customer replaced. Companies that work hard at retaining customers can reap major benefits. For example, one financial services organization increased renewal rates by 45 per cent and added over $9 million to its bottom line by identifying potential lapsers and targeting them through its call centre.

Developing an understanding of the components of customer lifetime value not only allows a company to measure the value of CRM, it also fosters a deep knowledge of how customers create (and sometimes destroy) value for an organization. If this understanding is turned into customer relationship management strategies, it can create real value for the company. This, then, is the real evidence that CRM pays off.

Does CRM create shareholder value?

To date, the evidence that CRM creates shareholder value has tended to be reported by segment or marketing activity, rather than by individual customer. One study, for example, reports the results of a customer profiling and targeting exercise by a retail bank: direct mail campaign costs fell by a third, yet response rates doubled; the number of new accounts increased by 33 per cent and the profitability of new accounts by 32 per cent; defection rates fell 5 per cent; and the lifetime value of customers grew by an estimated 20 per cent (Dorman and Hasan, 1996). Another study reported on the use of a customer information database at AT&T. In 1994, AT&T attracted more than 1.2 million accounts, whilst reducing acquisition costs by more than US$3 per customer. By 1994, 50 per cent of the dollars invested in acquiring new customers led to a customer acquisition, as opposed to 5 per cent in 1990 (Grant and Schlisinger, 1995).

Other results are reported in terms of overall company profit or performance. There are several examples of potential and actual performance improvement based on CRM. A Canadian grocery store, for example, estimated that it could increase future gross profits by 300 per cent if it expanded its customer base by 2 per cent, reduced defection rates by 5 per cent, and substituted two own-brand items for two branded purchases per customer visit. When Taco Bell found that 30 per cent of its customer base accounted for more than 70 per cent of volume it focused on these customers. Sales increased from US$1.6 billion in 1988 to US$4.5 billion in 1994, and earnings increased more than 300 per cent over the same period (Grant and Schlisinger, 1995).

Improving customer relationships through CRM increases revenues from current customers as well as increasing retention rates and customer lifetimes. Indeed, one underlying premise of CRM is that share of loyal customers rather than share of market maximizes profitability. An American retail bank, for example, found that it could generate an incremental US$25 million after tax over three years by cross-selling each customer an additional 1.5 products. A 1999 survey of more than 900 executives across various manufacturing industries in Canada, undertaken by Deloitte Consulting, provides yet more evidence on the positive impact of CRM. The survey revealed that manufacturers who had adopted a CRM strategy exceeded their targets for sales growth by 65 per cent on average, whereas companies without such plans exceeded their targets by only about 17 per cent. Those with a CRM strategy exceeded their targets for new product revenues by more than 60 per cent, almost twice that of manufacturers without customer-centred strategies (Saunders, 1999).

One of the most important and, for many companies, astonishing revelations from information generated by their CRM systems is the high proportion of their customers that are unprofitable. For example, contrary to popular belief within the banking industry, banks do have many unprofitable customers. Research has showed that a quarter of new customers each year for American banks never generate enough revenue to offset what it cost to acquire them, and an additional 30 per cent never generate enough income to make a positive contribution to profits (Dorman and Hasan, 1996). Improving customer profiling can therefore be highly beneficial. The American retail bank cited above found that after a customer profiling exercise, its direct mail campaign costs fell by a third, yet response rates doubled. Surprisingly, most banks are not carrying out effective database-driven targeted marketing: research shows that only one in eight banks adopts targeted marketing using an enterprise-wide strategy. It may be that this is changing. U.S. Bank, for instance, has recently changed the way it views customers and now scans all of its customers for value, risk, attrition, and propensity to buy; Banco Central Hispano uses its CRM system to identify propensity to purchase. The response rate from mailings using this criterion is almost six times greater than the traditional mail shot.

However, the picture is not all positive. Indeed, in Chapter 1 we identified the downside of poorly thought-through CRM projects as 'massive investments with questionable return'. There are indications that some CRM investments are failing to deliver or, possibly, that customer expectations are increasing faster than the ability of companies to keep up.

The American Customer Satisfaction Index (ACSI) is a quarterly survey of American customers' satisfaction with the goods and services that they buy.[1] At its inception in 1994, the index stood at 74.5 (out of 100). Between 1994 and 1997, despite a growth in spending on CRM software, services and customer-service applications from $200 million to $1.1 billion, the ACSI fell to 70. Between 1998 and 2000 the index climbed back to just under 73 but resumed its long-term decline during 2001. While ACSI scores have improved for some companies and industries, customer satisfaction overall is not keeping pace with spending on customer-oriented technology. This is particularly bad news for companies because consumer spending seems to have broadly followed trends in the ACSI since 1994 (*Financial Times* 2001).

The sheer scale of major CRM projects puts them into the category of major IT investments. IT spending per white collar worker tripled between 1980 and 1993 and was projected to grow a further 60 per cent by 1999, accounting for 9.9 per cent of revenue. Investment in IT now represents 70 per cent of all capital investment. However, the return on this vast expenditure is by no means clear.

For instance, the returns on data warehouses are apparently not well documented and, where measured, they often turn out to be poor. A survey of 1500 companies in six European Union countries found that only 27 per cent of those who had implemented a data warehouse could identify a quantifiable financial benefit, while 40 per cent did not even know the costs they had incurred. However, most expected to obtain non-financial benefits from their data warehouse – about 80 per cent of respondents were only able to identify non-financial benefits, but most thought that these benefits would be substantial. The same survey found that, although the increase in revenue resulting from a data warehouse was approximately in line with expectations, cost reductions were significantly lower than expected and the time taken to implement data warehousing was considerably longer than anticipated. Sixty per cent of respondents expected to implement their data warehouse within six months, but only a quarter succeeded in doing so (OTR Group, 1997).

There seemed to be three main problems associated with this apparently poor performance: company data are not properly understood, leading to cost under-

[1] ACSI is a measure of consumer attitudes towards some 200 companies in 35 industries based on an annual survey conducted by the University of Michigan Business School, the American Society for Quality, and Arthur Andersen.

estimates; pilot systems 'transform themselves' into production systems so companies lose track of costs; and complex, bespoke and/or combination software causes more difficulties than anticipated (OTR Group, 1997).

For this reason, payback on CRM investments has become a more visible issue for companies in recent months and is likely to remain high on the corporate agenda for the foreseeable future. One way in which companies can accelerate the payback on CRM projects is by containing the costs of the project. Some organizations, for example, now prefer to generate a short-term return on their CRM investment by using data marts, smaller data warehouses targeted to a single line of business or single department. Others have backed away from expensive bespoke solutions tailored precisely to the needs of their organization alone, favouring cheaper solutions based on standard off-the-shelf products with minimal tailoring. These measures do seem to be working: a 1999 study found a more positive payback on IT projects, ranging from $1 million to $50 million, with payback periods of between six months and three years.

Other ways in which CRM can create value

Our discussion so far has focused on different ways of building the business case for a CRM investment and on the importance of customer lifetime value. We have argued that it is the lifetime value of a customer relationship that is important and that changes in lifetime value are the best indicators of successful CRM. However, there is some evidence that customers create value for organizations in other ways, as well as directly through their purchasing. These activities on the part of customers occur as a result of the relationship and have therefore been called 'relationship benefits' (Ryals 2002). There are two types of relationship benefit. Some customers act as reference sites and/or make word-of-mouth referrals, and such customers make it cheaper and easier for companies to acquire new customers. Other customers may test out new products or (in a business-to-business context) share information, benchmark processes, or become involved in joint ventures. These activities can have a profound impact on the overall sales or profits of an organization.

CRM can help companies achieve relationship benefits and measure how extensive those benefits are. Some companies are beginning to combine the results of market research surveys on which customers are more likely to act as reference sites or make word-of-mouth referrals, and then use data mining to find other similar customers in their data warehouse. They can target these customers with special offers to encourage referral. Really advanced CRM companies sometimes use sophisticated data matching techniques to look for patterns of referral/referred customers in their data warehouse. They may target influential customers – the opinion formers in their social circles, for example –

for their reactions to new products or services, to help spread the word of mouth to other potential customers. Customers who bring in other business through word of mouth are regarded as more valuable than equivalent customers who do not make recommendations.

Other leading-edge CRM measurement techniques explore the value to companies of sharing information, innovation and learning. Conventionally, these would be regarded and valued as independent projects, but this ignores the value contributed by a customer who is prepared to participate. Some companies are looking to apply advanced valuation techniques in these situations. One such technique recognizes the value of flexibility in some projects like these. Working with a customer to develop a new product, for example, may bring the added benefit of early feedback that would allow the company to scale up – or, if the product is unsuccessful, scale down – its investment. This flexibility is intrinsically valuable, not least because it allows the company to postpone major commitments until the market picture becomes clearer. It also increases the options available to the company, and a technique known as 'real option valuation' can be used to value this flexibility (Luehrman 1998).

Valuing the entire customer relationship is a fascinating new field, in which innovative approaches to measurement combine with data obtained from CRM systems to provide new ways of thinking about the value of CRM. There is still much to be done in the whole area of measuring the returns from CRM, and most companies are still struggling to understand the basic profitability of their customers. However, more sophisticated measurement of the value of CRM is likely to lead to more sophisticated CRM strategies being developed which will maximize the potential value locked up in a company's customer base.

Summary

CRM is not just a 'can do', it is a 'must do'. Customers expect better and better service, and companies without CRM systems will struggle to manage more than a few customer relationships effectively and profitably.

Yet, although CRM projects represent a major investment for most companies, many fail to measure the returns. Not only can CRM improve customer satisfaction and company performance, it can also boost productivity and efficiency. Moreover, organizations sometimes focus on the hardware and software costs of CRM investments, while failing to recognize the costs involved in time, training and so forth. Sometimes firms will find it difficult or impossible to assess the benefits of CRM using traditional accounting measures, and may need to turn to Activity-Based Costing (ABC) to help them weigh up the costs and benefits of their different marketing activities.

The case studies in this book suggest that CRM has an impact not just on the marketing department and on customer management strategies. As Chapter 2 reveals, there are implications too for organizational structure and for the skills that marketers need. Some companies have already been forced to recognize that to maximize shareholder value from their CRM projects, they need to change the structure of their organization from a products focus to a customer focus. Such organizations are creating multi-functional teams to serve certain highly profitable customers or customer segments. What's more, in order to understand the complex data that are generated from CRM IT systems and turn these into customer relationship management strategies, marketers are having to work closely with their IT departments and develop new data manipulation skills. We explore these developments in organizational structure and marketing skills and practice in more detail in Chapter 9, where we ask a selection of CRM opinion leaders for their views on the future of CRM.

References

Dorman, J. and Hasan, M. (1996) Turning lead into gold. *Bank Marketing*, **28**(11), 28–32.

Financial Times (2001) Customers get no satisfaction. *Financial Times*, 23 May.

Grant, A. W. H. and Schlisinger, L. A. (1995) Realize your customers' full potential. *Harvard Busness Review*, **75**(5), 59–72, September–October.

Hallberg, G. (1995) *All Customers Are Not Created Equal.* Wiley, New York.

Kutner, S. and Cripps J. (1997) Managing the customer portfolio of healthcare enterprises. *The Healthcare Forum Journal*, **40**, 52–54.

Luehrman, T. A. (1998) Investment opportunities as real options: getting started on the numbers. *Harvard Business Review*, 51–67.

OTR Group (1997) Do the benefits of data warehousing justify the costs? Report published by OTR Group, London.

Ryals, L. J. (2002) Are your customers worth more than money? *Journal of Retailing and Service Studies* (forthcoming).

Ryals, L. J., Knox, S. D. and Maklan, S. (2000) *Customer Relationship Management: The Business Case for CRM.* Financial Times/Prentice-Hall: London, Management Research Report series.

Saunders, J. (1999) Manufacturers build on CRM. *Computing Canada*, **25**(32), 17–18.

Chapter 9

The future of CRM: What opinion leaders think

As the cases in this book illustrate, companies embarking on customer relationship management are on a steep learning curve. Many must feel they take one step backwards for every two steps forwards. Yet they should be applauded. They are pioneers of using closer relationships with their customers to achieve differentiation and competitive advantage in a world that is increasingly commoditized, competitive and characterized by ever more demanding customers.

As these businesses struggle heroically to implement CRM, we asked some of the long-time advocates of CRM, the opinion leaders, for their views on what companies need to do to enhance the benefits they reap from CRM. We also asked them to predict how CRM might change over the next few years.

We spoke first to 'one-to-one marketing' guru Don Peppers. Peppers and his partner Martha Rogers are highly respected pioneers of relationship marketing, who maintain that competitive advantage and profit derive from 'treating different customers differently'.

Peppers believes there are five main reasons why companies' CRM efforts fail. One, they tackle the issue from a supply-side push rather than a demand-side pull perspective. They see CRM as a technology that will help them sell more faster, rather than as a way to improve customers' lives through delivering a better product or service. 'Most companies talk a good game', says

Peppers 'but for the most part, customers are adversaries.' Without a fundamental culture change, companies' CRM efforts are doomed. The second pitfall is that companies only measure the cost of CRM, rather than the benefits. The third challenge is managing the issue of customer 'governance' which arises when you start treating different customers differently. 'Whose job is it to make the decision of how the enterprise, across all of its divisions, will treat any one customer?' asks Peppers. The other two key challenges are managing channel conflict and planning for a CRM implementation that doesn't happen all at once.

The main thrust of comments from the other three opinion leaders – consultant Dave Fagan, BT Major Business marketing head Simon Kelly, and Phill Robinson, marketing chief of CRM software supplier Siebel – is the need for pragmatism. As Fagan says: 'CRM is not rocket science. It just needs someone with a good plan, the ability to look at the customer value proposition, and to execute against it. The best companies have been doing it for the past 2000 years.'

In similar vein Kelly says: 'Customer relationship management should do what it says on the tin. It is part of marketing, and is all about anticipating and meeting customers' needs profitably. But many people forget the absolute basics of understanding customers, their industry, their particular needs, and of offering them value propositions accordingly.'

Robinson concurs: 'There has been a real goldrush of people climbing on to the bandwagon in search of benefits without being prepared to do the basic groundwork ... you need executive buy-in, phased implementation, user buy-in and a clear understanding from the beginning just what the benefits are.'

Marketing chief of Siebel he may be, but even Robinson acknowledges the misguided faith many businesses have in CRM technology. 'Someone who expects to buy our software, unwrap it and install it is bound to be disappointed', he says. 'CRM is not just about software; it is a strategy, a process, a cultural change, and software enables that change.'

Looking to the future, Peppers predicts that the only successful companies will be those that carve out a place for themselves as the 'relationship stewards' of their customers. Given that companies will not want relationships with more than a handful of companies, which companies will consumers trust to act in their best interests? Working out how to treat each customer the way you would want to be treated if you were that customer is, says Peppers, 'a tremendous challenge' and one that 'even the most advanced companies are only now beginning to get to grips with'.

Fagan believes the name CRM should be dropped because it is too closely associated with technology, and has become tainted with failure. Kelly believes the single most important requirement for CRM now and in the future will be integrated channel management in order to 'give the customers the touchpoint to interact with the company when and how they want to'. And Robinson believes that while companies should be realistic about what benefits they want to achieve from CRM, they could be more ambitious in their targets. As he points out, CRM is one of the few initiatives designed to grow revenue rather than cut costs, but too many business cases are justified on the basis of cost reduction. CRM is all about generating revenue from customer relationships, so, he maintains, 'organizations should be more upfront about the real net benefit'.

Those who feel daunted by the array of advice, technology and techniques on offer should take comfort from Simon Kelly's words: 'I think people have tried to over-complicate CRM. It should essentially be about translating the individual personalized service you would get in your corner shop across a wider platform.'

Don Peppers

Don Peppers, and his partner Professor Martha Rogers are perhaps the world's best-known pioneers of one-to-one marketing. Their seminal 1993 book, *The One-to-One Future*, which coined the term 'one-to-one marketing', is still a valued reference for academics and practitioners alike. Peppers and Rogers Group is an international consulting firm that helps leading companies figure out how to execute Don Peppers' oft-repeated motto 'treat different customers differently'. Peppers and Rogers have co-authored several best-selling follow-up books, including *Enterprise One-to-One*, *The One-to-One Fieldbook*, and *The One-to-One Future*.

'I recently came across a shocking statistic. Only one in five sales people believes that the new CRM technologies forced upon them in the past year are worthwhile. If this is true, then this is an incredible waste of capital investment and a real missed opportunity for their companies. I don't believe the problem lies with the technologies. Most of the technologies work as advertised. The main problem is that companies have not addressed many of the fundamental business issues that are raised whenever a company tries to make a transition to treating different customers differently. Treating different customers differently is the quintessential definition of relationship marketing, CRM, call it what you will, and it leads to a lot of problems. At my company, we tend to talk about the five major challenges in implementing CRM.

The number one mistake that most companies make at the beginning of the process is to ask the wrong question: "How can we use this new technology to sell our customers more stuff?" The question they should be asking is: "How can we use this new technology to make our customers' lives better; how can we make our product or service more convenient, faster, cheaper, more tailored or more appropriate?"

Failing to view the whole process from the right perspective is, in fact, an indication of the first challenge, that is, the culture of the organization and the people who make decisions on behalf of the customers. We dedicated *The One-to-One Manager* to General Robert McDermott, the man credited with turning around USAA, by transforming the once stodgy and bureaucratic insurer into an icon of customer service. When I asked him how he managed this change, he told me that when he first got there, he made everyone aware of his "golden rule of customer service" – to treat each customer as you would want to be treated if you were the customer. It was a culture change.

Most companies talk a good game. We often say things such as "the customer is always right". But for the most part, customers are adversaries. They represent the obstacle to overcome in achieving our profit objectives. The ultimate transition is made when a company models itself as the trusted agent of the customer. You know you have achieved this when your customers trust you to make recommendations in their best interest, not yours. Even when there is a short-term financial sacrifice, you are willing to invest in some customers for the value of the long-term relationship. Of course, this immediately brings up two questions: how much to invest, and with whom? A lot of companies fund their marketing budgets by counting how many customers are acquired, paying little attention to the types of customer acquired.

Therefore, the second challenge for most firms implementing CRM is measurement. Consider, for instance, the simple problem of evaluating the benefits of increased customer loyalty. In strict economic terms, increased loyalty translates directly to an increased net present value of future purchases. But companies don't report the benefit of increased customer loyalty, only the increased cost of investment, systems and manning levels. We don't have a good way to gauge our success, our return on investment. We need metrics for the value of the customer base. In the future, firms will accept that their customer base is their central productive asset and they will want to continually measure its potential future value. Companies will want leading indicators that measure the health of that customer base so they can make intelligent decisions regarding their core asset.

In *One-to-One B2B* we describe a computer services outsourcer that is developing "technological entanglement" measures for each customer to assess customers' investment and commitment to the relationship. When its customers' processes are tightly integrated with its own, the customer is less likely to leave that relationship, because to do so would entail incurring the costs and risks of rebuilding these processes with a new supplier. Customers that are locked into your processes are more valuable to you than those that are not. Ranking customers by the degree to which they will remain committed to you provides a more insightful segmentation than purely ranking customers by last year's sales volume and profitability.

The third challenge is customer governance. When you begin treating different customers differently, you immediately create a governance issue. Whose job is it to make the decision about how the enterprise, across all of its divisions, will treat any one customer? Does it happen by accident or is it a strategic and informed decision? Let me give you an example of a company in the airline industry that runs a popular web site that dynamically serves content to millions of individuals. It uses a set of business rules, no more than one or two hundred at a time, to permit a nearly infinite number of permutations. Creating those rules is a strategic activity and vital to the development of differentiated customer treatment. Moreover, these rules should not apply just to the web site. The airline should really apply its online business rules at its reservation call centre, its check-in desk, and even on the plane. But whose role is it to write and maintain these rules, which together determine how different types of customers are treated in different situations? Most organizations simply don't have a clearly appropriate place where this role "belongs".

The fourth challenge, and currently the most discussed issue in CRM, is channel conflict. When companies begin interacting directly with end-user customers, one senses at first an almost gleeful rush to cut out the middleman, or so-called "disintermediation". Yet, if you visualize your business differently, there are roles for these middlemen. Let me give you a hypothetical example of what is possible in the airline industry. Nine out of ten airline web sites have no role for travel agents, because no airline wants to pay travel agents commissions on transactions that they will now generate directly with the fliers. But imagine the following scenario: an airline company sends out a letter to its agents, saying: "Here is a list of your customers who booked tickets with us in the past two years. Enclosed is a PIN number that we wish you to send these customers and invite them to use on our web site. We will give these customers a frequent flyer mileage bonus when they sign up, and we'll give you one per cent of the value of their purchases over our web site for the next ten years. You won't have to write the tickets, you won't even have to answer the phone." Wouldn't the agents welcome that?

The reason the airlines have not done this is that they are adapting new technology to their existing transactions-based business model. Serving your best customers better and better is more like a subscription business, and relationship marketing should be managed as a subscription model. In this business model, you reward channel partners for recruiting subscribers. This will drive traffic to the web, and into deeper relationships with your company, quickly and profitably. So thinking about your business as a relationship business not only creates major changes for marketing to the end customer, it also forces you to think about your channel model very differently.

The fifth and final challenge that I want to highlight is planning for a CRM implementation that doesn't happen all at once, but over some period of time. You need to plan for what we call "transition states". You can't merely flick a switch and have all the governance issues resolved. In our client work, almost all the successful implementations are the result of rolling out from a series of pilot projects. We "picket fence" some small parts of the customer base, providing selected groups with the desired customer experience, and build from these successes. If you want to solve the customer governance issues, you pick a few key customer segments, appoint customer managers for each group, and provide them with the authority to really change the way the company manages those customers. This may mean giving them control over such areas as pricing – for *their* customers. Of course, you need to have good measures of return – it is easy to create loyalty by giving your products away. You must hold customer leaders accountable, and this presumes that you will also be measuring the right things.

As to the future, Martha and I are convinced that computers will become so small and so cheap that they will go into everything – literally every product you buy will have a microchip. You will walk out of the store and your account will be charged automatically, the chip on the shirt will regulate how it is washed, and so forth. Within five to ten years, every adult in the world with any disposable income at all will be more or less continuously connected to an intelligent product of some kind, and every manufacturer will therefore have the potential to be in nearly continuous contact with their consumers. In this scenario, the only successful companies will be those that can carve a place for themselves as the relationship stewards for their customers. But think about it: a consumer will not generally want more than maybe half a dozen relationships. The vendors with whom they choose to maintain relationships will take care of various core areas of their life, such as managing the household, their finances, and travel and leisure. Companies must learn to handle a large number of consumer interests across a constellation of activities that solve a customer problem. This is where the money will be. Every one else will be selling commodities. We wrote about such agents in *The One-to-One Future*. The agent will be the customer's representative on the market, getting the best offers through managing information about their individual wants and preferences, while protecting their anonymity and privacy.

So the real issue is whom the consumer will trust to act in their best interests, which brings us right back to General McDermott's "golden rule" – "treat each customer as you would want to be treated if you were the customer". This is a tremendous challenge that even the most advanced companies are only just starting to get to grips with.'

Dave Fagan

Dave Fagan is business development manager at Ideas to Interconnect BV (i-to-i), a company that provides consultancy and project management to enterprises to help them successfully complete CRM and e-business solutions. He previously worked at BroadVision and Oracle.

'Companies which do CRM well understand that the customer must be at the centre of their efforts. That may sound obvious, but many companies adopt CRM to make life easier for themselves, and they make life more difficult for their customers as a consequence. It's hardly surprising that many consumers see CRM as mass victimization by companies who are essentially saying: "tell us more so that we can pester you even more". The most obvious example of companies putting their own needs ahead of their customers' is call centres, which, as any irate consumer who's ever been trapped in a voice mail loop will testify, are largely tuned for the company's efficiency rather than to make life easier for their customers.

Many people automatically associate CRM with call desks, and many people think that by implementing a call desk they have implemented CRM. But CRM has to be applied at every contact with a customer. Call desks have their place, but so does other technology.

Some of the best technology solutions for CRM involve running the call desk and a website together. Customers who want to serve themselves can use the web to find what they need and resolve certain issues how and when they want to. But if they need to resolve more complex issues, you can encourage them to use the call desk.

This type of solution can reduce the workload of the call desk by up to 80 per cent, allowing more time to be spent with customers that require real help.

You may well need lots of information on your customers, but you can gather that information gradually rather than by bombarding customers with requests for information all at once. What's more, you can design your questions so that it is in the customer's interests to answer you. Both the way you elicit information and the timing are very important.

Take American Airlines, for example. It asks its passengers very gentle questions. When you first visit its website you don't have to register. They ask you where you normally fly from. When you book your first flight they ask you which seat you would like and whether you would like them to hold that seat as your default preference on future flights. They make it easy for you because you only have to click on yes or no. So they drip feed you questions and each answer is relevant to the next step of the interaction.

The US company Home Depot, the biggest DIY chain in the world, is also very good at CRM. They invite you into their site by asking what task you want to do – whether building, decorating, installing, or whatever. The site is very task-centric and a very good example of how to design business interactions on the internet. They guide you from the beginning. If you wanted, for example, to install a stop cock in a toilet, they would show you pictorially how to do it, tell you what equipment and tools you need, the level of experience required, and how long the job is likely to take. If you wanted to paint a room, they would ask you the size, the number of windows and doors and so on, and estimate the amount of paint or other materials the job requires.

Initially, Home Depot wanted a web presence, but time pressures meant it had to start with an information-only portal, and added the ability to transact e-commerce later. But it found that while its customers preferred to research their purchases via the website, they chose to actually shop and purchase in a store. So Home Depot is now making it easier for customers to do just that. By linking the website to the individual store stock control systems, it is enabling customers to not only research their DIY requirements but also to check which stores near them have the items they need actually in stock. In essence, what Home Depot has done is modify the way it does business to suit its customers.

The lesson Home Depot learnt is a very important one for companies implementing CRM. It realized that focusing on the transaction on the internet was not the best thing to do, because transactions focus on price rather than the relationship or the decision-making process. The most sensible place to focus is the decision-making process – or "collaboration" – when the customer is doing their research and discussing things with the vendor. Once they are armed with information gathered from the internet, most customers actually want to go into the shop and see and touch things before they buy.

There's a lot of hype about customers buying cars over the internet, particularly in the US, but the reality is that they do their research over the internet, then, armed with lots of knowledge, go into the dealer to actually make the purchase.

I don't think any single company has done CRM properly or completely, but many are trying very hard. One of the problems many of them are having to contend with is that they jumped in with both feet, and are now having to rein back and consolidate, because not only have IT costs spiralled, but they have lost central control over the brand and the quality of the customer relationship.

Some big companies have as many as 350 customer facing websites, but no control over the quality of information, pricing, the value proposition or the offer.

I believe CRM works best if it is run as a virtual company within a company, rather than handled by a cross-functional team. CRM needs to be flexible and responsive, and offer a single face to the customer. It needs to be held together by oil, not glue, and you need to work at "the speed of business". Cross-functional teams often work like committees, which slows things down, and encounter problems trying to drive things through. You just need to get on and do CRM.

You don't actually need many people to run an e-business. You could do it with two full-time people or five part time, for instance. But it is more effective to have people dedicated to the task rather than being compromised by legacy, preconceptions and prejudices.

Building the business case for CRM is one of the most difficult, yet important, things a company has to do. Most companies have no idea how to forecast what return they are likely to get on their investment. They turn to people like us to guarantee it for them, which is as ludicrous as asking the construction company which built their office block to guarantee what profits they will make. But we have conducted some detailed research over the past year, which we are building on all the time, as to the kind of RoI different types of companies in different types of situations might expect. I mean RoI in the sense of, for example, increased market share, customer satisfaction, customer churn and so on. There are no cast iron guarantees, but at least it provides an indication of the level of RoI customers might expect.

But you have to focus on the right things, as I mentioned earlier. The internet bubble has burst. Larry Ellison of Oracle was both right and wrong when he famously claimed that the internet changes everything. Yes, you can go cross border, 24 hours a day and have a never-ending supply of "digital" products. Companies like Philips and Hewlett-Packard can load a piece of software once and deliver it 3 million times. But the internet changes nothing when it comes to the fundamental principles of doing business.

The area where real competitive advantage lies is in "e-marketing" – what we describe as "the seduction process", or the "collaboration" I referred to earlier. The results are there for all to see. In June 2001 American Airlines won yet more awards for its fantastic site. On one day alone, 26 June 2001, it had over 830 000 visits to the website, generating over $6 million of revenue.

CRM can't be divorced from e-business, and it is very important that both have a champion at board level. CRM shouldn't be seen as an IT project carried out by a programmer who reports in to the CIO [Chief information officer]. The person who is effectively VP CRM should report straight in to the chief executive.

The people best suited to the role tend to be business/technical hybrids – highly technically competent, but commercially aware and open to new ideas. There are very few of them around, but if you can identify them and put them in the right place they can become very successful. The most fertile hunting ground is probably among very business-competent CIOs.

These people should be responsible for the presentation of the brand, the image, the value proposition and the actual proposal of the company to customers and vendors. Marketing isn't doing that at the moment. Marketing does the frilly CRM stuff, but it does the old stuff too, and it is still trying to maximize its own rather than its customers' efficiency.

For example, we believe that good CRM can target people much more effectively than traditional direct marketing, which mails 10 000 people in the hope of getting three or four hundred responses. We believe that if you mail three or four hundred people in the right way at the right time they will all respond. But you need radical change within companies to break the legacy.

If CRM is to evolve and develop, I think the name CRM should be dropped. It has become too closely associated with technology, and has become tainted with failure and by too close an association with technology vendors. This is not meant to be a slight on technology vendors: it's just that people believe that by implementing a technology solution they have completely implemented CRM, which they haven't.

CRM is not rocket science. It just needs someone with a good plan, the ability to look at the customer value proposition, and the ability to execute against it. The best companies have been doing it for the past 2000 years.'

Simon Kelly

Simon Kelly is head of marketing at BT Major Business. Part of BT Retail, BT Major Business turns over £4 billion and provides sales and service, led by marketing, to the company's top government and corporate clients. The division comprises some 5000 people who are responsible exclusively for client relationships.

'Customer relationship management should do what it says on the tin. It is part of marketing, and is all about anticipating and meeting customers' needs profitably. But it has become so closely associated with companies such as Siebel and Oracle, and with software solutions, that many people forget the absolute basics of understanding customers, their industry, their particular needs, and of offering them value propositions accordingly.

CRM has been clouded by an over-emphasis on technology. Technology should be an enabler rather than an end in itself. I also think people have tried to over-complicate CRM. It should essentially be about translating the individual personalized service you would get in your corner shop across a wider platform.

To provide good customer relationship management, you need a deep understanding of the key issues affecting customers, in order to be able to present meaningful offers to them. At the end of the day, you can have a great CRM technology package, but you will struggle unless you have a client-needs orientation at the heart of your business.

We have a programme called Insight Interactive, which involves asking 35 000 clients about the business issues that are important to them, and shaping our offering to them based on their responses. A lot of what we've done is repackaging what we sell in a more compelling format, but the business benefit is clear: the programme brought in an additional £50 million-worth of business last year.

But though we are dealing with BT's top clients, because of falling prices and increasing competition, we can only hand craft a service to our most profitable customers. We provide account management for our major customers, with the emphasis on face-to-face interaction. But the people providing that service are trained to understand the customers' industries and particular requirements, rather than just flogging them a product. In fact, the service we provide to those clients is more akin to consultancy with a solution implemented at the end.

Further down, we look to mass customize what we offer. The four principal issues concerning businesses today are CRM, supply chain management, organizational effectiveness and knowledge management, and we present all our offers to that tier of customers in that context.

We have recently introduced a major programme offering clients a choice of channels when dealing with us. You don't have to manage all customer relationships face to face, and customers don't necessarily want that either. So some interactions will be desk based, some telemarketing from one of our call centres, and customers increasingly want to use the e-channel. This year we will be fully integrated around more channels to market.

The channel choice programme has allowed us to review the service we offer and to take a lot of cost out of the way we do business. For example, we have halved the number of people working on account management. Also, we used to have more than 900 people providing customers with installation and maintenance services. Now we have separated order processing from order handling, because people spent only about one fifth of their time interacting with clients when they were processing an order or a fault. Now 400 people interface directly with clients, 400 have moved into client fulfilment, and 91 have moved elsewhere in the business.

Building a business case for CRM is becoming more and more problematic. Two years ago people were throwing money at e-channels, and now you have to prove return on investment in every channel you use, which is equally crazy. Things have moved from the sublime to the ridiculous, when what's required is something in between. The business case should be based on channel mix, as most e-channels cannibalize revenue from existing channels, because customers see them as a lower-cost alternative. So the business case has to consider how much you are saving elsewhere to fund this new channel.

We are all looking for models to help us work out our thinking on the best way to build a business case for strategic CRM. But you need to justify your channel mix by demonstrating that it represents the way customers want to do business with you, based on sound, predictive research, show how much it will cost, and show how you will move lower-value business to a lower-cost channel.

My division of BT has funded two CRM awards, and all the winners were single-channel players – online banks, for example. Very few companies do fully integrated channel management, which, given the difficulties, is not surprising.

In the end you should be offering the customer whatever channel choice they want, which, arguably, should be most profitable for you. If anyone has the answer to how you resolve that conflict I'd like to hear from them.

But doing nothing is not an option. Companies need to get to grips with the whole multi-channel arena, because customers are increasingly going to want to access services how they choose, and companies have to work out how to meet that expectation profitably. If you don't have channel reach, nimbler competitors will get in on the act and steal advantage. Some, of course, might decide they don't want to provide a particular channel because it isn't cost-effective, despite the potential loss of revenue.

EasyJet, for example, has actively forced customers down the internet channel. That might put off customers who want a direct interface with the company, but the airline is more profitable than it would be if it offered several channels. And there will be other businesses like that, where the economic benefit for customers of using the lower-cost channel coincides with the economic benefit to the organization.

At the moment, you have to be economical with the truth to get investment for CRM, because these things just don't pay back over two years. Perhaps companies should be considering other measurement criteria – such as "return on relationship" for example: if you invest x what will be the impact on the relationship with your customers and overall customer satisfaction? At BT we see very clearly the value of understanding our customers and delivering products and service against that understanding, as evidenced by the additional revenue we have made from Insight Interactive. That, in turn, leads to customer satisfaction. One of the criticisms of the old BT was that while customers were largely satisfied with our billing and service, they would have been more satisfied if we'd really understood what they were all about.

Having a CRM champion in the company really helps. My job has been a lot easier here since Pierre Danon joined as chief executive of BT Retail at the beginning of 2001. He has pushed out a very customer-centric internal vision which drives home the importance of a client-centric strategy and has forced us to remodel customer satisfaction measures. His passion for customer centricity has infected the entire organization. But while he is an enabler, creating the environment and providing the leadership, people have to shape their own strategies and executions.

We have a new idea every day about what to call CRM and how to differentiate ourselves in the marketplace. But, going forward, whatever CRM looks like or is called, what will be of critical importance is having the technology that gives customers the touchpoint to interact with the company when and how they want to. A state-of-the-art software system or fantastic database will count for nothing if customers can't actually do business with the company. I believe integrated channel management is a bigger part of CRM than most people realize.'

Phill Robinson

Phill Robinson is vice-president, international marketing, for Siebel Systems. Siebel Systems is the world's leading provider of e-business applications software, with 50 to 60 per cent of the e-business and CRM software market. It counts blue chip companies such as ABN Amro, Prudential, BT, Deutsche Telekom and NPower among its clients.

'The idea that competitive advantage derives from the four P's of product, price, place and promotion has fundamentally changed. The key to revenue growth these days is customer relationships. CRM enables companies to enhance their relationships with their customers and make more money out of them by meeting their needs more specifically. It does that by creating a single relationship and a single view of the customer across the entire organization, allowing the customer to do business any time, any place and anywhere they choose through whatever channel they choose.

The customer can traverse the different channels – branch, call centre or internet, for example – based on their immediate needs. The challenge for every organization is to identify the customer immediately and personalize its service based on that customer's previous interactions. That is the key to improving customer satisfaction and what we call "customer relationship equity".

However, most companies are a long way off. For example, when you buy a car, you might go to the website to get information and look at the colour and spec of the car you want. The next day you go into the dealer for a test drive, but the dealer has no idea what spec of car you have chosen. The next day you ring the call centre for some technical data and they don't know anything about the test drive. CRM should be able to integrate those channels, allowing the organization to build on each interaction to improve the quality of the customer experience and increase their likelihood to buy.

There have been some outstanding successes with CRM, despite the claims of some of the market pundits that CRM projects are not delivering the expected benefits. Every six months Siebel Systems surveys its customers' levels of satisfaction. The survey, which is independently audited, helps us develop new products for our customers and incentivize employees, whose bonuses are based upon the results.

That survey tells us that among our 3000 customers around the world we have 96–98 per cent loyalty. We also ask about the benefits the CRM implementation has created. On average, companies have seen customer satisfaction rise by 20 per cent, revenue rise by 12 per cent and employee productivity rise by 20 per cent. Those figures represent the best return on investment I've seen of any software implementation in the 20 years I've been in this business.

So, how do we reconcile those sorts of results with the gloom of market analysts? Well, we view the glass as being half full, rather than half empty, so rather than focusing on what others are doing wrong, we seek to help clients replicate the success we have achieved elsewhere.

We are very pragmatic. We sit down at the beginning with customers and set realistic targets. If their expectations are realistic they have more chance of being successful. There has been a real gold rush of people climbing on to the bandwagon in search of benefits without being prepared to do the basic groundwork. Because while there are compelling benefits to CRM, you can't rush it. The same universal principles apply to CRM that have applied for software implementations for the past 30 years, and people forget that. For example, you need executive buy-in, phased implementation, user buy-in and a clear understanding from the beginning just what the benefits are. Someone who expects to buy our software, unwrap it and install it is bound to be disappointed. CRM is not just about software; it is a strategy, a process, a cultural change – and software enables that change.

The results of the American Customer Satisfaction Index (ACSI) from the University of Michigan, which measures customer satisfaction across the spectrum of industry and commerce, suggest that customer satisfaction is improving only ever so slightly, or even decreasing. That makes the results we can achieve even more remarkable. But the competitive advantage these organizations have achieved has not come about because of a piece of software, but because of the initiative they have taken to become customer-focused, which, in turn, has driven lots of benefits. To become customer-focused you need people, process and strategy. If you are not customer-focused any CRM initiative will fail.

Cross-functional working is essential to customer focus. The link between employee satisfaction and customer satisfaction is proven. Indeed, so important is employee buy-in that we have recently launched an employee relationship management (ERM) solution too, and we see this as a potentially bigger area even than CRM. ERM is designed to harmonize employees around a set of values and principles that go towards creating customer satisfaction, as well as enhancing cross-departmental communication. Again, software is an enabler. Around 18 months ago we launched a similar service for a company's business partners – partner relationship management, or PRM.

But despite the strides that have been made, companies still struggle when trying to create a business case for strategic CRM. Perhaps more businesses need to look at some different key performance indicators. R & D as a percentage of turnover, or days sales outstanding (DSO) are typical KPIs for many businesses. But if customer satisfaction and customer equity are acknowledged to be increasingly important, why not add in measures such as customer satisfaction as a percentage of turnover, or rate of churn, as some of the more customer centric businesses are starting to do.

But having said that, CRM is a very good example of an initiative designed to grow revenue rather than cut costs. Most traditional IT projects are inwardly focused and concerned with generating internal efficiency by driving costs out of the business. And we've all got pretty good at that, with initiatives such as business process reengineering and downsizing paring companies down to fighting weight.

But you get to a point where you cannot get any leaner and you actually need to generate more revenue to drive profits. So IT projects now have an external focus, and CRM is all about generating more revenue from customer relationships. Companies ought to be able to build a business case based on that. Too many business cases are two-sided: because increasing revenue is speculative, they are justified on the basis of cost reduction, with the expectation that they will also increase revenue. It's a pragmatic approach, but organizations should be more upfront about the real net benefit being to increase revenue.

You have to be careful with CRM. Handled wrongly, it can damage relationships with customers. Personalization is a very important component in customer satisfaction, but you have to be sensitive to both when and how you use it. For example, when Sainsbury's first introduced its reward card scheme, checkout staff would hand it back to the owner, thanking them by name. Fifty per cent of people loved that level of personalization, but 50 per cent hated it and thought it was an invasion of their privacy.

Having a board level champion, with the vision to drive the business benefits and get buy-in from the rest of the organization, is crucial to successful CRM, and the most successful projects tend to be those with CEO buy-in.

I think there has never been a better time for companies to look at investing in CRM. Everyone realizes that this recession could last for some time, and in a contracting marketplace it becomes increasingly important to sell more to existing customers in order to keep making profits. Customers will only keep buying if they are happy and satisfied, so the argument for investing in CRM becomes even more compelling, though it may feel counter-intuitive at a time when profits are under pressure. We have been very successful in the European telecoms market over the past 12 months, for example. Some telecoms companies have come under fire from the media and their shareholders because of all the money they've invested in third generation licences, but they know that they have to protect their customer base in order to be able to sell them the new 3G phones in three years' time.'

Index